Socialism in France

Also published in association with the ASMCF, *Elites in France: Origins, Reproduction and Power*, edited by Jolyon Howorth and Philip G. Cerny.

Socialism in France
From Jaurès to Mitterrand

Edited by

Stuart Williams
Wolverhampton Polytechnic

St. Martin's Press, New York

Printed in Great Britain
First published in the United States of America in 1983

Library of Congress Card Catalog Number: 83-42532

ISBN 0-312-73667-3

CONTENTS

Abbreviations

AFSP	—	Association Française de Sciences Politiques
CDP	—	Centre Démocratie et Progrès
CERES	—	Centre d'Etudes de Recherches et d'Education Socialistes
CFDT	—	Confédération Francaise Démocratique du Travail
CFTC	—	Confédération Francaise des Travailleurs Chrétiens
CGC	—	Confédération Générale des Cadres
CGT	—	Confédération Générale du Travail
CIR	—	Convention des Institutions Républicaines
CNIP	—	Centre Nationale des Indépendants et Paysans
CNPF	—	Centre Nationale du Patronat Français
ENA	—	Ecole Nationale d'Administration
FEN	—	Fédération de l'Education Nationale
FGDS	—	Fédération de la Gauche Démocrate et Socialiste
FO	—	Force Ouvrière
IDC	—	International Division of Labour
IFOP	—	Institut Français d'Opinion Publique
INSEE	—	Institut National des Statistiques Economiques
LCR	—	Ligue Communiste Révolutionnaire
MNC	—	Multinational Company
MRG	—	Mouvement des Radicaux de Gauche
PCF	—	Parti Communiste Français
PCI	—	Parti Communiste Internationaliste
PCML	—	Parti Communiste Marxiste Léniniste
PME	—	Petites et Moyennes Entreprises
PS	—	Parti Socialiste
PSU	—	Parti Socialiste Unifié
RFSP	—	Revue Française de Sciences Politiques
RI	—	Républicains Indépendants
RPR	—	Rassemblement pour la République
SFIO	—	Section Française de l'International Ouvrière
SOFRES	—	Société Française d'Enquêtes par Sondages
UDF	—	Union pour la Démocratie Française
UGSD	—	Union de la Gauche Socialiste et Démocratique

Preface and acknowledgements

It is not too much of an exaggeration to say that the September 1982 conference of our Association for the Study of Modern and Contemporary France (ASMCF) ended with the participants 'ready for more'. This book is the next stage in the process, giving, in black and white, the many valuable ideas and references introduced by the speakers. It is varied in subject and style, reflecting our membership and all our conferences. Some of the contributions have been translated, by the editor unless otherwise stated.

I should like to thank the chairmen of the conference sessions, Maurice Larkin, Sian Reynolds, Dennis Ager, Nicholas Hewitt, John Frears and Douglas Johnson for their organisational contributions and their aplomb (in the positive English sense). I should also like to thank heartily all the contributors for responding to all my demands so promptly, thus allowing the book to appear within a few months of the conference. Finally, I should like to thank David Bell for his advice and Lindsay Wilson for her secretarial support.

Stuart Williams
Wolverhampton Polytechnic.

Introduction

DOUGLAS JOHNSON

When the Socialists were elected to power in May and June 1981, their victory re-kindled an interest in French socialism. There were certain obvious reasons for this. In Great Britain it was seen as important that a near continental neighbour should have a government which rejected the most widely accepted methods of dealing with the economic crisis, which envisaged unemployment as the prime target and which sought to spend and invest rather than to continue with an austerity programme of spending cuts. The entry of four Communist ministers into the government was not only a break in French tradition since 1947, it represented a change in the assumptions of the West. The very fact that the opposition had come to power and was no longer the opposition for the first time since 1958, suggested the possibility of considerable change and it seemed essential to discover what form this change would take.

But there were other reasons, more closely associated with the history of socialism in France. It had to be recognised that the electoral victories of Mitterrand's Parti Socialiste were more extensive than any which had been won in preceding times. After the municipal elections of 1977 and the presidential and legislative elections of 1981, all power was with the Socialists. The constitution of the Fifth Republic ensured that the President was the supreme figure in France, with a power than was unequalled in any other democratic country, and since this power was buttressed by an absolute Socialist majority in the Assembly and by Socialist control of an unprecedented number of large towns, it seemed as if there were no obstacles to prevent the Socialist administration from doing whatever it wished; a striking contrast to the traditional history of French socialism, which told the story of failure.[1]

At first, it appeared that the only obstacle was the internal divisions existing among the Socialists and it was remembered that such divisions were a natural and perpetual part of French socialism. They had always been associated with different personalities, whether one thinks of political theorists or of the leaders of the different political factions. Thus, before the 1914 war Guesdistes, Blanquistes, Possibilistes, Allemanistes and Centristes Indépendants represented different Socialist ideas and plans; between the wars Léon Blum established a dominant position alongside his organisational chief, Paul Faure, but they were frequently at odds and he often also had to face up to the criticism of groups led by Marcel Déat, Marceau Pivert and Zyromski. After the war, Blum's designated heir, Daniel Mayer, was ousted by Guy Mollet, and although Mollet has been described as someone who wandered from one end of the political spectrum to another in his actions,[2] his leadership was sometimes opposed, notably by Gaston Defferre, and was frequently criticised by the political clubs that flourished in the late 1950s and 1960s. When the Socialists were on the point of electing Mollet's successor they seemed hopelessly divided. Mitterrand's final victory in 1971, over Alain Savary, was by the narrowest of margins, and from time to time opposition to his leadership continued to surface. Prior to the presidential elections of 1981 when, possibly for tactical reasons, Mitterrand allowed a doubt to foster as to whether or not he would be a candidate, the possibility arose of having two Socialists in contention for the Presidency, the one Michel Rocard, representing the right, the other Jean-Pierre Chevènement, representing the left wing (CERES, the Centre d'Etudes de Recherches et d'Education Socialistes). with Pierre Mauroy, the leader of the powerful Fédération du Nord, always remaining another possible contender. It was no wonder then that the new opposition, the Giscardians and Gaullists, claimed that after May 1981 the pluralism that had characterised French politics hitherto still existed, but was not localised within the Socialist party.

A further danger of disruption within the governmental coalition arose from the attitude of the Communists. After the breakdown of the alliance in 1977 and after the Communist attacks on the right-wing tendencies of the Socialists during the presidential campaign, for how long would the Communists agree to be the junior partners, in danger of losing their identity to a social democracy they both feared and detested?

The fact that Socialist activity has actually been constrained by economic factors, both national and international, and by the evolution of the international scene, does not invalidate these considerations concerning the unity of the Parti Socialiste and the governmental coalition.

Other aspects of the nature of French socialism were also uncertain in 1981. It had often been said that traditional French socialism relied for support upon the peasant vote but that this peasantry, possibly radical in the sense of being republican and anti-clerical, was nevertheless a bastion of the bourgeoisie and one of the principal obstacles to any Socialist revolution.[3] By 1981, since the number of peasants had dramatically declined and much of the pattern of the French agricultural economy had been modified, it was not clear how French socialism would react to this changed situation.

In the past there had been a curious relationship between the theories of socialism, which were often utopian in character, and the syndicalist nature of much worker action. This had been particularly true of the period of the Second Republic.[4] But by 1981 the Parti Socialiste could not be said to have any theory of socialism at all. *Le projet socialiste*, which was approved in 1980, contains certain points of doctrine, but it was essentially a practical document and lost its importance when Mitterrand drew up his own election manifesto. The result is that French Socialists appeared in 1981 only to have a programme to organise production and thereby overcome the crisis in unemployment. After eighteen months in power Maurice Duverger could define French socialism as 'un socialisme de la production, axé sur le progrès économique, seul moyen de développer le progrès social'.[5] And while it can be argued that this is in accordance with a Marxist conviction that the state would necessarily be a more efficient producer than private capitalism, it is also clearly in accordance with the long-standing French tradition emphasising the role of the state in economic matters. The election result also exposed the problem of relations between the Socialists (and their Communist associates) and the trade unions, a problem which has become acute because the Socialists have often been accused of thinking of themselves as a parliamentary party, engaged in the task of legislation, distinct therefore from the workers in their unions. In the 1980s, as a number of trade unions consider that their action should not be confined to a limited form of social action, but should be extended politically, in terms of a concern for worker rights in general and in order to achieve a new organisation of labour, then these problems will be revived.

The integration of the working class into French society has long been an issue. It has been said that the French working class has been integrated politically, and has often played a political role in alliance with that part of the bourgeoisie that, for historical and cultural reasons, accepted revolution in the nineteenth century and radical reform at certain moments of the twentieth century. But the working class has never been integrated socially. Hence, it is claimed, the relative slowness with which social legislation has been achieved in France, and the tendency for the working class to identify itself culturally with those incidents, such as strikes, or those institutions, such as the Communist Party, which emphasise its social exclusion.[6]

The Association for the Study of Modern and Contemporary France, in its third conference, held at Wolverhampton in September 1982, obviously did not study all the problems relevant to the coming of the Socialist party to power. The chapters which follow were among the papers that were delivered to the Conference, and they are testimony to the very real interest that these recent events have caused among all those concerned with French studies.

> Douglas Johnson
> Professor of French History,
> University College, London.
>
> President of the Association for the Study
> of Modern and Contemporary France.

Notes

1   See, for example, the comments of Tony Judt, *Socialism in Provence*, Cambridge, Cambridge University Press, 1979, p. 281ff.
2   Frank L. Wilson, *The French Democratic Left 1963–1969*, Stanford, Calif., Stanford University Press, 1971, p. 65.
3   N. Poulantzas, *Les Classes sociales dans le capitalisme d'aujourd'hui*, Paris, Seuil, 1974, p. 355.
4   Rémi Gossez, *L'Organisation ouvrière à Paris sous la Seconde République*, La Roche-sur-Yon, 1956 (or for a later period, Michel Perrot, *Les Ouvriers en grève*, Paris, Mouton, 1974.)
5   *Le Monde*, 21 December 1982.
6   See the remarks of Jacques Julliard in Alain Touraine (ed.), *Mouvements sociaux d'aujourd'hui: acteurs et analystes*, Paris, Les Editions ouvrières, 1982, pp. 165–9.

PART I   HISTORY

1   From the bourgeois republic to the social republic

JOLYON HOWORTH
University of Aston

La République en France a ceci de particulier: que personne n'en veut
et que tout le monde y tient.

Gobineau

One of the greatest problems of the French Left since the end of the nineteenth century has been its inability to reach consensus about the historical
nature, the political value and the tactical usefulness of republican institutions. French socialism has always declared itself to be 'revolutionary', has
always set itself as an objective some sort of rupture with the economic,
social and political institutions of the republican bourgeoisie.[1] At the same
time (and this is where the problem begins), it has been virtually unani-
mous in asserting that the only institutional context in which such a
rupture could be planned and organised would be the bourgeois Republic
itself.

The problem stems from the fact that the various components of the
French Left have never clearly addressed the issue of what it is they value
in the bourgeois Republic; nor have they resolved the contradictions
between that assessment and the stated intention of overthrowing it. Such
an analysis involves supplying the answers to several sets of questions. First,
what is the historical nature and function of the bourgeois Republic?
What is the political and social reality behind its democratic institutional
facade? Second, given the answers to those questions, what tactical
approach should the Left adopt in its political relationship with the
Republic? To what extent are the 'formal' freedoms of which the Republic
claims to be the guarantor an invaluable asset in the Socialists' own
struggle, and to what extent are they, on the contrary, a trap or a form of
co-optation? These two sets of questions lead logically to a third one, the
most important of all: what is the historical relationship between the
bourgeois Republic and the social Republic? Is the latter merely a
'quantitative' improvement on the former, or is it in fact fundamentally
different in 'qualitative' ways?

1

In this chapter I have a twofold aim. First, to argue that the intense debate generated at the close of the nineteenth century by the 'republican crises' associated with two military officers named Boulanger and Dreyfus and one Socialist minister named Millerand, secreted three quite separate approaches to the various questions raised above. These three lines were formulated by the three main leaders of the Socialist party: Jean Jaurès, Jules Guesde and Edouard Vaillant. My second aim is to show that right up until the end of the Third Republic (and perhaps beyond) these three lines were constantly recycled, in one form or another, by the various tendencies on the Left, without there ever being any resolution of the contradiction that they posit at the level of Socialist tactics. If all philosophy is footnotes to Plato, to a very large extent all of French left-wing thought on this particular issue is footnotes to Jaurès, Guesde and Vaillant.

The nature of the bourgeois Republic

At the risk of oversimplification (for it is an enormously complex issue) one might say that there are, ideologically, two discrete roots to the republican question in French left-wing thought. The first, from 1789, asserts that the republican *form* (even if the institutions remain solidly bourgeois) is an adequate if not necessarily ideal context within which to struggle for socialism and the social Republic. This *linear* analysis has had many advocates on the French Left, but it was perhaps most eloquently stated by Jean Jaurès in 1903 when he described the Republic as

> . . . a great act of confidence: to institute the Republic is to proclaim that millions of individuals will be able to work out for themselves a common set of rules for their mutual intercourse; that they will succeed in reconciling liberty and law, movement and order; that they will be able to struggle without tearing each other apart; that their quarrels will not lead to the chronic fury of civil war.

And Jaurès went on to conclude that the republican political form had become 'the durable law of the nation, the definitive shape of French life', perfectible still and above all to be extended to the economic and social fields.[2] The logic of this position led Jaurès to envisage the social Republic as an infinitely improved version of the bourgeois Republic.

The second root to socialist republicanism in France takes its sustenance from a Marxist source. Marx always asserted that the French Republic was the ideal arena in which the proletariat should struggle for its emancipation.[3] In the *Communist Manifesto*, he had originally assumed that it would be sufficient for the proletariat gradually to take over the institutions of the bourgeois Republic and to use them to hasten the advent of the social Republic. After the failure of the Paris Commune, he modified this line, arguing that since those institutions had been custom-made to serve the interests of the bourgeoisie, they could not be operated by the proletariat in its own interests and should consequently be smashed.[4] In Marxist theory, therefore, it appears that the final passage from the bourgeois Republic to the social Republic must involve a violent rupture, a qualitative leap and wholesale destruction of the earlier republican forms. This interpretation of the nature of the two Republics I have called dia-lectical as opposed to linear. Unfortunately for his disciples, Marx neglected to comment on the precise value of the bourgeois Republic in the period prior to the social revolution; the result has been a plethora of different comments from Socialists considering themselves to be Marxist. I shall return to this problem in a moment.

There seems to be a major ideological contradiction between the 'linear' and the 'dialectical' interpretations of the Republic. What makes matters worse is that upon examining the texts, traces of both analyses are found in all three of our protagonists. Jaurès was perfectly capable of making important concessions to the dialectical approach,[5] and Guesde occasionally paid more than lip service to the linear view.[6] Vaillant was the man who attempted to promote both at once. It should nevertheless be made clear that at the level of theory, none of these leaders, not Vaillant, not even Jaurès, and still less Guesde, ever succeeded in formula-ting a satisfactory synthesis of the two interpretations.[7] The debate was essentially about tactics, and it was therefore on the basis of an uncertain and inconclusive response to my first set of questions that the early Socialists began to formulate responses to the second set. It is to these second, tactical questions that we must now turn our attention.

The crisis of the Republic: a question of tactics

The tactical question facing the socialists during the years 1898-1904 was, briefly, this: could the Party allow itself to lay down the weapons of class struggle and form a political front with the republican bourgeoisie in order to prop up the apparently tottering republican form?

Jules Guesde is a highly complex figure and is easily misunderstood and misrepresented. If Jaurès was like an intellectual butterfly, constantly flitting from one attractive notion to another in an earnest quest for truth and unity, Guesde was more like a political chameleon, changing his colours to match the environment in which he found himself. Any attempt to pin down the 'real' Jules Guesde is bound to fail. There are many signs however that in his heart of hearts Guesde's feelings towards the bourgeois Republic were a mixture of suspicion, resentment and hostility. On regular occasions during the republican crisis, the Guesdists argued that the regime simply was not worth 'saving', that there was, from the workers' point of view, no difference between the French Republic and the German Reich.[8] The ambivalent attitude of the Guesdists towards republican reforms is well documented[9] and there is no need to retread well worn ground. What is necessary, however, is an analysis of the implications of the various contradictory positions adopted by the Guesdists on this issue of republican tactics.

Their first main position was a variant of the Marxist 'dialectical' line. Guesde took Thiers's dictum ('the Republic is the form of government which divides French men least') and, in fine Marxist style, stood it on its head, arguing on the contrary that 'it brings into direct conflict the collective antagonism between the classes'.[10] But what are the political and tactical consequences of this classic Marxist formulation? Was it true, as Guesde frequently claimed, that the workers 'had nothing to gain'[11] from the bourgeois Republic? Or did the Marxist approach, on the contrary, imply that the bourgeois Republic as an arena for active struggle could allow the Socialist movement to strengthen itself constantly through thousands of minor skirmishes, to educate itself and achieve political maturity in such a way and to such an extent that the 'qualitative leap' referred to earlier would happen gradually and almost imperceptibly? This latter interpretation, as we shall see, was that adopted by Edouard Vaillant. The Guesdist position, however, was very different.

Quite frequently, the Guesdists argued that the value of the Republic was that it proved to the workers in practice that all reforms within the system were illusory, and that this was not just a question of misfortune but of inevitability.[12] In his debate with Jaurès at Lille in 1900, Guesde, addressing the issue of republican reforms, stated overtly: 'nothing at all has changed in present society and nothing at all can change as long as capitalist property has not been abolished'.[13] In other words, according to this position, the Republic would eventually frustrate the workers so totally that they would rise up in revolt against it.

But this revolutionary fatalism was only one side of the Guesdist speech; at the same time, they peddled another line on this issue, which in fact claimed the opposite of the first. According to this second line, the Republic was essentially an instrument of co-optation which would succeed in sending the workers off to sleep. As early as 1883, in their *Programme du Parti Ouvrier*, Guesde and Lafargue had argued that 'in capitalist society, reforms, even working-class reforms, benefit the capitalists and it is this feature of them which allows them to be passed'.[14] In this way, if the managers of the Baccarat glassworks allowed child-workers to take a lunch break, this, according to Guesde and Lafargue, was 'in order to produce, for the present, alert little workers and, in the future, reasonably healthy adults'. In the same vein, when the Socialist lawyer Alexander Millerand was offered a ministerial job in the 'bourgeois' government of René Waldeck-Rousseau, Guesde and Lafargue both detected in this event a cunning bourgeois plot to 'send the workers off to sleep'.[15] So terrifying to them was this prospect that they did not hesitate to say that if this offering of soporific cake began to work, and if the exacerbation of naked class struggle began to be muted by republican confidence tricks, then 'the Republic would become the worst of all possible governments',[16] in which case, suggested Guesde, it should, like the *ancien régime* before it, be swept away lock, stock and barrel: 'the bad and the good, the good with the bad'.[17]

According to the Guesdists, therefore, the bourgeois Republic appears to be doubly flawed: either it offers nothing whatever to the workers, or, by offering them something, it douses their revolutionary ardour. In either case (and herein lies the explanation for this apparent contradiction) the real purpose of these positions is to prove to the workers that their main objective must be the destruction of the regime.

It was this type of 'revolutionary' logic, totally depriving republicanism of any positive usefulness, which underpinned the arguments put forward by Marcel Cachin (a former Guesdist) at the Congress of Tours. Responding to accusations that Bolshevism constituted a break with French republican tradition, Cachin specifically pointed to Guesde's line on the Republic as evidence that Bolshevism was, on the contrary, the true heir to the French revolutionary tradition.[18] Other parallels abound. The article in the first number of *Bulletin Communiste* in which Souvarine drove home the lessons behind the Tours split, reads in part like a redrafted version of the 1899 manifesto in which Guesde analysed the reasons for the split with Jaurès and the ministerialists.[19] The arguments used during the 'class against class' period in the late 1920s and early 1930s were informed by precisely the same negative ambivalence towards the Republic and positive simplicity towards proletarian revolution as those which characterised the Guesdist speech in the period 1898-1905.

But it was not only the Communists who inherited this tradition. Within the SFIO, there were two tendencies that shared the Guesdists' attitudes towards the bourgeois Republic. Jean Zyromski and Marceau Pivert and their friends tended to look upon the Republic with suspicion.

This suspicion was based, in the two cases, on different premises, the former seeing it as a dangerous source of co-optive temptation, the latter as a hypocritical absurdity that could be dispensed with at no cost to the Socialist movement.[20]

Such a line has all the strengths and all the weaknesses of simplicity. By hitching the party waggon to the single horse of class, the anti-republicans in the French Left were able to drive home a message that was easy to formulate, easy to understand and (at least on the face of it) easy to implement. It was, of course, a message not entirely devoid of truth, but its fatal flaw was that it flew in the face of French history. It ignored the fact that the Republic in France, as Maurice Agulhon has shown,[21] had been the one objective not only of all progressive political movements since 1792, but also of a deep-rooted popular culture. However much the average Socialist militant might fulminate against the inadequacies of the Republic, he knew that it nevertheless represented the major tangible fruit of a century-long struggle.

Jean Jaurès was from the beginning to the end of his career in no doubt about that. I have already outlined Jaurès's view of republican progress towards the social Republic, and his theories are in any event widely known.[22] There is no doubt whatever that during the years of 'republican crisis' (1898-1905), Jaurès identified himself wholeheartedly with the 'linear' view of republicanism, arguing that the presence of a single Socialist minister in government was a logical and inevitable consequence of parliamentary action, and that such a presence would accelerate and intensify the rhythm of progressive republican reforms. For Jaurès and his associates there appeared to be no 'qualitative' dividing line which marked off those republican pastures in which Socialist seeds might thrive and flourish from those in which they would, on the contrary, be strangled by bourgeois republican weeds. Each step, from the passage of a reform to the election of a Socialist councillor or deputy, to the appointment of a Socialist mayor or minister, was essentially the same as every other. Jaurès clearly saw the republican state as a potentially neutral force, arbitrating impartially between the different classes and collective interests.[23]

This position is not without its logic and its merits. It accepted the indivisible nature of republican politics and the implicit responsibilities that came with participation in them. It valued most highly the opportunities for political education and democratic training that republican institutions and the republican ethos bestowed upon the working class. It placed the highest value on the free exchange of human reason and reflected an unswerving faith in the immanence of social justice. But it also neglected another aspect of French history as deeply-rooted in the popular conscience as was the affection for the Republic mentioned above. That aspect was the French revolutionary tradition and the almost instinctive awareness, on the part of the Socialist militant, of the reality of class struggle. But perhaps its greatest weakness as a political line throughout the Third Republic was that, in 1905, Jaurès himself decided to abandon it. There is no doubt that what Jaurès agreed to on accepting the terms of Socialist unity was the repudiation of the 'linear' republicanism for which he had pleaded so eloquently over the preceding seven years. At the level of official party texts, the SFIO of 1905 was, without the slightest equivocation, a 'revolutionary' party.[24] However many reservations Jaurès may have had about the word 'revolutionary', he did subscribe, sincerely and steadfastly, to the notion that the final transition towards the social Republic would have to involve some qualitative (possibly violent) rupture.[25]

Despite Jaurès's eventual rejection of his own logic, that logic refused to lie down and die. It was taken up again by his contemporaries, Millerand, Viviani and Briand, all of whom were destined for rich ministerial careers. It was the line adopted throughout the 1920s by men like Pierre Renaudel and Joseph Paul-Boncour on the right of the SFIO. But so complete had been the disavowal of these principles in 1905, that all these individuals, by espousing them, merely succeeded in talking themselves out of the party. After 1905, at least at the level of official ideology, there was simply no place for such notions within the unified party.

Why did Jaurès abandon the apparently coherent 'linear' line on the Republic in favour of an attempt to synthesise it with the other, more 'dialectical' one? The reasons are many and complex: internationalist discipline, intense desire for unity, recognition of the deep-rooted nature of the revolutionary tradition, disillusionment with the Millerand experiment, the need to move on from these ideological squabbles to more practical matters (in particular the struggle against war). But I suspect that his decision was facilitated by his conviction that in the ideas of Edouard Vaillant was to be found a way of fostering that synthesis, if not at the level of ideology, then at least at the level of praxis.

Vaillant's was the third line on the Republic. It was different not only from that of Jaurès, but also (and this is less widely realised) from that of Guesde. With Socialist unity, it did receive the blessing of Jaurès, but it was never to meet with the approval of Guesde. Vaillant considered the republican form (even under bourgeois hegemony) to be the 'indispensable principal condition for the conquest of all our rights',[26] the most precious result of the entire revolutionary tradition. In the very speech which helped topple Prime Minister Dupuy and thus generate the Millerand 'crisis' in June 1899, he stated that the bourgeois Republic contained within it 'the preliminary state of the social Republic'.[27] For Vaillant, republican freedoms and rights were neither bourgeois nor proletarian: they were fundamental *human* rights and they constituted the *sine qua non* for the transition to the social Republic. Without this vital training in the use of political freedoms offered by the bourgeois Republic, the social Republic was, in his view, not only beyond the reach of the proletariat but also premature, and to that extent, even undesirable. He was at one with Jaurès in seeing the Republic as, first and foremost, a 'great act of confidence'.

But the practice of republicanism also involved political risks, and it was at the level of the tactical use of republican institutions that the basic difference between Jaurès and Vaillant came into play. Vaillant believed that it was precisely because those institutions were so precious to the party that the dividing line between the bourgeois Republic and the social Republic should be kept crystal clear. That all-important frontier was less institutional than ideological: for the bourgeois, republican liberty allowed the individual to pursue his own private interests, in contradistinction to (and, if necessary, in opposition to) those of the collectivity; for the socialist, that same liberty allowed the individual to fulfil himself through conscious harmonisation of individual and collective interests. For the bourgeoisie, republican democracy meant the imposition of the wishes of the majority through the delegation of power, representative government and the rule of elites. For the Socialists, it meant a quest for consensus, the popular 'general will' through a process of mass participation in direct democracy.[28] The fundamental antagonism between these two approaches needed, in Vaillant's view, to be fully understood and constantly underscored.

It was precisely because of the importance he attached to the bourgeois Republic that Vaillant felt the need to keep that distinction clear. For the Socialists were not only the sole genuine descendants of the nineteenth-century republican tradition, but also the only true ascendants of the ultimate republican ideal. 'We are', he said in 1908, 'republicans such as are not to be found in the other parties calling themselves republican, but which, not being Socialist, cannot desire the fulfilment of the Republic.'[29] Never did Vaillant suggest (even less believe) that reformism and parliamentarism might be harmful to the social movement. Never did he imply that there might be some danger (either through co-optation or disillusionment) in utilising to the full the institutions of the Republic. On the contrary, he saw this as an unparalleled opportunity for political education: 'in the past, it was the ruling-class which imposed a government on the country; today the government is chosen by the people. They still make mistakes and choose wrongly very often, but less and less so as their political education progresses as a result of those very mistakes.'[30]

For Vaillant, therefore, there was not the vestige of a doubt: when the Republic was in danger, it had to be defended. He declared unequivocally, during the vital debate with Jaurès in Amsterdam in 1904, not only that he and his friends were 'ready to sacrifice their life . . . to save and defend [the Republic]', but also that they continued to see in republican institutions, 'the essential and indispensable framework' for social emancipation.[31] On this, he was at one with Jaurès. The difficulty arose over the political price the two men felt it was necessary to pay to achieve this objective. Jaurès, by openly and unconditionally supporting the Waldeck-Rousseau government or the Bloc des Gauches, by concluding political alliances with representatives of the bourgeoisie, had blurred that all-important dividing line between bourgeois and socialist republicanism. And for that alone, Vaillant was prepared to break dramatically with him for he believed that such a price tag was unnecessarily high. There was simply no need, he reiterated on every occasion, to commit the party to anything, to sign formal agreements or to contract alliances. Republican defence, he insisted, would be conducted all the more successfully by the socialists if it were done 'without commitments, without lasting attachments, in total freedom and independence'.[32] Moreover, if the campaign for republican defence were organised by a unified Socialist party, it would be infinitely more effective than if it were the work of only one half of a weak and divided movement. What he reproached Jaurès with was having engaged battle 'in confusing and disastrous conditions', whereas, he claimed, 'the victory of the Republic and of socialism was guaranteed on the one condition that the struggle . . . remained, visibly and integrally, the struggle for the Republic, the working class and socialism.'[33]

It is beyond dispute that the line eventually enshrined in the Declaration of Socialist Unity in 1905 was this Vaillantist line. Uninterrupted pursuit of republican progress and reforms went hand in hand with an almost pathological fear of 'ministerialism'. The almost obsessive repetition, in the party's official documents, of the 'revolutionary' mission of socialism was similarly a reflection of this vital tactical necessity of maintaining a clear distinction between the two visions of republicanism.

But there were, alas, two problems with this line, and they were to grow more and more acute with the years. The first was that it strikes such a fine balance between the linear and the dialectical interpretations of the Republic that it was devilishly difficult to implement under almost any circumstances. The second was that it was, to some extent if not wholly, predicted upon the belief that the revolutionary apocalypse would precede the advent of a socialist parliamentary majority. Léon Blum was the man who had to cope with these two problems, many years later.

In anticipation of those problems, Blum had elaborated, in the early 1920s, his celebrated distinction between conquest of power, exercise of power and support without participation. On close examination, this is merely a revival, through juxtaposition, of the arguments of Guesde (conquest), Jaurès (exercise) and Vaillant (support without participation). It is instructive to consider the arguments used by Blum in his defence of these notions. At the Tours Congress, Blum's speech was constructed around the two main axes formulated by Vaillant and accepted by Jaurès in 1905: unfailing defence of the Republic and its political culture, but rejection of ministerialism in the name of class struggle and the revolutionary objective of the party. But the ideological justification for this dual articulation (which Blum used throughout the 1920s and 1930s) was similarly informed by the debates of the earlier period. First, that a unified socialist party could be of more assistance to a progressive republican government as a united outsider than as a divided insider. Second, he constantly stressed the necessity of maintaining intact the ideological dividing line between radicals and socialists. Third, he argued that this stance was essentially motivated by political tactics rather than by ideological principle.[34]

On different occasions, Blum also felt the necessity of providing an ideological justification for the notion of exercise of power. To do this, he returned to the speeches of his master, Jaurès, and argued that ministerialism was the logical consequence of a linear process of which electoral and parliamentary participation were but earlier manifestations. He also presented ministerialism (as Jaurès had done) as being likely to accelerate the process of progressive reforms within the bourgeois Republic.[35] To a British mind, this looks less like dialectical wizardry and more like trying to have one's cake and eat it. It is hardly surprising that it failed to work.

To complete our survey of the republican options taken out by the French Left in the twentieth century, there remains the line adopted by the PCF after May 1934, in the period which Brower has characterised as the 'new Jacobinism'. It would be foolhardly to attempt to characterise the bases of that line in a few sentences. It seems, however, that Maurice Thorez summed it up nicely at the Communist Party Congress in 1936. The PCF, he argued, by rallying to the defence of the Republic but refusing to participate in government, had 'avoided the dual error of Jaurès and Guesde at the time of the Dreyfus Affair'. Jaurès, he explained, 'had jumped on the bandwagon of the democratic petty bourgeoisie, and had

lost sight of the specific interests of the working class and of the independence of his party' while Guesde, 'with his lack of tactical subtlety, had
somewhat lost contact with a struggle which had mobilised considerable
sections of the popular masses'.[36] But in order to legitimise this case,
Thorez chose not to cite its genuine (French) author (Vaillant being out of
favour with Communists because of his position in 1914). Instead, he
attributed the source of this tactical wisdom to the fertile mind of a
bicephalous Soviet thinker called Lenin-Stalin.

The republican dilemma survived the collapse of the Third Republic,
and even survived Vichy. In 1947, Léon Blum addressed the issue of
conquest/exercise of power before the students of his *alma mater* in the
rue d'Ulm. Referring to the ambiguous and contradictory tradition which
had asked the former Prime Minister why he had agreed to take office in
impossible task facing any government of the Left, he recalled a conversa-
tion he had had several years previously with Ramsay MacDonald. Blum
had asked for former Prime Minister why he had agreed to take office in
1924 when the Labour Party had only a minority in the House of
Commons, adding: 'surely you knew that such a government is not viable?'
MacDonald had replied: 'yes I knew that, but I considered it necessary . . .
to smash the prejudice of aristocratic government'. In response to Blum's
question, he explained that what he meant by that was that 'the great mass
of English people, including the workers, [believe] that only one social
class is worthy of the mission of governing Great Britain. I therefore took
office in order to prove that when power slipped out of the hands of the
ruling class . . . the earth would not suddenly open up.' to which Blum
replied: 'do you realise that, with us, the problem is exactly the reverse?
You say: we must take office in order to show the country that when we
are in government nothing will change. For us, on the other hand, the
problem is to show that everything will change.'[37]

And he went on to enumerate all the arguments that must be deployed
in France in order to counter charges that the Socialists in power are either
traitors to the Revolution or traitors to the Republic. The contradictions
spawned in the period 1898-1905 have still found no satisfactory solution.
A good case could be made for arguing, at the time of writing, that for
want of such a solution the government of François Mitterrand is being
seen increasingly as a traitor to the Revolution *and* the Republic. Perhaps
it is time to bury the ideology of the past.

Notes

1   The 'Declaration of Socialist Unity' which formed the basis, in 1905 for the
     creation of the SFIO stated (article 1): 'The Socialist Party is a class party

whose aim is the socialisation of the means of production and exchange, that is to say the transformation of capitalist society into collectivist and communist society [. . .] the Socialist Party, while pursuing the enactment of immediate reforms demanded by the working class, is not a reformist party, but a party of class struggle and revolution.' — *Parti Socialiste: ler et 2e Congrès nationaux*, compte rendu analytique (Paris,n.d.), pp. 13-14. In the introduction to the Socialist Party's 'Socialist Project' of 1980, we read: 'our wish is to establish as precise and concrete a method as possible for moving from one economic, social, cultural and hence political system to another, from the capitalist system to a socialist society in France. . . We situate this project within the logic of revolutionary rupture. . . *Projet Socialiste pour la France des années 80*, Paris, 1981, p. 10.

2   Jean Jaurès, *L'Esprit du Socialisme*, Paris, Gauthier, 1964, pp. 56-7.

3   Karl Marx, 'The Class Struggles in France: 1848-1850', in *Surveys from Exile*, Harmondsworth, Penguin, 1973, p. 43.

4   Marx had already hinted at this in the final section of the 'Eighteenth Brumaire of Louis Bonaparte', ibid, p. 238. He stated it most explicitly in his letter to Kugelmann of 12 April 1871 and in *The Civil War in France*, 1871. It was repeated in the Preface to the 1872 German edition of the *Communist Manifesto*. This rectification is, however, the subject of ongoing debate in Marxist circles and it is by no means clear that Marx himself realised the implications of his own thought.

5   'I do not claim that the Republic, simply because it is the Republic, is a principle of progress. If democracy, even republican democracy, were not constantly kept on the alert and urged on by the class action of the proletariat, it would remain stagnant.' *Sixième Congrès Socialiste International tenu à Amsterdam*, compte rendu analytique, Bruxelles, 1904, p. 180.

6   In April 1898 at the height of the Dreyfus agitation the *Conseil National* of the *Parti Ouvrier Français* (Guesdist) called on the workers to value 'the great republican tradition' as 'this essential instrument of your emancipation', *Le Réveil du Nord*, 16 April 1898. Between 1893 and 1898, the Guesdists seemed to have adopted the 'linear' line in its entirety. See, on this question, Claude Willard, *Les Guesdistes*, Paris, Editions Sociales, 1965, p. 187.

7   The man who probably came nearest was Jaurès in his debate with Guesde at Lille in 1900 published under the title *Les Deux Méthodes*. See text in Jean-Jacques Fiechter, *Le Socialisme français de l'Affaire Dreyfus à la Grande Guerre*, Geneva, Droz, 1965, pp. 231-58.

8   During the Boulanger crisis, Guesde had written: 'the structure of power is irrelevant; it all depends on who wields it', *Le Cri du Peuple*, 24 April 1888. For Guesde's argument that the French Republic was no better for the workers than the German Reich, see 'Un Congrès modèle' in *Le Petit Sou*, 19 September 1900. Jaurès considered the content of that article to be so scandalous that he published it himself in *La Petite République*, 22 September 1900. This same argument was also used by Bebel at Amsterdam in 1904 when he argued that German workers had in fact had a far better deal from the Reich than the French workers had had from the Republic (*Sixième Congrès Socialiste International*, op cit., pp. 85-7 and 151-2). Jaurès, at Amsterdam, insisted that the difference was that the French workers had won their rights through struggle, whereas the Germans had had theirs handed down from on high. Here, the Guesdists, in siding with the Germans, were running into another hopeless contradiction since they too had always argued that the only 'valid' reforms were those won through struggle.

9   Willard, op. cit., pp. 181-97 and 553-6. See also Charles Rappoport, *Jean Jaurès, l'homme, le penseur, le socialiste*, Paris, Emancipation, 1915, pp. 352-72.

10   *Sixième Congrès Socialiste International*, op cit., p. 201.

11   Jules Guesde, *Le Socialisme au Jour le Jour*, Paris, Giard, 1899, p. 310.

12   *6ᵉ Congrès national du Parti ouvrier*, tenu à Roanne du mardi 26 septembre au dimanche 1 octobre 1882, sd, s.l., p. 19.

13   Fiechter, op. cit., p. 255.

14   Jules Guesde and Paul Lafargue, *Le Programme du Parti ouvier, son histoire, ses considérants, ses articles*, Paris, s.d. (1883), pp. 85-6.

15   *Congrès général des organisations socialistes français*, compte rendu sténographique, Paris, 1900, p. 186 (Guesde) and p. 114 (Lafargue). It is worth noting that they added that a more likely outcome would be that the workers would be so disgusted and alienated by the Republic that they would rush to 'le premier sabre venu' (ibid., pp. 184-6). In light of events from 1936 to 1940, this may well have been prophetic.

16   *Sixième Congrès International*, op. cit., p. 201.

17   Fiechter, op. cit., p. 254.

18   *XVIIIᵉ Congrès national du Parti Socialiste*, Paris, 1921, pp. 189-91 and Annie Kriegel, *Le Congrès de Tours*, Paris, Julliard, 1964, pp. 56-7. It is perhaps significant that Frossard, in his speech at Tours, put forward very different arguments in favour of the Third International. Although he pointed to the failure of the pre-1914 tactics as a reason for joining the Comintern, he nevertheless glorified the French republican tradition, which he presented as an unbroken chain from Babeuf to Jaurès and Vaillant. Not surprisingly, Frossard lasted only three years in the PCF.

19   Souvarine text in *Bulletin Communiste*, 1 (1 janvier 1921) — cited in Nicole Racine and Louis Bodin: *Le Parti communiste français pendant l'entre-deux-guerres*, Paris, Colin, 1972, pp. 28-9. The manifesto 'A la France ouvière et socialiste' in A. Zévaès, *Le Socialisme en France depuis 1871*, Paris, Charpentier, 1908, pp. 311-13.

20   See Nathanael Greene, *Crisis and Decline. The French Socialist Party in the Popular Front Era*, Ithaca, Cornell U.P., 1969, pp. 48-9 and 56-9; Jean Rabaut: *Tout est Possible: Les 'Gauchistes' français, 1929-1944*, Paris, Denoël, 1974.

21   Maurice Agulhon: *La République au Village*, Paris, Plon, 1970.

22   See, above all, Harvey Goldberg, *The Life of Jean Jaurès*, Madison, University of Wisconsin Press, 1962.

23   Goldberg, op. cit., p. 313.

24   See note 1.

25   See in particular his speech to the Congress of Toulouse in 1908, in which he specifically denied that the arrival of a majority in the Chamber of Deputies would be sufficient to help inaugurate the new Socialist order: 'it is possible that at some stage in this on-going process, in a crisis brought on by the resistance or the criminal stupidity of the bourgeoisie, the proletariat will be called upon to resort to violent insurrection; but we are not so childish as to imagine that an insurrection would suffice to set up and organise the new regime. On the morrow of the insurrection, the capitalist order would still persist and the proletariat, apparently victorious, would be impotent to use and build on its victory if it had not already been prepared to make use of it through the development of all sorts of institutions [of its own]. *Parti Socialiste: 5ᵉ Congrès national tenu à Toulouse*, compte rendu sténographique, s.l., s.d., pp. 313-14.

26   See Jolyon Howorth, *Edouard Vaillant: la création de l'unité socialiste en France*, Paris, Edi/Syros, 1982 (Troisième Partie, 'République et Révolution').

27   *Journal Officiel*, Chambre — Débats, 12 June 1899, p. 1641.

28   'We believe that humanity will go on developing, that there is no limit to this infinite development and that . . . the time will come when, as a result of the concordance between each individual volition and the general development,

a communist regime will establish itself in which individual liberty will be total at the same time as the resurgence of the collective energies of humanity will be boundless' *Journal Officiel*, Chambre — Débats, 10 February 1894, p. 179. See also ibid, Chambre — Annexes, No. 1748, 23 January 1898, p. 24.

29   *Parti Socialiste: 5ᵉ Congrès national*, op cit., p. 159.

30   Vaillant, 'Législation directe' in *Le Petit Sou*, 16 November 1900.

31   *Sixième Congrès International*, op. cit., pp. 104-5.

32   Ibid, p. 104.

33   Edouard Vaillant, 'Œuvre de salut et d'honneur socialiste', *Almanach de la Question sociale*, 1900, p. 18.

34   Léon Blum, *Œuvre*, 3 Part 1 (1914-1928), Paris, Albin Michel, 1972, p. 387. See also Joel Colton, *Léon Blum, Humanist in Politics*, New York, Knopf, 1966, p. 70. One should also note that the necessity of preserving this demarcation line was the motivation behind much communist propaganda during the 'class against class' years. See André Ferrat, 'Nouvelle période, nouvelle tactique', *Cahiers du Bolchevisme*, janvier-février 1929, pp. 18-20.

35   Léon Blum and Paul Faure: *Le Parti socialiste et la participation ministérielle*, Paris, 1926. For a discussion of Blum's thoughts on this, see Colton, op. cit., pp. 71 ff. and Jean Lacouture, *Léon Blum*, Paris, Seuil, 1977, p. 206.

36   Maurice Thorez 'Rapport au VIIIᵉ Congrès du PCF', in *Une Politique de Grandeur Française*, Paris, Editions Sociales, 1945, p. 87.

37   Léon Blum, 'Exercise et Conquête du Pouvoir', *La Revue Socialiste*, 15, novembre 1947, pp. 389-390.

2 Party practice and the Jaurésian vision: the SFIO (1905-1914)*

MADELEINE REBÉRIOUX
University of Paris

The period I wish to consider constitutes the immediate sequel to the years that were dominated by the Millerand Affair and by the political debates between Jaurès, Guesde and Vaillant. My analysis will concentrate on the nine years between socialist unity and the Great War, and will address the issue of the practice of the SFIO in general and the vision of Jean Jaurès in particular.

Amazingly, very little is actually known about these years. There is a dearth of published work on this period, both in France and abroad. There are three reasons for this and they are worth pondering over. The first is that Socialist unity in France did not produce that euphoric upturn in party fortunes anticipated by those members most devoted to the cause of unity. Not until the very eve of World War I did the SFIO begin to take off, both in terms of members and in terms of electoral support. And even then the results were hardly spectacular. Between 1906, when the dust finally began to settle on the process of unification, and 1914, membership figures only doubled, rising from 44,000 to 90,000. At the same time, electoral support grew by about 60 per cent, from around 880,000 in 1906 to 1,400,000 in 1914.[1] The massive surge of support expected as a result of unification simply did not appear.

The second reason why this period is so little known is that our vision of the infant party has been deeply coloured by the tragedy of 1914. August 1914 ruled out any attempt to 'glorify' the years prior to the war, and seemed to demand a quasi-teleological approach to the early history of the Socialist Party. Historians tended to study these years in order to explain the failure of the party's peace crusade and to comment on its eventual acceptance of 'Union Sacrée.[2] It is far from certain that this teleological approach is the best way to study a new-born organism. It is certainly not the only way, and it clearly inhibits any genuine autonomy of historical approach. The third reason is that when in 1971 the new Socialist Party came into being at Epinay, the modest efforts it made to

* Translated and edited by Jolyon Howorth

discover some historical roots, in order — quite legitimately — to differen-
tiate itself from the Communist Party, tended to stress the Léon Blum
tradition of 1919-20, rather than the years of unity prior to 1914. The
problem at this level is compounded by the fact that, from around 1906
until 1914, Blum abandoned his active commitment and played absolutely
no role whatsoever in the SFIO. There were, therefore, various tempta-
tions to eschew the study of the party's infancy and to give priority to the
period which began with the emergence of Léon Blum as a major political
leader.

Our ignorance of these years nevertheless constitutes an enormous
obstacle to any real understanding of French socialism. It leads, in particular, to a gross underestimation of the difficulties many socialists were to
experience when they finally found themselves in power. Indeed, from
1905 onwards, to a very large extent as a reaction against Millerandism,
the prospect of governmental responsibility was officially ruled out, as
was any coalition with other parties, particularly the Radical Party. This
was called '*Bloc des Gauches* phobia' and it was kept very much alive by
the vigilance of Guesde and his friends, by Vaillant in a more restrained
fashion, and by the small band of Allemanists who, despite their disappear-
ance as a national political force, nevertheless maintained a public presence
through a number of individuals of national stature. These various groups
constantly reiterated the impossibility of ever going back to the practice
of political agreements with the radicals.

Since the party had little hope of electoral victory on its own, and since
barricades and armed insurrection were implicitly excluded (despite occasional words of bravado from Guesde or Lafargue) the Socialist Party's
prospects became somewhat unreal. In the absence of any immediate
governmental ambition, all that remained was to 'propagandise',[3] to
'develop the idea' (as both anarchists and socialists used to say) and to
concentrate on the education of the electorate. This idea that the voters
had to be educated and that through this process of education the party
would eventually win a parliamentary majority, was the driving force
behind party practice in these years, even if 'D-Day' was acknowledged
to be far ahead in the distant future. This pre-eminent concept stamped
an entire generation of activists with its mark. Socialist unity, born of the
aspirations of the rank and file, and of the political will of Jaurès and
Vaillant, may not have attracted the very young (for reasons I shall return
to) but it did allow for the promotion of new, younger party officials.
One has only to consider the names of the federal secretaries in 1905 and
those in 1914 to appreciate the far-reaching turnover of personnel which
took place in these years. One has only to study the names of the delegates

to the national congresses to comprehend the wholesale renewal of the rank and file activists. There is, of course, a feeling that it was always Jaurès, Guesde and Vaillant who delivered the major speeches, but the emergence of a new generation of activists was a phenomenon of profound significance. The recent new edition of the Congress of Tours[4] has shown that, despite the bloodletting of the war, which claimed many of them for ever, large numbers of those who came to socialism in the years after unity were still very much in evidence in 1920. Habits were formed in those early years. The rank and file was trained in a certain mould. Those habits and that mould were to last for a very long time and were to leave their stamp indelibly on the party's practice, which is why it is so important to study these years, if only as a guide to understanding what happened later.

Out of this background emerged the charismatic figure whose un-disputed leadership was finally accepted not only by the party's supporters but also – and this was much more difficult for him to secure – by the active rank and file. Jaurès's socialist vision went far beyond the horizons of his comrades, including those of his closest friends, who made up what was known as the 'Jaurès tendency'. Jaurès had wanted unity (even if it looked as though it were in fact imposed upon him) and little by little he came to be its major political beneficiary. Hence the title of this chapter and its two constituent parts.

Approaches to the study of the SFIO (1905-1914)

Before dealing with specific aspects of the SFIO's practice, I should like to make three suggestions about possible lines of approach. First, methodology: at what level should the study of such a party be situated? To remain focused on the speeches of the leaders is to miss a good deal. I see four possible levels, but there are certainly others. To begin with, we need to study the functional operation of the party at the topmost national level – the debates, modes of propaganda and political campaigns – all within the institutional framework of the statutes of 1905, the veritable Charter of the SFIO, the political compromise which made unity possible. Secondly, we should analyse the federal (or departmental) life of the party. This is all the more important in France in that the 1905 statutes consecrated the enormous diversity of the departmental federa-tions. These federations had their own statutes, they selected their own electoral candidates and enjoyed considerable autonomy. So strong was this autonomy that even proposals (such as those regularly formulated by the Guesdists) for training regional delegates to act as links between the departmental federations and the national hierarchy were rejected with predictable regularity.

The third level at which to study the party is that of the groups and tendencies. The distinction is important. The tendencies (*tendances*) were officially instituted in the SFIO in 1907, reflecting both the continued existence of the 'old' parties and the recent emergence of new problems. They began to disappear, however, by 1912. They were 'officially instituted' in the sense that they were represented on the permanent administrative commission[5] in proportion to their voting strength in the key debates at party congresses. The groups are quite different. Pressure groups in one sense, these were not officially recognised by the party, but their impact was nonetheless very real. There were the groups of 'friends' . . . of Jaurès, or of Guesde. There was the group of *normaliens*[6] around Robert Hertz, a sociologist later to be killed in World War I. Hertz's group, the *groupe d'études sociales*, was to play a vital, though marginal, role in the life and especially the thought of the party between 1908 and 1914. The fourth level of study is that of the individual, grass-roots militants.

Whichever way one approaches it, however, the fact remains that the practice of the party was conditioned by the phenomenon analysed elsewhere in this volume by Jolyon Howorth:[7] that the unified party, mainly as a result of the political debate which gave rise to unity had become an organisation perhaps most easily defined negatively – non-social-democratic. This is the second potentially fruitful line of approach. The cardinal feature of the SFIO was that it was not a social-democratic party. The political space occupied in central and Western Europe by social-democratic parties was seen by French socialists as alien territory. They were also totally opposed to the idea of the 'vanguard party', a function fulfilled within the Second International by the SPD. This 'non-social-democratic' party, the SFIO, was deeply rooted in the French republican tradition. Little by little, it came to accept the principle of the political institutions emanating from that republican tradition. This can be seen at three levels between 1905 and 1914. First, there was the rapid marginalisation of those who liked to stress the dangers – essential or substantial, in the etymological sense – of parliamentary activity – men like Paul Lafargue, or Hubert Lagardelle and his socialist workers' group, or the Allemanists. Lafargue was soon eclipsed. He was in any event isolated politically, however fascinating he may have been as an individual. As for Lagardelle, his socialist worker group was collapsing by 1908 and was burnt out by 1910, at least with respect to its opposition to parliamentary activity. The Allemanists by this time were down to a handful of politically active individuals.

The second level at which one can recognise the extent to which political institutions had ceased to be an issue is the total absence of any proposals for new institutions under socialism. In our period there were masses of texts of a quasi-utopian nature (political essays or even political 'codes'[8]) in which the vision of the future was clearly spelled out; yet nowhere was there the slightest reflection on the political institutions of the future. Future society was to be different in terms of economics and industry, of daily life and production. But at the level of politics, there appeared to be consensus with the status quo. This is not to say that republican institutions were not subject to certain criticisms, especially with regard to the way they operated, but their essence was beyond discussion.

The third level that revealed the emergence of political institutions was the incorporation of the parliamentary group into the heart of the party. Despite the statutory precautions taken in 1905,[9] the parliamentary group played an increasingly important role in the party, becoming in one sense its principal driving force. These three phenomena underscore the degree of consensus for acceptance of republican institutions that emerged within the SFIO.

At the same time, and this is the third approach, owing in part at least to the considerable measure of autonomy enjoyed by the departmental federations, the republican references displayed by the SFIO were of a particular type: Girondin and Proudhonian rather than Jacobin and *conventionnel*. Moreover, by giving priority to the local section as the basic unit of the party (followed closely by the departmental federation), and by eliminating any form of collective membership,[10] the SFIO saw itself much more as a citizens' party than as a proletarians' party. This feature was reinforced by the absence of discussion within the party of matters connected with industrial organisation or labour struggle. Furthermore, the notion of 'citizens' party' was highlighted by the fact that individual or personal links between the world of politics and the world of organised labour were minimal. They were not unknown. Many syndicalists who were also members of the SFIO made important contributions when issues affecting the working class were being discussed.[11] But in general socialists who were also syndicalists tended to keep the two worlds separate. Personal links between the two worlds were few in number, skin-deep and uncommunicative. Any communication between socialists and syndicalists tended to go on outside the party. This was because the CGT, overtly ever since socialist unity, but in reality since the Millerand affair, was at war with the SFIO. The CGT's socialism was quite different from that of the party and while, at one level, this conflict created monumental problems for the SFIO, an another level it enhanced its function as a citizens' party by foreclosing the option of transition towards a proletarians' party.

The political practice of the SFIO between 1905 and 1914 therefore emerges from the features I have just outlined. One obvious element is the central role attributed to the electoral process. This was at the heart of most discussion at both national and departmental congresses. It is worth commenting on only to the extent to which it consigned almost to oblivion two groups of individuals who had the misfortune not to be citizens: women and young people under the age of twenty-one. If need be, their energies could be mobilised to stick up posters but there seemed little reason to mobilise their intelligence, or even to solicit their opinion, in a party whose main function was to gain power through catching votes. To be without a vote was to be a non-citizen. The party was a party of men, of adult men over the age of twenty-one, and this can be seen in every aspect of the party's organisational existence.

But the citizens urgently needed training and education; consequently the basic activity of the party lay in this area. To propagate 'the idea' was the main function of the party, the one which, sooner or later, would enable it to scale the electoral ladder, to become the majority party, and, eventually, to seize power. Socialist education demanded a sustained effort. It was the only activity for which the party, with its meager resources, was prepared to make a genuine sacrifice. The director of the SFIO publishing house was a full-time paid official. (He did very little work, but he did get paid!) There were also paid delegates for the organisation of progaganda. (They, on the contrary, worked themselves to the bone!) With the exception of Louis Dubreuilh, the general secretary, these were the only real permanent officers of the party.

And yet, as the years passed by, the traditional forms of propaganda required critical reappraisal. Was the spoken word still the most efficient means of getting the message across? Attendances at public meetings were falling off; what could be done? The party publishing house distributed all the paraphernalia of revolutionary ritual: rosettes and badges, songs, postcards — in short, all the essential elements for an understanding of socialist culture. Soon there were to be socialist recordings and, after 1912, socialist cinema. But what about reading matter, written texts, education by the book? They appear to have been rather neglected. Ten-cent pamphlets and almanacs sold far better than 200- or 250-page books. But more serious was the fact that party brochures were few in number and the collection grew at a snail's pace – no more than three or four new pamphlets per year. And all the efforts of Jean Longuet to set up a publications sub-committee to print the selected works of Marx came to nothing. The sub-committee met for a year (1909-10) and then fizzled out. Such a modest project for such failure! Yet it was the same story with the Socialist School, founded in 1909, which hobbled along until 1914 with virtually no impact whatsoever.[12] The net result was that propaganda, which everyone recognised as a vital element, gradually became a serious problem, except at election time. The most perceptive party leaders were acutely aware of this, but were unable to find a solution.

An awareness of these defects gradually gave rise to the third aspect of party practice I should like to discuss. Questions about how to prepare the party for power – one day – other than via the limited and increasingly problematic vehicle of propaganda, produced the notion of 'mass action'. The notion that mass action could be the answer to the problem of training, the belief that activists could train themselves through activism, through struggle, led to an effort to mobilise the entire party, especially among the social classes it hoped to influence. Meetings, petitions and mass demonstrations became the new forms of a new party practice which took shape after 1910 with the campaign of solidarity for the striking railwaymen. The mass campaign in 1911-12 over the cost of living, and above all the campaign against the three-year military service law in 1913 were extremely important manifestations of this new strategy. This transformation was promoted by a handful of exceptional individuals, foremost among whom, in my opinion, was Jean Jaurès.

The Jaurésian vision

Today, Jean Jaurès is relatively well known. The *Société d'etudes jaurésiennes* has been hard at work for twenty years.[13] There is every reason to believe that Jaurès's own vision went way beyond his party's, while nevertheless remaining an intrinsic part of it. I wish to discuss three aspects of that vision which seem to me to be of fundamental importance.

The first is his perception of socialism as an essential force for change in the world. For Jaurès, the political function of socialism within the framework of republican institutions was never in any doubt, but it underwent a major reappraisal in his mind as a result of the Millerand affair. The beauty of Jaurès was that he never ceased to learn – which is more than can be said for Jules Guesde. Despite the fact that Jaurès was entirely at home in the world of republican institutions, they never represented for him the be-all and end-all of socialism. He was a republican, and he was devoutly attached to republican institutions. But there was also a specifically Jaurésian vision of socialism within the Republic.

For him, socialism in the Republic implied that the working class had a vanguard role to play in French society, and that if the working class ever wished to come to power, it would have to engage itself – explicitly and openly – in the politics of class alliances. The entire question of class alliances lies at the heart of the Jaurésian vision of the working class as the basic motive force behind the Socialist movement. One aspect of Jaurès's political originality is the fact that he was the only French Socialist before 1914 who attempted to study the meaning of class alliances. It is a commonplace to say that within the SFIO everybody agreed that the working class was the driving force of socialism. But nobody else really thought about what was involved in class alliances and in practice nobody, with the exception of Jaurès and Vaillant, ever really thought about what was *meant* by the statement that the working class was the motor of socialism.

For Jaurès, from 1905 onwards, the concept implied full recognition of the function of the CGT and of its importance in French social life. This vision is diametrically opposed to the Guesdist conception of syndicalism as little more than the corporatist defence of workers' material interests. For Jaurès, there was no ranking as between the CGT and the SFIO. He believed that the strength of French syndicalism derived precisely from the fact that the CGT was socialist in its objective (the abolition of salaried labour) and in its basic method (the organisation of the world of labour for a confrontation with capitalism) and in its potential for education through action. For all these reasons, he regarded the CGT as socialist. As such, it was an integral part of the overall socialist project: the coming to power of socialism in France. This is where there is a fundamental difference between Jaurès and the vast majority of the pre-1914 SFIO. Although Jaurès succeeded in persuading the party to tolerate his views, there is little evidence that the SFIO as a whole subscribed to them.

For Jaurès, in any case, syndicalism represented the immediate, proletarian form of socialism, its class foundation, without which alliances with other social groups were meaningless. Those alliances he saw as essential and this belief permeated all his speeches on the subject both inside and outside the party. It is important to understand this peculiar Jaurésian contribution to the SFIO of his time, but also, in a broader framework, to the history of French socialism, as well as to what might one day become the socialism of the present in its widest sense.

The second element of the Jaurésian vision is the strengthening of the socialist project in preparation for ultimately coming to power. Far from happening with the ease and simplicity which, in the 1890s, seemed almost beyond question (for Jaurès and for everybody else), this project came up against new forms and structures of capitalist power, some of which Jaurès was quick to spot in the very way in which the Millerand experiment collapsed. His analysis of the deep-rooted reasons for this collapse helped him accept what Jolyon Howorth has called the 'rejection of his own logic'.[14] I disagree with that formulation. With Jaurès, the problem was constantly to make sense of new developments at a given moment in the history of humanity. Through Millerand, he understood that the transformations taking place under capitalism were in fact making the triumph of socialism more difficult and more complex, rather than easier and more manageable.

It would, of course, be wrong to imply that he saw, as clearly as we can see them today, the contradictions and consequences of the forms of transformation which capitalism was undergoing at the turn of the century. He remained quite unaware of most of them, but he did perceive some, and with immense clarity. He observed, among other things, towards the end of his life (and in a way which has profound relevance today) the cultural poverty and deprivation of those social groups in France which were nevertheless regarded as educated and 'cultivated'. This cultural poverty was, in his eyes, as great as or even greater than that afflicting the working class. This brings me to my third point: Jaurès's cultural vision.

The displacement of the political (in its narrowest sense) by the cultural (in its widest sense) is a novel feature of those pre-war years. Jaurès isolated two fundamental defects in French culture at the turn of the century. Firstly, a feature he had noticed all along, but which he came to see more and more clearly: unbridled individualism. He considered this to be the reverse side of what he saw as the positive features of capitalism: its daring and its spirit of initiative. On this, he was wholeheartedly in agreement with the group of socialist *normaliens* (with whom, on other issues, he disagreed totally). He saw the necessity for a remorseless ideological struggle against, not so much the Radical Party, which remained in his eyes an important political ally, but rather that aspect of radical culture which Clemenceau was by no means alone in epitomising: the cult of individualism. He yearned for a collectivist culture with which to replace it. But how?

The second vice which he saw spreading all around him, and which he had not noticed before about 1905, was the frivolousness of a certain Parisian society, its superficiality and its fragility, its blissful unawareness of the forces of barbarism which were mustering on the horizon and which, in their way, reflected the crisis of capitalism. And here he was at one, not with the *normaliens*, but with the thought of the young Jean-Richard Bloch who, in 1909, became secretary of the departmental federation of Vienne, a man tormented by the decadence of artistic life and the sclerosis of French society and social culture. In 1910, Bloch launched a fascinating little review called *L'Effort*, which he published in Poitiers and which aspired to promote, in his own words, a 'revolutionary civilisation'.[15] Like Bloch, Jaurès pleaded in favour of a fortification of cultural values, their reinsertion into working-class culture, the culture of 'the real France', many aspects of which were to be sought, where Jaurès was concerned, in the region of Occitania.

But this reinvigorated culture was not to be inward-looking, was not to be centred on France or even on Europe. In this respect, Jaurès was a true pioneer in France, the more so in that he had advanced considerably from the days when he too shared the widely held belief that outside of France and perhaps Europe, there was no real culture. It was between 1910 and 1914 that he parted company with his own certainties about the cultural superiority of France and began to discover other cultures: the splendours of Arabian culture, which he saw being desecrated in Morocco under the French occupation; the culture of Latin America, which he discovered during his long trip in 1911; the culture of the Far East and China, which he encountered during Sun Yat Sen's visit to Europe; the culture of Turkey, which he considered to be vital for the regeneration of Europe.[16] Was this just dreaming, a form of escapism? By no means.

This leads me to the third aspect of the Jaurésian vision: his intense desire to achieve, to accomplish something important and real. Perhaps, one day, this might mean government if that was necessary in order to achieve his ideal. But he had no illusions. Millerand had been the minister in 1899, not Jaurès. Millerand had taught him that socialism could lose its soul if it tried to accomplish too much too soon. Its aims could only be realised by a great, united party, solidly wedded by multiple organisational links to the working class, and associated with other social groups, meshed with the Second International, fully conscious of the new requirements of a complex, plural world. Only such a party could govern successfully. Jaurès had no time for idle formulae: exercise of power, conquest of power. Such concepts would have been meaningless to him, utterly devoid of interest. What mattered to him was to build up French socialism into a force sufficiently strong to assume, sooner or later, the responsibility of power. This implied a serious analysis of the evolution of the political situation, as well as the articulation of various different forms of political action.

These analyses led him to the recognition that French socialism was not ready in this period, that it would have to wait; but also that it would have to act upon the present in every conceivable way. Action meant the promotion of meaningful reforms, ones which would fortify the working class and give it the means to gain administrative experience, through co-operatives, through *syndicats* and various other economic and social institutions – to learn to be more than a mere front for refusal. The other aim of these reforms was, of course, to weaken the bonds of capitalist society by devising forms of production that would be harbingers of the new, future order: nationalisations, of course, which were advocated prior to 1914 not by the CGT but by the SFIO. And finally, his object was to prevent the victory of barbarism by winning the race against war, through the organisation of an entire panoply of inter-class activities, chief of which was to be the political mass strike, an invention, as he put it, of 'working-class genius'. On this issue he was in total harmony with Vaillant.

Such were the various elements of Jaurès's strategic vision. They were predicated on the availability of time. Alas, time was the one element which was not available, not for Jaurès, nor for French socialism nor for the human race. That is why, I believe, none of the subsequent warring factions of the French Left can claim for itself the totality of the Jaurésian legacy. But that is also the reason why his presence at the heart of the French Socialist movement in its widest sense must remain the object of knowledge and of historical reflection, and not merely an object of admiration or veneration.

Notes

N.B. Most of the following have been added by the translator as elements of explanation. Where the note is derived from Mme Rebérioux's text, this is indicated thus: (MR)

1   Because of the official system of vote-attribution, and because of the complex configuration of political allegiances, the figures for electoral support are very difficult to establish with precision in this period.
2   The 'Sacred Union' of all parties and political forces in France which, in August 1914, pledged an end to internal political struggle for the duration of the war.
3   This is a literal translation of *'propagandiser'*, the term used quite widely at the time.
4   *Le Congrès de Tours*, édition critique, J. Charles, J. Girault, J. L. Robert, D. Tartakowsky, C. Willard (eds.), Paris, Editions Sociales, 1980.
5   The *commission administrative permanente* was, as the title implies, the principal executive body in the SFIO. It comprised twenty-two members elected directly by the National Congress. Deputies were debarred from membership.
6   Former or current students of the Ecole Normale Supérieure of the rue d'Ulm.
7   See above, chapter 1 by J. Howorth.
8   The SFIO occasionally drafted 'Codes' (along the lines of the Napoleonic

Codes) for the organisation of the future society (MR).

9   Apart from being debarred from the *commission administrative permanente*, deputies were also prohibited from sitting as individuals on the National Council (*Conseil national*), although, under article 23 of the party statutes, they were entitled to collective representation on that body.

10   For example, *syndicats*, co-operatives or editorial collectives were debarred from collective membership of the SFIO. The only exception to this rule was the Fédération des Ardennes, which was regarded as a special case (MR).

11   As, for example, in 1910, when the socialist Luquet spoke up in defence of the CGT position on workers' retirement pensions despite his serious disagreements with the CGT on many other issues (MR).

12   This was not the case, however, with the 'Propaganda School', which was started in 1911, under the direction of Poisson, to teach the art of oral propaganda (MR).

13   The *Société d' études jaurésiennes* was founded in 1959 on the occasion of the centenary of Jaurès birth. It has published a quarterly journal, the *Bulletin de la Société d'études jaurésiennes* since 1960. Address: Gilles Candar (Secretary), 33, rue de Fresnes, 92160 ANTONY.

14   See above, chapter 1 by J. Howorth.

15   Jean-Richard Bloch was a friend of Romain Rolland, of Elie Faure and of Roger Martin du Gard and many others. He was a great novelist whose work has been, regrettably, entirely overlooked. (MR).

16   During the Balkan wars, he spoke out strongly in favour of maintaining Turkey as an integral part of Europe, as the gateway to and for the cultural riches of Arabia and the Middle East (MR).

3 The Popular Front*

JEAN-NOËL JEANNENEY

I am asked to go back in time and recall the Popular Front of 1936, and I must say that this is an exercise that we have all been rehearsing for the last year. This is especially true in France, a country thirsty for, not to say intoxicated with, history. From different sides of the political scene different pictures would emerge. So a person from the opposition would be told that after all the Popular Front did not last very long. A person from the Left could be told that 1936 was a great moment in history. For each group and tendency has its own history and that history is partly mythical; often the reality of events counts less than the idea that people have of them.

Also ideas about the past vary according to present circumstances. I am not going to delve into all these varied and changing views but we could consider simply the historical attitudes of the last Presidents of the Republic. Those of us who were aged twenty to thirty in the 1960s saw de Gaulle relating the sometimes unexpected events of his presidency to his own idea of his and his country's history. After 18 June 1940 everything acquired a retrospective significance, though not everyone accepted his interpretations. His successor Georges Pompidou also had a vision of French history in part contrasting with his political mentor's vision, for example in the matter of his irritation at current ideas about the Resistance which he wished, but did not quite dare, to sweep away. Then came Valery Giscard d'Estaing with a quite different view and a sense that 1974 represented a break with the past. (And since he was reading a biography of Louis XV, who knows what he foresaw for the coming era?) Finally we come to the present President of the Republic who chose to inaugurate his presidency with a series of ceremonies and speeches. He went to the Pantheon and placed roses at the foot of three tombs: of Victor Schoelcher as a symbol of emancipation from slavery; of Jean Jaurès as a symbol of ongoing socialist tradition and of Jean Moulin as a symbol of French resistance to invaders and occupiers. On the same day there was a little

* Translated and edited by Stuart Williams.

27

noticed exchange of speeches between François Mitterrand and Jacques Chirac, Mayor of Paris and one of the opposition leaders. Both of them indulged in the stylistic exercise of recalling the history of Paris and I was struck by the disparity of the histories. They quoted one name in common, that of Charles de Gaulle. The Mayor had Sainte Geneviève, Henri IV, Etienne Marcel of course, since he led the merchants' opposition to the national government. Chirac then skipped the intervening period and came to de Gaulle. François Mitterrand quoted at length the various revolutions as well as Victor Hugo, Jean Jaurès and Léon Blum. I think I am right that he referred to Blum, if he did not, he ought to have!

For it is clear that the Popular Front is the major precedent for what is happening now. Guy Mollet is not a hero of the Socialist pantheon even though there are groups within the party who remain faithful to him. The government of 1945 was important also, especially with reference to the nationalisations, but it was not purely left-wing. I could also mention the *Cartel des Gauches* of 1924-6 [1], which at the time represented an important renewal of left-wing thought but is not referred to now because the government had no socialists in it and the radicals who led it are not thought to belong to the left. So there remains the Popular Front as the last very significant advance in social progress, with Léon Blum, perhaps not the heavyweight that Jean Jaurès was, but nevertheless a figure of moral nobility and great intellect and someone to whom François Mitterrand often refers.

Some years ago he celebrated Blum's birth with an important speech at the *Mutualité*. Also Mitterrand's Prime Minister, Pierre Mauroy, if he was not a *faucon rouge*, was certainly involved in activities directed by Léo Lagrange, secretary of state in the Popular Front. Curiously enough the right wing also refer to Léon Blum, as someone who was 'reasonable'. Of course, the right will also argue that the Popular Front caused the 1940 defeat. It constantly re-enacts the Riom trial[2] at which the Vichy regime accused the 1936 leaders of causing the defeat of 1940. Recently an RPR backbencher, Gabriel Kaspereit, surprised the chamber by saying to the Prime Minister and his colleagues, 'Gentlemen, you should be silent. You were responsible for the defeat in 1940'. To which the Prime Minister replied that he was in short trousers at the time.

Many references to 1936 appear in the form of allusions, as when Jacques Delors, Finance Minister, spoke of a 'pause', referring to the pause of early 1937. One felt that in so doing he injected an emotional charge into the technical debate. On another occasion Pierre Mauroy referred to an '*embellie*' whereupon the *Monde* commentator wrote that a promise of a 'brief period of sunshine between two storms' was not very appealing.

But, as several readers at once pointed out, this was a quite specific allusion to Léon Blum's saying, in more or less these words, 'I did not often leave my office when I was Prime Minister, but when I saw those workers on their tandems with their matching pullovers, proving that the idea of leisure had awakened a kind of coquetry in them, I felt that I had let a *ray of sunshine* into their difficult and obscure lives'. The remark once made by Bracke-Desrousseaux, one of Blum's friends, is also regularly quoted, 'at last, at last the difficulties are beginning!' (I have also heard this attributed to the period of the *Cartel des Gauches*). Finally, with the problems of unemployment, inflation and confusion in the money market, you hear references to the Gnomes of Zurich replacing the *Cambistes* and the *Mur d'Argent* references heard in 1924 and 1936 — a modern version of a supposed international businessmen's plot against our currency. Of course the makers of these allusions can be deceiving themselves, like Louis Philippe: 'in February 1848 Louis Philippe had been misled by the deceptive light that the history of the past throws upon the present'.[3]

In the assessment that follows I shall have difficulty in offering the reader any new material, for paradoxically the 1970s have been less productive with regard to the Popular Front than the 1960s, which gave us the works of Annie Kriegel on the Communist Party and the unions and Antoine Prost on the CGT; Georges Lefranc, Ziebura and Colette Audry (who blamed Blum for not going far enough). In the 1970s, except for foreign policy, less work has been done on the period. I will summarise some of the conclusions in a recent, interesting work by Robert Frankenstein on the question of whether the Popular Front caused the 1940 defeat.[4] On the other hand the opposition to the Popular Front has been studied and we now have a less caricatured view of the right-wing and business milieux.

1. A precarious and ambiguous victory

The radicals were more tied to the Left after the 1936 election since they were almost all elected by vote transfers of Communist and Socialist electors. The new majority was 370 strong (previously 322) with rather fewer radical deputies (116 as compared to 159); the Union Socialiste Républicaine with 26 deputies (previously 45); the SFIO with 146 deputies (previously 97 and now the biggest group); a negligible Parti d'Unité Prolétarienne broken off from the Parti Communiste, which had 72 deputies (previously 10). So the question is what were the electorate indicating by this swing? A first factor to be noted is the climate of violence and political insecurity which existed for some years and which caused the political machine to jam (although it had never run very smoothly). The Stavisky affair had shown politicians in a bad light, particularly the centre-left, the radicals. Also there had been the rise of the Leagues, but fortunately for democrats, divided among themselves. Then there had been the 6 February 1934 events, which ironically had facilitated the beginning of a reunion between Communists and Socialists fourteen years after the Congress of Tours. There were street fights between students and, much more disquieting, an attack on Léon Blum himself in February 1936 at the time of the funeral of the historian of *Action Française*, Jacques Bainville. It was a chance affair, Blum was recognised in a car driven by his friend Georges Monnet, he was struck and injured, and could have been killed. The impression given is that the political and parliamentary system cannot deal with these challenges; Daladier's resignation seems to prove the point, although he justified his actions on the grounds of avoiding further bloodshed. The attempt to reform the state made by Gaston Doumergue of the centre-right (fetched from his village of Tournefeuille) was an almost complete failure. The system thus proved that it could not reform itself.

The second disquieting factor was the economic recession, for France having rejoiced at being spared the effects of world crisis, had now been affected later than the rest and was stagnant while the neighbouring states were recovering again. So prices in France were 20 or 30 per cent too high compared with other countries. In response to this Paul Reynaud on the right proposed devaluation, but most of the right and a good many of the left considered this a crime against the country. (Observers and activists often think the thermometer is the cause of the high temperature!) So instead, with Laval, the deflationary solution was tried, attempting in 1935 to reduce the money supply and certain debts, even reducing civil servants' salaries – which was courageous but electorally stupid. Anyway if failed because prices continued to rise particularly because of an agricultural shortage.

The third element in the situation that the Popular Front inherited was the perilous international scene. I need only recall the rise of the dictatorships with the novel tripolarity of Stalin, Mussolini (who had come not too badly out of Ethiopia) and Hitler (who remilitarised the left bank of the Rhine in March 1936, with no more than a protest from the interim government of Albert Sarraut). Of course, the progress of Stalin and Hitler had a certain charm for the extreme Left and Right in France. I am bound to remark at this juncture that one of the most glaring differences between today and 1936 is the prodigious consensus concerning the rules of the political game that exists now. This is one of the most important facts of

May 1981 whereas in 1936 nearly half of the French wished to change the regime and the rest were not prepared to die defending it. In foreign affairs Barthou, assassinated in October 1934, had been the last minister to seek a French foreign policy that was not perpetually following behind the English governess. These were some of the difficulties and ambiguities facing the Popular Front at the beginning of its term.

2.   The strong momentum masks the problems

The attentive observer can discern the ambiguities in for example the great wave of factory occupations and seizures by the workers of plant and equipment, though they were very respectful of it, maintained it carefully, destroyed nothing. It was the sign for all the working class that a heavy load had been lifted from them. (Simone Veil has left us some magnificent pages about the atmosphere of the time.) Yet the events embarrassed the government in its dealings with the Centre-left and Centre-right and such was the ambiguity of those occupations that it has often been asked who provoked them, whether some agency made use of the latent rivalry between the two recently reunited union groups, the CGT and the CGTU. In a note written during the war, Ramadier, formerly a socialist and who became one again later, explained that there was no doubt about German agents provoking the factory sit-ins. I do not at all believe in this thesis and there are more people who believe that the Communist party through the CGTU wished by this means to have a guarantee that the government would carry out what it desired.

Thus there was considerable uncertainty in the alliance between the PCF and the SFIO, and the radicals' tendency to take fright added to the problem. Their electorates were often rural and suspicious of the goings-on in Paris and in working-class circles. The socialists also, despite Blum's personal authority, were swept by strongly divergent currents; there was the Paul Faure group among whom one could already discern the beginnings of the great split when he sided with the Vichy regime in 1940. And there were the extreme Left groups with Marceau Pivert and Zyromski;[5] their followers thought that all was possible immediately. In a way, Blum was able to arbitrate these differences but only with considerable activity (and without the constitutional advantages that the President has today). One is led to consider the personality of such a leader: more than sixty years old; entering politics late (over forty); an activist and intellectual professing revolution in his youth but choosing later to be the party's lawyer; a man who loved the theatre, his family life, certain pleasures of living; not at all a hesitating Hamlet as he has been painted but capable of great willpower and courage, yet doubting at times his own ability to lead. There is an astonishing speech of his on film made to the National Council of the SFIO: 'No, he will not refuse to take power. No, I will not say to you [he puts his hands over his eyes] take this cup away from me. No, we wish it for we wish the victory of socialism'. ('Very good', says Bracke sitting behind him.) The fact that he spent ten minutes wondering whether he was the most suitable person to lead was both an indication that he was something special and a cause for some to doubt him. In March 1937 in a moment of great fatigue and depression, he said to Monnet, 'Georges, take my place'. This fragility was largely masked at the beginning by the wave of feeling as a great portion of the French population, the workers, realised that the tacit alliance of the middle classes and the rural milieux (France was still half rural in those days) was broken and they were no longer on the outside. I refer you back to those thrilling days described by Simone Veil and others, to Bastille day 1936, a few days before the bell sounded for the war in Spain.

The people around the Bastille in 1981 shouted *'Elkabbach ou placard!'*[6] but French trade unionism does not seem to have gained many members whereas they flocked in in 1936. The ministerial team still had some old radical 'crocodiles' who seemed unlikely persons to bring about change; Yvon Delbos was at Foreign Affairs and a good but rather weak character, Daladier himself was at National Defence. There were also young Turks, new figures like Pierre Cot whom the Right called *'le galopin sanglant'* since he wanted to help the Spaniards in their war. Jean Zay was a great Minister of Education and Georges Monnet a very good Minister of Agriculture, even if socialist historiographers play down his role because of his subsequent break with Blum. There were also three women in ministerial posts, who did not last long but who were nevertheless the first women in government in France at a time when women did not yet have the right to vote.[7]

The pace of events was also rapid; this was a period in politics when action could be taken although the term *'etat de grâce'* (honeymoon period) was not used in 1936. The Right was afraid and the Left was full of hope; the clay was still soft and could be worked. The Right would accept some measures since they were more symbolic than concrete. In any case the Left could say, 'we had to do this because of the situation we inherited from you'. Later, as in all post-electoral situations, the leaders of the opposition could begin to say 'if things do not go well, it will be entirely your fault'. Léon Blum realised that he had to act quickly and so the gains of the first days of the Popular Front are important and virtually the only measures that have lasted. Not only the progressive wage rises, which could be eroded by inflation, but also the structural reforms which were of a type that could not be reversed: the Matignon agreements, the forty-hour week, the paid holidays (perhaps the reform of greatest symbolic significance), the collective agreements, the compulsory arbitration, a little later the Corn Office, the nationalisation of some armaments factories. Not much was made of nationalisation and the Communists, for example, were largely against it.

3. Decline

Thus was the glorious dawn of the Popular Front and then came, on 18 July, the tragic news of the Spanish civil war. This would be a tragedy for the Popular Front and for Blum personally. Now the Popular Front was faced with an intrusion of foreign problems; 'should we or should we not help our republican friends in Spain? Great Britain was opposed to intervention in Spain as were the French radicals. Blum therefore had the realistic choice of remaining in power without intervening openly in the Spanish conflict or resigning. In my opinion Jean Lacouture in his biography criticises Blum unfairly.

In the matter of national defence the Popular Front was criticised for immobilism and for 'losing the war' in 1940. The view of Robert Frankenstein was that the Popular Front's leaders were hardly more farsighted than their predecessors in strategic terms; he quotes the famous interview between de Gaulle and Blum and recounted by both of them.[8] As far as armaments are concerned, Frankenstein's careful argument essentially reduced the blame sometimes attached to the Popular Front. Indeed Blum's government did expand aeronautical production and at considerable political cost.

Added to these problems were the economic problems resulting firstly from the devaluation at the end of the summer, which came too late because of socialist opposition to both deflation and devaluation and general opposition to measures affecting gold. Secondly, with regard to the forty-hour week, the well known arguments of Alfred Sauvy[9] have been newly stated by Jean-Claude Asselain in an article in *Histoire*. On the whole the criticisms of this too rigid measure are not called into question by recent historiography. Thirdly, there was great statistical ignorance so that all decisions were to a large extent taken in the dark.

In 1937 in the public mind the Popular Front was failing and this image counted more than the real, if small, recovery taking place at the beginning of that year. Politically the extreme Left fell away, the PCF kept its distance and the radicals (strong in the senate) became more and more wary. Gradually the leaders became demoralised as a result of the implicit pause of October 1936 and the explicit one of February 1937, the suicide of Salengro,[10] the delayed universal exhibition, the punch-ups in Clichy, the gold transfers abroad, the resignation of various experts and finally Blum's failure in the senate.

There are certain clear differences between 1936 and 1981. France was different then, still considerably rural.[11] The international environment was quite different, as we have seen, and the state institutions were different. Nevertheless, the memory of the Popular Front has exerted an influence on the events of 1981-2 and maybe the recollection of certain failures in the past has influenced certain policies of the present. For example, the thirty-nine-hour law is much more flexible than the forty-hour law of 1936, though I am not so sure about the 'purchasing power' policy.

In other respects it seems to me that the Socialist leaders of the eighties might well have looked more closely at the reality of history and not accepted mythological versions. For example, they need not have regarded the employers as hostile, univocal and an inseparable bloc. Also in general they seem to me to underestimate the complicated make-up of their opponents and fail thereby to take advantage of a latitude that exists and that might, as history shows, result in permanent gains.

Notes

1   See my book *Leçon d'histoire pour une gauche au pouvoir* published a month after the split between Socialists and Communists on 21 September 1977, (Paris, Seuil).
2   February 1942. In particular Blum, Daladier and General Gamelin were on trial.
3   de Toqueville, *Souvenirs*, Paris, Gallimard, 1964.
4   *Le Front Populaire a-t-il perdu la guerre?*, Editions de la Sorbonne.
5   The latter leading a group called (after its journal) La Bataille Socialiste.
6   Jean Pierre Elkabbach, TV journalist. One of the most detested spokesmen of the Giscard regime.
7   Under-secretaries of State Mme Léon Brunschvicg, Irène Joliot-Curie, Susanne Lacore.
8   In 1936. See for example Blum, *Mémoires*, Paris, Albin Michel, 1955, p. 114.
9   *Histoire économique de la France entre les deux guerres*, Paris, Fayard, 1965-75.
10   Roger Salengro, Minister of the Interior, slandered by some of the press, committed suicide in 1936.
11   In particular Senator Joseph Caillaux harped on this theme. See for example Pierre Barral, *Les Agrariens français de Méline à Pisani*, Paris, Fondation nationale des sciences politiques, 1968.

4 Ideological parallels: 1936 and 1981

TONY CHAFER and BRIAN JENKINS
Portsmouth Polytechnic

The drawing of historical parallels is always a hazardous exercise, even when confined to the experience of a single nation across a relatively short time span. For if the political culture of a nation often produces a distinctive political vocabulary and style which persist through time, the social and ideological substance of that culture cannot remain immune to the historical process. Any comparison of the recent Socialist victory with that of the Popular Front in 1936 must therefore take full account of the impact of forty-five intervening years of rapid social, economic and political transformation. The temptation to emphasize the recurrent themes of French political life must be qualified by the awareness that continuity of *form* may disguise fundamental changes of *content*.

The analogy with the thirties is none the less an inviting one. Given that the French Left collectively regards the Popular Front as the only valid historical precedent of a government brought to power by the progressive social forces of the nation (the era of tripartism from 1944 to 1947 being tainted by its associations with Gaullism and Christian Democracy), popular nostalgia was inevitably reawakened by the 'second coming' of 1981. These recollections are no doubt strengthed by certain apparent similarities in the circumstances that accompanied these two electoral triumphs of the Left. In both cases, after periods of relative prosperity and optimism, the country was faced with a major economic crisis and a serious deterioration in the international climate. And whereas in many other countries the mood of pessimism and insecurity favoured political experiments of a very different character, in France on both occasions it was the Left that was able to present itself as the relevant response to such circumstances. In 1936 as in 1981 the Left was able to win support for a radically different approach to the economic problems of the day, one which leant towards an interventionist strategy in contrast to the more liberal stance adopted by preceding governments.

These resemblances have reinforced the temptation to see the Popular Front as a storehouse of lessons and examples. Will the *Mur d'Argent* neutralise Socialist economic policy as effectively as it did forty-five years ago? Will the relative shortage of natural political allies on the international front circumscribe Mitterrand's policy options and leave him as isolated as Léon Blum once was? Will the traditional divisions of the Left, which eventually reduced the Popular Front to impotence, find ways of undermining the apparent impregnability of the new Socialist parliamentary majority? [1]

It is not, however, the intention to address such questions here. Our concern is with a rather different analogy, namely possible parallels in the *ideological* climate that preceded each of these election victories of the Left. The contention is that on both occasions France experienced what may be described as an 'ideological crisis'. This can be detected in the decline of established political orthodoxies, in 'the effervescence of intellectual activity in the field of politics', in attempts to recast the framework of ideological debate. This process in turn reflected a growing conviction in certain circles that existing ideological perspectives were inappropriate in the light of radically new social and economic circumstances.

Such developments within the ranks of the intelligentsia would not, of course, be significant (or even possible) unless they reflected an identifiable change of mood at the more popular level. Here, the symptoms must be sought in patterns of collective behaviour rather than in the articulation of specific objectives, but they are none the less clear. As already suggested, both the thirties and the seventies were marked by a climate of growing pessimism and insecurity, but they were also marked by major shifts of political allegiance. Fear and doubt may generate confusion and disillusionment, but that in turn may breed a new responsiveness to political innovation. In such times, when political organisations can no longer count on the traditional loyalties and reflexes tending to operate in calmer years, the role of ideology as a tool of persuasion, as an agent of mobilisation, and as a means of securing political legitimacy is greatly enhanced.

Before proceeding to examine this analogy in more detail, we must define the precise time-scale of this process of ideological upheaval experienced in the two periods under consideration. In the case of the 1930s, the phase to which we refer dates from 1932-3, and thus precedes the Popular Front victory by only a few years. In the contemporary case the gestation period would seem to have been much longer, for though the worsening economic climate since 1974 must be seen as a contributory factor, the origins of the process of ideological innovation may more accurately be set in the events of May 1968.

Within this framework of enquiry, three questions must be asked. First, what is the evidence for the existence of what we have called an 'ideological crisis' in either period? Second, were the ideological innovations that emerged in these two periods comparable to any significant extent? Finally, what implications did these innovations have for the subsequent exercise of power by the Left in 1936 and 1981?

Symptoms of ideological crisis

The origins of the ideological upheavals of the 1930s in France can be traced back at least to World War I. The heavy financial burden of war and reconstruction made France a debtor nation. The dual effect of this was to link her into the international economy and thus undermine her defences against world recession, and to give French governments in the twenties monetary and budgetary difficulties that helped to weaken the credibility of parliamentary institutions. The emergence of the Soviet Union and of Mussolini's Italy also sowed the seeds of future discord, by lending a new ideological dimension to international relations and by providing new ideological reference points in domestic politics. The impact of these changes was softened by the illusions raised by the military victory of 1918 and the industrial growth and relative international calm of the 1920s. However, this merely ensured that popular opinion would be all the more embittered and disillusioned when problems surfaced in the thirties. The onset of the world economic depression and the worsening international climate that followed the Nazi victory in Germany presented France with a fundamentally new challenge.

If the established political practices of the Third Republic had managed to muffle the warning signals of the 1920s, here was a set of problems that required a more radical response. The continuing instability of the government process[2] and the failure of the main political formations to develop a credible approach to these new circumstances set in train an increasing popular alienation from the political options offered by the regime. The rise of the right-wing leagues, the Paris riots of 6 February 1934 and the mass strikes of June 1936 expressed a pattern of extra-parliamentary activity and political violence which was to last until the end of the decade. On the Right, the tone of conservative opinion was increasingly set by the more strident sections of the right-wing Paris press and by the authoritarian perspectives of La Rocque's PSF and Doriot's PPF.[3] The orthodox parliamentary Right, for fear of being outflanked by such developments, was itself more and more critical of the institutions of the Third Republic.[4] On the Left, disenchantment with the established channels of political activity was exemplified in the extra-parliamentary dimension of the Popular Front campaign, in the June 1936 strikes and sit-ins and in the greatly increased Communist vote at the 1936 elections. Finally the Radical Party, for so long the backbone of parliamentary politics in the Third Republic, began an inexorable decline after Daladier's resignation on 7 February 1934, and this was symptomatic of the decreasing credibility of the regime itself. In the last six years of the Republic's life, Parliament voluntarily renounced large areas of its law-making functions for a total of thirty-four months, allowing governments to rule by decree.

These major shifts in the pattern of political allegiance at the popular level were reflected in the sharpness of ideological conflict in political and intellectual circles. The fading Radical Party spawned its generation of 'Young Turks.'[5] The heightened factionalism of the SFIO produced the 'neo-socialist' split of 1933, which sent leading former Socialists like Déat and Marquet on the path to eventual collaboration with the Nazi occupation.[6] Right-wing deputies colluded openly with the extra-parliamentary leagues, and even a respectable moderate politician like André Tardieu, frustrated in his hopes of reforming the regime, found his way to a position on the extreme Right.[7] Most curious of all, Jacques Doriot, a leading Communist and Mayor of Saint-Denis, took most of his federation out of the party in 1934 and eventually became the architect of the avowedly fascist Parti Populaire Français. This drama unfolded against a background of intellectual turbulence, with the proliferation of marginal political groups, reviews, periodicals and speculative political programmes. The vacuum left by traditional political formulae and practices was filled by a variety of ideas, some inherited from France's own ideological experience, some gleaned from foreign experiments, some indeed anticipating future national developments by more than a decade.[8]

France was unable to develop an indigenous solution to her problems in the 1930s, and the military defeat of 1940 was in part prepared by a growing sense of political impotence. The 'ideological crisis' thus persisted throughout the decade. The period 1932-4 is, however, of special significance. In these years an attempt was made in certain intellectual circles to develop a comprehensive critique of the existing social and economic order and of the politics of the Third Republic. This reflected a general dissatisfaction with the performance of political parties and with the existing terms of ideological debate. What was being identified was something akin to a '*crise de civilisation*', as indicated by the titles of some of the key works of the period: *Le cancer américain* (Robert Aron and Arnaud Dandieu); *La révolution nécessaire* (Robert Aron and Arnaud Dandieu); *Le monde sans âme* (Henri Daniel-Rops); *Le rajeunissement de la politique* (Henri Daniel-Rops); *La crise est dans l'homme* (Thierry Maulnier).

The slogan 'ni droite ni gauche'[9] was no doubt naive, and after February 1934 the rapid polarization of political forces dispelled the illusion that this kind of ideological synthesis could be achieved. The so-called 'non-conformistes des années trente'[10] were driven back into the Left–Right framework by the growth of the Popular Front, the drift of the Right towards authoritarian perspectives, the growing impact of foreign policy choices on French domestic politics. It is, however, in this brief phase of attempted ideological renewal between 1932 and 1934 that the contours of the political and intellectual crisis of the thirties are most sharply defined. We shall return later to a consideration of the specific terms in which this debate was framed. First, however, we must examine the contention that the period since 1968 in France similarly corresponds to a phase of 'ideological crisis'.

It would be wrong to expect the symptoms of 'ideological crisis' in the contemporary setting to be identical to those of the 1930s. As is shown in the next section, the historical circumstances differed in important respects and popular attitudes have changed in the interim. Especially significant in this regard is the consensus which has emerged around the political institutions of the Fifth Republic, and the general decline in levels of party political militancy which seems to be an essential by-product of advanced capitalist society. Of course, the events of May 1968 represent a dramatic exception to this more muted pattern of political expression in France and in Europe at large. But that extraordinary upsurge of direct action may itself have contributed to the relative political 'demobilization' of the subsequent period, especially as the 'events' failed to achieve the degree of change that their scale appeared to warrant. Thus, though the period of the 1970s saw fundamental shifts of political allegiance, the decade was not marked by the feverish and often violent political activity of the thirties. The features of 'ideological crisis' are to be found rather in the electoral decline of political movements that had previously enjoyed unquestioning loyalty, in the development of what Alain Touraine has called 'social movements'[11] outside the traditional framework of political activity, in the birth of an alternative political culture and in the failure of political ideologies to generate more than a relatively unstable electoral appeal.

It would be impossible in this brief essay to examine in detail the various implications of the upheaval of May 1968. In different ways it manifested a hitherto suppressed popular disaffection both with the Gaullist establishment and with the parties of the mainstream Left.

Arguably it also implied a questioning of the social rationale of advanced capitalism, and the economic crisis of that system in the 1970s has clearly reinforced such doubts. What is evident, however, is that the events, though their immediate impact was limited, had a profound effect on subsequent political developments. How far May 1968 hastened de Gaulle's resignation as President is debatable, but it certainly undermined the Gaullist consensus on which the key economic transformations of the 1960s were based. With the succession of Pompidou, Gaullism progressively lost the image of a 'movement' with cross-national appeal and became an identifiable 'political party' of the Right. In the course of the 1970s the Gaullist Party successively lost the Presidency, the office of Prime Minister and its dominant position within the parliamentary majority. Finally in 1981 it found itself in opposition.

The first beneficiaries of this process of decline were the independent Centre and Right groups who rallied round the banner of the Giscard presidency and who in 1978 formed an electoral federation (UDF) that achieved near parity of parliamentary representation with the Gaullists. But the process has also contributed to the extraordinary renaissance of the Socialist Party, which emerged from a state of near-extinction at the end of the sixties to achieve eventually in 1981 the largest parliamentary election vote ever recorded by a political party under the Fifth Republic. Furthermore, this electoral transformation has left its marks elsewhere. In the 1960s André Malraux had said that between the great movements of Gaullism and Communism there was a political 'void'. The decline of traditional Gaullism has been accompanied by an even more dramatic decline in the fortunes of the Communist Party. Regarded for so long as the natural 'tribune' of the oppressed, deeply entrenched in working-class loyalties and better organised than any of its political rivals, the Party has seen its electoral base steadily eroded by the Socialists and was reduced in 1981 to its lowest vote for forty-five years.

These changes may be partially explicable at the purely electoral and circumstantial level. But it should be recognized that Gaullism was the political expression of a particular model of social and economic development, whose social rationale was challenged by the May 1968 upheaval and whose economic viability has been thrown into doubt by the recession of the 1970s. The optimistic modernising ethos of traditional Gaullism associated as it was with rapid economic growth, was no longer appropriate in the depressed economic climate that followed the 1973 oil crisis, and this helped create something of an ideological vacuum.[12] Though often disguised or distorted by the pursuit of electoral advantage, the quest for ideological credibility has thus been a major preoccupation of the principal political formations in recent years.

One sign of this is that the Gaullist Party itself, under Jacques Chirac, presents a radically different image from the one it displayed in the 1960s. The blend of right-wing populism and neo-liberal monetarism which it has now espoused has no place in the Gaullist tradition of economic interventionism and the pursuit of social consensus. This conversion has involved deliberately ideological initiatives through the formation by Chirac's supporters of *clubs de pensée* like the Club de l'Horloge and Club 89. It is noticeable too that Giscard d'Estaing's attempts to weld the independent Centre and Right groups into a coherent political federation has involved significant ideological pronouncements, though there is some debate as to whether 'Giscardism' really does point the way to an 'advanced liberal society' rather than to a form of paternalist elitism, a technocratic version of Vichy.[13] The sudden emergence of the Nouvelle Droite into public consciousness in the summer of 1979, although of only limited importance in terms of breadth of influence, was further evidence of the new significance attached by the Right to ideological issues, of a fresh quest for credibility in the wake of the decline of Gaullism.

The ideological disturbances of the Left have been no less profound. It would be hard to explain the dramatic decline of the Communist Party without some reference to its chronic ideological sterility, and this failure to adapt its doctrine and strategy to changing circumstances has been the key factor in the alienation of so many of its leading intellectuals in the last five years.[14] Finally, the remarkable regeneration of the French Socialist Party in the last ten years cannot be separated from its project of ideological renewal, the successful development of an image of social modernism and economic radicalism which contrasts strongly with the opportunism and traditionalism of the old SFIO.

In many ways it would seem that the Socialists were more attentive than any other party to the lessons of May 1968, and were thus better placed to profit from the growing economic discontent and political disillusionment of the 1970s. It would be naive however to suggest that they have thereby resolved the 'ideological crisis' where the Popular Front once failed. One of the features of the May 1968 legacy has been the development of forms of social protest that fall outside the normal framework of party politics – the ecologist and anti-nuclear lobby, the women's rights movement, regional separatisms, a variety of campaigns on specific social issues. If the ideological crisis of the 1930s was translated above all in 'political' effervescence, the contemporary one is located more squarely in so-called 'civil society'. In so far as this reflects popular disillusionment not just with the existing framework of political debate but with

'politics' as such, the challenge may arguably be even greater than that of
the 1930s. The rejection of contemporary political debate as sterile, of
the Left-Right divide as archaic, is to be found in the discourse not just of
the Ecologists but also of the Nouveaux Philosophes and the Nouvelle
Droite.[15] The mood of *crise de civilisation* finds frequent echoes in
intellectual circles, and even those sympathetic to the political Left have
indicated the need for a fundamental revision of the terms of ideological
debate, as these recent titles indicate: *Pour une nouvelle culture politique*
(Pierre Rosanvallon and Patrick Viveret); *Adieux au prolétariat* (André
Gorz); *L'Après-socialisme* (Alain Touraine); *Pour sortir du XXe siècle*
(Edgar Morin).

Despite the considerable differences both in the historical circumstances and in the way in which problems were perceived at these two
stages of French history, we would therefore propose that on both occasions the Left came to power against a background of political disillusionment and ideological confusion, and was faced with the challenge of
breaking the mould of established economic and political practice. The
next section looks more closely at the precise nature of the 'ideological
crisis' in these two periods.

The nature of the 'ideological crisis'

It should be said that certain factors which weighed heavily in the ideological debates of the 1930s have been largely absent in the contemporary
period, and of these the first might appear to be a paradox. We have
already noted a certain political 'demobilisation' in the recent period as
compared with the thirties, evident both in a greater political passivity and
in the diversification of activity in 'civil society'. But alongside this there
has grown a degree of consensus around the institutions of the Fifth
Republic that was markedly absent in the closing years of the Third.
Perhaps this is itself a symptom of the new political mood, a greater
concern with social and economic realities rather than with the fetish of
constitution-building. In contrast, it certainly was the case that between
the wars one of the main areas of discontent was the Third Republic's
failure to generate stable majority government, and projects for constitutional reform thus occupied a central position in many of the
ideological propositions of the 1930s.[16] The survival of political traditions
hostile to parliamentary democracy and the appeal exercised by authoritarian experiments in other countries combined to weaken the political
consensus on which any regime depends, and this lent to the political
conflict of the 1930s a dimension of constitutional dissent which is not

present to anything like the same degree under the Fifth Republic.

The second factor which makes comparison more difficult is the contrasting international climate. Though recent years superficially recall the thirties with their heightened international tension and uncertainty, the issues at stake and the nature of their repercussions for domestic politics are profoundly different. There is, of course, still an 'ideological divide' in world politics but its character has greatly changed. The super-bloc system has become the unbending reality of international politics, progressively reinforced by the strategic imperatives of geo-political rivalry and military co-existence. The models of social and political development exemplified by the great powers no longer inspire enthusiastic ideological emulation. They have simply created a framework of international relations that firmly circumscribes the foreign policy options of every other nation. This remorseless logic may lead other nations to a simple acquiescence born of a sense of impotence or, as in the case of France, to a reassertion of the aspiration to *national* independence. Thus, in France, whereas in the 1930s the ideological confrontations on the world stage had a profoundly divisive internal effect, today the attempt to develop at least the image of an independent foreign policy has generated considerable cross-party support. Thus, however much the international climate may still affect the public mood, its capacity to divide political loyalties on the domestic front is greatly reduced.

It would be wrong to underestimate the importance of these dissimilarities in the political and international contexts of the two periods, or indeed to pretend that they may be discretely separated from other areas of comparison. This is especially true in any discussion of 'ideology', where the notion of interdependence is paramount. It is nonetheless the case that ever since World War I, the domestic politics of most industrially developed countries have been dominated by social and economic issues, and it is to that area that we now turn.

The period 1932-4 represents a critical phase in the decline of the Third Republic. These years saw the first effects of the world depression in France, the beginnings of sectional social protest, the victory of Nazism in Germany. They also, as we have seen, saw a chronic destabilisation of the political process. The mood of these years was one of political eclecticism and ambiguity, with dramatic political defections and strange convergences of dissident opinion.

It was against this background that a process of ideological innovation was initiated by groups of Paris intellectuals, often from Catholic backgrounds. The group of writers known as the Jeune Droite, the coteries around reviews like *Esprit* and *L'Ordre Nouveau*, projects like the

Plan du neuf juillet brought together a wide variety of political dissidents in an attempt to forge a general critique of the contemporary social and political order and to propose an ideological alternative that would break the deadlock of existing political orthodoxies.[17]

At one level this involved a rejection of what were seen as the sterile doctrines and issues that dominated the parliamentary politics of the time. The Right was castigated for its pursuit of narrow class interests to the exclusion of any project of social reform. The Radicals were seen as a moribund force, constantly re-enacting old battles that had already been won. The Socialists and Communists were in their different ways trapped by their dogmatism and materialism. Behind this, however, there lay a deeper philosophical critique.

The essence of this was a simultaneous disavowal of the doctrines of both economic liberalism and Marxist collectivism. The former was condemned as an irrational distortion of the principle of private property. Far from enhancing the social well-being of humanity, it had created the tyranny of credit and parasitic capital, the growth of monopolies, the ethic of production for production's sake, the dehumanisation of labour.[18] Economic liberalism had in fact crushed man as a social and spiritual being beneath the weight of selfish materialism, just as *political* liberalism had reduced man to the status of an atomised individual voter, manipulated by the political class and faced with artificial issues and sterile choices.[19] On the other hand Marxism was seen as a simple derivation of laissez-faire liberalism, equally locked within a materialist logic. By placing the struggle for socialism on the basis of materialist class interest Marxism paved the way either for the *embourgeoisement* of the working class or for a new form of soulless economic tyranny. If the popular imagination was to be mobilised for the transformation of the social order, the ethical and spiritual bases of socialism must thus be reasserted.[20]

This body of thought was the product of a brief convergence in the early thirties between right-wing thinkers seeking to incorporate a 'social' dimension into conservative thought, and a more libertarian tradition seeking to purge socialist thought of what was seen as the rigid determinism of orthodox Marxism as expressed by the Third International. These diverse groups were in fact engaged in an exploration of the ideological space between economic liberalism and Marxism, and momentarily they alighted on a series of formulae which created the illusion of some sort of ideological synthesis. The doctrine of so-called 'personalism'[21] proposed that existing economic and political antagonisms could somehow be transcended by a new form of social organisation based on 'corporatism'. This concept, which became one of the most fashionable economic projects of the 1930s, envisaged a corporate organisation of employers and workers within the industrial enterprise and the effective incorporation of economic and professional interest groups into the legislative and executive functions of the state.[22]

The unity of this whole discourse was soon to be undermined. It was founded on a moral and philosophical illusion that, because so many of the conventional political disputes of the Third Republic were apparently artificial, there was no real rationale for *any* of the social and political conflicts that mark modern industrial societies. The sentimentality of this dream of social harmony attained through moral persuasion, echoing both the utopian socialists and the Social catholics of the last century, could not survive the harsh political realities of the post-1934 period. Those involved in these debates soon found themselves drawn in radically different directions.

The reactionary implications of 'corporatist' ideology are well enough known. It rests on the notion of a communality of interest between employers and workers, and thus denies not only the existence of class conflict but also the reality of capitalist social domination. In the hands of those who, like the group known as the Jeune Droite,[23] were simultaneously recommending a thoroughly authoritarian political regime, it is not surprising that such ideas found their greatest appeal in extreme right-wing circles in the course of the 1930s. Gibrat and Loustau of *L'Ordre Nouveau* helped draw up the programme of La Rocque's *Croix de Feu*, while Jean-Pierre Maxence performed the same service for the league, Solidarité Francaise.[24] Maxence and other members of the *Droite* group like Drieu La Rochelle and Thierry Maulnier eventually joined Doriot's fascist PPF, and their corporatist notions, along with the technocratic concepts developed by Jean Coutrot[25] and the neo-socialists around Marcel Déat, formed part of the ideology of Vichy's *Révolution Nationale*.

However, this was not the only current to emerge from the ideological debates of the early thirties. For many of those who had sought their inspiration more in Proudhon and Sangnier than in Maurras and Barrès, the political polarisation after 1934 required a very different response. Mounier's Esprit group was eventually driven to identify itself, albeit critically, with the Popular Front Movement. Three of its erstwhile leaders – Caley, Izard and Humeau – eventually joined the SFIO, while two figures who were formerly close to *L'Ordre Nouveau*, Philippe Lamour and Pierre-Olivier Lapie, fought the 1936 elections as Popular Front candidates, the latter becoming an under-secretary in Blum's Government.

In these circles the earlier slogan of *'ni droite ni gauche'* was progressively abandoned as a reactionary 'blind alley', and corporatist doctrines were converted into more specifically socialist proposals. Groups like Esprit, Troisième Force, the review '*Plans*' and later the CGT attempted in the second half of the decade to popularise the notion of economic planning within an only partially collectivised economy, the control of key financial and industrial enterprises by public associations of managers, workers and consumers, and Keynesian economic management.

These latter propositions, which pointed the way to the establishment of the apparatus of French social democracy, were further elaborated in the Resistance movement and finally found political expression in the Liberation period. Clearly they might be expected to have made some ideological impact on the Popular Front experiment, and we return to this question in the final section of the chapter. First, however, we attempt to situate the contemporary 'ideological crisis' in relation to that of the thirties.

The ideological conflict of the 1930s revolved essentially around the concept of the state. The social implications of the world economic crisis could no longer be ignored in countries where the masses had achieved some access to the political process. In this situation the prevailing ethos of economic liberalism inevitably came under attack in favour of some degree of state intervention in the economy, though for many the extreme alternative of Marxist collectivism on the Soviet model was equally unacceptable. Hence the proliferation of projects for social and economic reform from a variety of political perspectives, momentarily creating the illusion of ideological convergence. The process was further complicated by the quest for constitutional solutions to the problem of political instability, and by the growing impact of the international ideological struggle on domestic politics.

In the forty-five years that have passed since the Popular Front experiment, many of the ideological confusions and ambiguities of the 1930s have been resolved. The sentimental illusions of Vichy have been exposed, along with the horrors of Fascism. In parallel with other Western societies, France has grafted onto the capitalist mode of production the apparatus of social democracy — Keynesian economic management, the mixed economy, social welfare and a degree of forward planning. In the economic recession of the eighties, this system too is called into question. However relevant it *might* have been to France's problems in the 1930s, however fundamental it *has* been to the revival of European economies since the war, the battery of institutions and techniques associated with the modern capitalist state is increasingly discredited. Traditional Keynesian remedies no longer have the same impact in the context of modern forms of inflation and unemployment and of the new international division of labour. The agencies of social welfare and public services are increasingly regarded less as a stimulus to economic growth than as a dead-weight on the economy. Fascist corporatism, Keynesianism, Social Democracy — the 'ideological space' between economic liberalism and Soviet Marxism appears to have filled up with corpses.

The gravity of the current ideological crisis has no better illustration than in the fact that, in many countries including France, sections of the Right have reverted to doctrines of monetarism, a dressed-up form of the economic liberalism that supposedly died in the 1930s. Where does this leave the Left? What now is the nature of the ideological space where new ideas and initiatives are being launched, and how relevant are they to the specific economic and social circumstances of the contemporary period?

The process of ideological renewal on the Left, confirmed and further accelerated by the events of May 1968, is a complex phenomenon that cannot be identified with any single political tradition. On the one hand it includes a current of so-called 'modernism' with technocratic overtones, socially progressive but anxious to establish the Left's managerial creden-tials. In this context, names like Mendès France and Rocard spring to mind, and for some of its critics it is no more than a 'leftish' version of Giscardism.[26] Another variant is the libertarian discourse developed above all in PSU and CFDT circles, a descendant of the Left Catholic doctrines first expressed in the 1930s and a major influence in the ideological regeneration of the French Socialist Party in the 1970s. Finally there is the whole area of debate which has opened up since the mid-sixties within and around Marxism itself, reflecting the decline of the Soviet model of Communism as an ideological reference-point for European Marxists.

Clearly each of these traditions offers different perspectives on the nature of socialist society and the strategy for transition towards it. However, they tend to overlap both in terms of their ideological impact and in terms of the new areas of social and economic debate to which they all address themselves. In this respect, three main themes may be identified.

The first involves a rejection of the prevailing model of economic development, whose rationale is seen as crudely productivist and 'con-sumerist'. Though this clearly implies a critique of the social and economic assumptions of advanced capitalism, it is similarly directed against the indiscriminate pursuit of economic growth that characterises the strategy of both the French Communist Party and the CGT. It focuses on problems like environmental pollution, dwindling energy supplies, structural unemployment, the alienation of the industrial workforce, the emergence of a leisure society. In response it invokes the concept of a 'new style of growth'[27] which should be qualitative rather than purely quantitative, which will question the finalities of industrial production and place the emphasis on industrial reconversion, the humanisation of the work process and the promotion of 'social growth'. Many of those issues emerged in the May events, but they have been given a fresh relevance in the economic climate of the 1970s. They are central to the discourse of not only the anti-nuclear movement and the ecology lobby, but also the PSU, and they have been taken up by certain elements in both the Socialist Party and the CFDT.

The second theme relates to the debate on the nature of socialism itself. If Soviet-style Communism inspires little allegiance, many sections of the French Left have similarly disavowed the whole model of Social Democracy constructed since the war. In their different ways both the May events and the demise of the old SFIO[28] confirmed this growing disillusionment, which has been further accentuated by the economic downturn of the 1970s. The existing agencies of state intervention have not proved capable, it is claimed, even of maintaining the small measure of social justice they initially secured.

The new ideological initiatives thus reject both Soviet Communism and Social Democracy, and find their fundamental rationale in a critique of the state. According to this, the abstract equation of 'State = the People' has led socialists into the blind alley of statism, technocratic in the capitalist world, totalitarian in the Soviet bloc. The debate has focused therefore on the mechanisms of popular control which could effectively democratise the key institutions of modern industrial society. The concept of 'autogestion', now general currency on the Left and even part of the vocabulary of the Communist Party, cannot be translated simply as 'workers' control' within the firm. It implies equally the development of consumer democracy, greater political autonomy for regions and localities, the democratic control of planning and technology.

This leads in to a third dimension of the current ideological upheaval. These new themes have risen to prominence largely from within 'civil society' rather than from the main political parties of the Left. They reflect the rise of social movements like women's rights, ecology and regionalism, the campaigns around issues like nuclear energy, Lip and Larzac,[29] the proliferation of consumer and self-help groups associated with the notion of '*la vie associative*'. This represents a fundamentally new challenge for any Government of the Left. Through the combination of a degree of disillusionment with established party politics and the emergence of new social categories, a powerful network of political activists now exists outside the normal political process, thereby enormously extending the field of ideological debate. The developing of 'alternative lifestyles' and social experimentation within civil society makes the task of integrating social aspirations and economic imperatives into a coherent political programme all the more difficult.

Conclusion

In retrospect it is possible to identify the nature of the challenge that faced the Popular Front Government. In essence it was the task of transforming the social and economic functions of the state in response to the crisis of liberal capitalism. This implied at least the adoption of interventionist measures like exchange controls, devaluation, social welfare and a public works programme, if not a more wholehearted policy of economic planning and public ownership. In the event certain of these remedies were applied, but in response to the tide of events rather than as part of a coherent Keynesian, let alone Socialist, package.

The Popular Front clearly faced enormous problems, quite apart from the difficult economic and international conjuncture in which it came to power. First it was confronted with the hostility of large sections of the financial and industrial establishment. Second, the Socialists, who were the pivot of the coalition, had few figures with the kind of experience and expertise in economic affairs that the situation required. Third, the political stability of the Popular Front alliance was permanently threatened by the conflicting interests of the three main parties on which it was based.

On this last point, it must be emphasised that the unity of the Popular Front rested largely on a vague commitment to defend the institutions of the parliamentary Republic, a regime whose credibility had been severely weakened, against the growing authoritarianism of the Right. Beyond this, the consensus was weak. Indeed, it would seem that the Communist Party was as indifferent to the task of structural economic reform for strategic reasons as the Radicals were for ideological reasons. Its main rationale for involvement in the Popular Front was the international struggle against Fascism and defence of the Franco-Soviet pact. It was thus on the Socialists that was placed the onus of responding to the challenge of economic depression, and it is not surprising in these circumstances that the task proved too great for a party that had never before participated in government.

This is not to say that the key ideological innovations of the 1930s found no disciples among the political leaders of the Left. But their failure to reach fruition in the brief life of the Blum Government has perhaps a deeper social explanation. No matter how irrelevant some of the political orthodoxies of the Third Republic may seem to have been when set against the economic realities of the 1930s, they still had strong roots in popular attitudes. Ideology is, after all, the product of social circumstances, and support for the kind of interventionist policies mentioned above was no doubt inhibited in the 1930s by the continuing economic weight of the agricultural sector and small-scale production. France had still not effected the transition to a fully industrial economy, and urban working-class aspirations had not yet displaced the deep individualism and suspicion of the state which characterised the still large category of small-scale independent producers. It took the shock of war and occupation to undermine the hold of these traditional attitudes.

There are those who would contend that the 1970s have seen the development of an economic and social crisis every bit as severe as that of the thirties, and that once again the French Left is faced with the challenge of adapting its ideological traditions to fundamentally new circumstances. It is at least clear that the oil crisis of 1973 marked the end of a period in which economic growth and rising living standards were taken for granted, and ushered in an era in which the traditional economic remedies for both recession and inflation have apparently lost their potency. The implication is that advanced industrial economies are faced with profound structural problems that require an energetic and radical response. Declining industries, dwindling energy resources, mass unemployment and environmental degradation do not necessarily point the way to the total disintegration or extinction of society, but they at least imply enormous economic problems. The prospects are all the more grim if it should happen that the grave social unrest created by this deterioration in the quality of human existence found no political outlet or direction.

The perspectives of industrial reconversion, production for social use, political decentralisation and worker democracy offer one kind of ideological response to the current crisis. Given the failure of more traditional remedies, it is hard to envisage any other alternative that would not involve a further concentration of industrial, technological and political decision-making in the hands of a narrowing elite — the emergence in fact of a new totalitarianism. In the long term, therefore, the ideological debates of today may well imply a fundamental choice about the kind of society that will evolve over the next twenty-five years, and this places a heavy responsibility on the Socialist Government in France.

In some respects the Mitterrand Government has certain advantages over that of Léon Blum. The election victories of 1981 were far more decisive than that of 1936, and the Socialists do not have to count on the parliamentary support of other parties, as they did on the earlier occasion. Furthermore the contemporary Left has had more time to prepare itself for power and, since 1972, has equipped itself with a degree of economic expertise that was not available to the leaders of the Popular Front. Finally the ideological innovations of the recent period have had time to win a measure of popular allegiance and have been disseminated through many political and social organisations of the Left. This is in marked contrast to the equivalent initiatives of the 1930s, which circulated only within fairly limited political and intellectual circles and did not acquire the kind of popular currency that might have made their impact more decisive. The present Government has less excuse for turning its back on the innovators than its predecessors of forty-five years ago, and the Socialists did indeed appear to have integrated many of the new themes into their programme before they came to power.

However, it would be wrong to underestimate the difficulty of applying new and untested ideas, especially when more traditional formulae continue to exert a strong electoral appeal. The Popular Front was always on stronger political ground with slogans like '*ni dévaluation ni déflation*' or '*défense de la République*' than it was with the more adventurous Keynesian measures being urged on it by a few far-sighted economists in its ranks. This reflected the problem raised by the social composition of the Popular Front electorate, a class alliance of industrial workers, the liberal professions and sections of the rural and urban *petite bourgeoisie*. This latter category was inevitably a brake on the introduction of inter-ventionist measures associated more with the demands of modern industrial society than with those of a rural or artisanal economy.

The present Socialist Government is also faced with the problem of resolving the social and ideological contradictions of a heterogeneous class base.[30] The new class alliance is one of industrial workers and the growing categories of so-called *travailleurs intellectuels*, which include the new middle classes exemplified by the *cadre* and the new working class broadly typified by the term '*technicien*'. If the new 'participative' ideology has made some inroads in these latter strata, it is less implanted in the ranks of the industrial proletariat, where aspirations to social justice are still conceived in terms of state intervention of the more traditional centralised type.

The challenge confronting the Socialists is therefore that of adapting the fundamental aspirations of socialism to these new ideological pers-pectives, and of producing from this blend a political programme that is relevant, coherent and credible. There are doubts as to the capacity of the Government to realise this objective. Early criticisms of the Socialists' performance in office have highlighted two central deficiencies — the apparent 'incoherence' of their legislative programme and their failure to 'communicate' the under-lying principles of their action to the electorate.

In seeking to remedy these shortcomings, the PS faces considerable obstacles. It does not enjoy the kind of mass working-class base afforded by trade-union affiliation, and it cannot yet count on the loyalty of its recently acquired and highly heterogeneous electoral following. A significant feature of the 1981 election campaigns was their tranquillity, their thoroughly 'electoralist' character. There were few hints of the popular enthusiasm that marked the 1935-6 campaign, culminating in the mass sit-in strikes of June 1936. The question must therefore be asked whether, without an energetic attempt to inform and mobilise its popular base, the present Government will be any more successful than that of Léon Blum in countering the resistance of entrenched capitalist interests, which in their modern transnational form continue to represent the greatest single obstacle to the success of any socialist experiment.

In this context, there is clearly a possibility that, like the Popular Front before it, the present Government will retreat to the lowest common denominator of its ideological base — that is, in the contemporary context, to economic concepts associated with traditional Social Democracy and whose efficacy in the climate of the 1980s is open to serious doubt.

Notes

1   Trouble may come, for example, through the internal factionalism of the *Parti Socialiste*, or as in 1947, through the Communists' control of the main trade-union confederation, the CGT.

2   Between the elections of April 1932 and the right-wing riots in Paris on 6 February 1934, which brought down the Daladier Government, France had no fewer than six governments!

3   Colonel de la Rocque's Croix de Feu were widely regarded on the Left as the most likely of all the right-wing leagues to lead a Fascist take-over in France. When the Blum Government banned paramilitary formations in 1936, the movement transformed itself into the Parti Social Français, which by 1938 had three-quarters of a million members and expected to become the largest parliamentary force on the Right at the general elections of 1940. Many deputies of the Right endorsed its programme, which was tinged with traditional conservative authoritarianism rather than with genuine 'fascism'. The Parti Populaire Français, led by the dissident ex-Communist Jacques Doriot, was however avowedly Fascist and regrouped many of the most extreme right-wing radicals of the earlier leagues. In 1938 it formed a 'Front de la Liberté' with the largest conservative group in the Chamber of Deputies, Louis Marin's Fédération Républicaine.

4   The Government of Gaston Doumergue, appointed in the aftermath of the 6 February 1934 riots, introduced an abortive proposal for constitutional reform which included measures to strengthen the presidential role. Many

deputies on the Right of the Chamber of Deputies had links with the extra-parliamentary leagues of the early thirties and, as note 3 above indicates, this convergence became more pronounced after the Popular Front victory in 1936.

5 The so called Jeunes Turcs were a group of Radical deputies who, in their different ways, hoped to modernise their party and rescue it from decline. They included some figures like Jean Mistler and Martinaud Deplat who were on the conservative wing, but more prominant was a Left current around Jean Zay, Pierre Cot and Pierre Mendès France.

6 In November 1933 an emergency National Council of the SFIO expelled Pierre Renaudel and six other Socialist deputies for voting against party instructions and for the Daladier budget of 1933. Thirty other deputies later followed the Renaudel faction out of the party. Behind the split lay the traditionally divisive issues of support for military expenditure and participation in Radical governments, the Renaudel group being favourable to both. Among those expelled were three figures whose 'revisionism' went rather deeper – Marcel Déat, Adrien Marquet and Barthélemy Montagnon. These self-styled 'neo-socialistes' called for the abandonment of the internationalist and democratic ideal in favour of an authoritarian planned economy founded on a nationalist mystique. Ironically, this was initially conceived as the necessary French response to the international threat posed by the rise of Nazism in Germany. The three neo-socialist leaders were all to end up collaborating directly with the Nazi occupation in Paris.

7 André Tardieu, twice Prime Minister in the 1928-32 Parliament, was one of the main architects of the constitutional reform package of October 1934 (see note 4 above). His frustration at the failure of these proposals led him into more radical positions. By 1936 he was contributing to the extreme-right periodical, *Gringoire*, and in May 1937 his own newspaper, *La Liberté*, came into the hands of Doriot's PPF. This and other evidence led some to associate Tardieu directly with the PPF in the late thirties.

8 Many of the constitutional proposals developed in the 1930s have since re-surfaced in the political institutions of both the Fourth and Fifth Republics. The Keynesian innovations of the 1930s along with the various reforms associated with Social Democracy (mixed economy, welfare state etc) all made their impact in France at a later date. The Gaullist movement of the 1960s finally gave political expression to another theme of the 1930s – the need for a conservative party with a social policy and mass appeal. Even the *'autogestionnaire'* ideology of the contemporary non-communist Left has antecedents in some of the dissident doctrines of the inter-war years.

9 This slogan was first advanced by Robert Aron and Arnaud Dandieu in the following terms: 'we belong neither to the Right nor to the Left, but if we must situate ourselves in parliamentary terms, we would say that we are halfway between the extreme Right and the extreme Left, behind the Speaker's chair and with our backs to the debating chamber'. Aron and Dandieu, *La Révolution nécessaire*, Grasset, 1933, p. 12 (authors' translation).

10 The phrase is borrowed from an exhaustive study of the dissident intellectuals of the period. J. Loubet del Bayle, *Les Non-conformistes des années 30*, Le Seuil, 1969.

11 For a definition of a 'social movement', see A. Touraine, *La Voix et le regard*, Le Seuil, 1978, p. 104. Alain Touraine and his team of researchers are currently publishing a series of studies of the major new social movements, of which three have so far appeared: *Lutte étudiante*, Le Seuil, 1978, a study of the student movements; *La Prophétie anti-nucléaire*, Le Seuil, 1980, on the anti-nuclear movement and *Le Pays contre l'état*, Le Seuil, 1981, the regional-ist movement in Occitanie.

12   The nature and effects of this ideological vacuum have been analysed by a number of commentators, notably recently by A. Touraine in *L'Après-socialisme*, Grasset, 1980.

13.   For a study of Giscardian ideology in this context, see T. Ferenczi, *Le Prince au miroir*, Albin Michel, 1981.

14   Apart from the late Aragon, virtually no nationally known intellectuals have remained in the Communist Party. Although exclusions officially ended in 1978, many intellectuals have either left the Party or 'put themselves out of the Party' and not had their cards renewed. These include for example Jean Elleinstein, Antoine Spire, Etienne Balibar, Raymond Jean and Hélène Parmelin. For further details, see E. Entwhistle, 'The PCF, the intellectuals and the failure of the Left in March 1978', unpublished dissertation, 1981, Cambridgeshire College of Arts and Technology.

15   See the ecologists' election programme *Ecologie: le pouvoir de vivre*, Eds de la Surienne, 1981, pp. 293-4; B-H. Lévy, *L'Idéologie francaise*, pp. 199-200; J-M. Benoist, *Les Idées à l' endroit*, Hallier, 1979, pp. 14-26. All explicitly reject the conventional Left–Right divide as sterile and archaic and claim their discourse is an attempt to explore the ideological space outside the traditional Left–Right debate. There are striking convergences between certain aspects of their discourse: all, for example, see themselves as political decentralisers, are in favour of regionalism, feminism and *'le droit à la différence'*.

16   This preoccupation with constitutional reform was not confined to political dissidents. Leading parliamentary figures were equally concerned, and the 1932 election manifestos of most parties included proposals for amendments to the Constitution. Léon Blum himself devoted a book to the subject (*La Réforme gouvernementale*, 1936), as did the leading conservative politician, André Tardieu (*La Réforme de l'Etat*, 1934). Further contributions came from Maurice Ordinaire, leader of the conservative Union Républicaine in the Senate (*La Révision de la Constitution*, 1934), from the national secretary of the progressive Catholic party, Démocrates Populaires, J. Raymond-Laurent (*Face à la crise*, 1934), from the right-wing historian and later Vichy 'National Councillor', Senator Jacques Bardoux (*Refaire l'Etat ou subir la force*, 1935), and from the Radical politician who later became a leading 'Left Gaullist', René Capitant (*La Réforme du parlementarisme*, 1934).

17   The group of writers known as the Jeune Droite had largely come under the influence of the royalist Action Française, but had found Maurras doctrines ill-adapted to the new social and economic challenges of the twentieth century. They included figures like Thierry Maulnier, Jean de Fabrègues, Robert Francis, Drieu la Rochelle and Jean-Pierre Maxence, who contributed to reviews like *Combat, Réaction* and *Revue du XXe Siècle*, but also to more widely circulated periodicals of the extreme Right like *Candide, Gringoire* and *Je Suis Partout*. *L'Ordre Nouveau* included Robert Aron, formerly involved in the surrealist movement, Arnaud Dandieu, a Proudhonian socialist, Jean Jardin from Action Française and Jacques Naville, an ex-Trotskyite. *Esprit* derived largely from the progressive Catholic tradition of Marc Sangnier, but was also influenced by the ideas of the Belgian revisionist Socialist, Henri de Man. It nonetheless included a former Action Française member, Pierre-Henri Simon, an ex-Communist Ramon Fernandez, and prominent future academics like François Goguel and Georges Duveau. The contributors to the *Plan du neuf juillet* included neo-socialists, Radical Young Turks, members of Croix de Feu and Jeunesses Patriotes, and trade-union militants.

18   This critique of economic liberalism was central to the whole debate, but see especially Robert Aron and Arnaud Dandieu, *Le Cancer Américain*, Rieder, 1931 and Henri Daniel-Rops, *Le Monde sans âme*, Rieder, 1932.

19   Thus Daniel-Rops wrote 'it is comical to think that our politicians can still expect to be taken seriously when they ask whether clericalism is still the main danger, or whether submarines or torpedo boats are defensive or offensive weapons'. *Revue Française*, April, 1933, p. 496 (authors' translation).

20   It is not surprising in this context, to find that the 'socialism' of these groups recalls the ideas of Fourier, Proudhon, Péguy and other Socialist thinkers who fall outside the Marxist tradition. The work of the Belgian, Henri de Man, with its similar emphasis on the idealist dimension in socialism, was also influential in these circles, H. de Man, *Zur Psychologie des Sozialismus*, Brussels, 1927.

21   This doctrine envisaged institutions that would reflect the complex realities of human existence instead of reducing man to the status of Abstract 'citizen' — institutions that would 'replace the citizen by the producer, the individual by the community, the abstract man of the Encyclopaedists and the French Revolution by the real man of the Industrial Revolution, in short, by a man who has not only an 'opinion', but also and above all a trade, a regional identity, a homeland'. Aldo Dami, *Esprit* no. 21 (June 1934), p. 371 (authors' translation).

22   The establishment of a Conseil Economique et Social representing organised interest groups and endowed with consultative or legislative functions was part and parcel of most of the projects for constitutional reform in the 1930s. As far as the trade unions were concerned, the CGT had been closely involved in the planning of the war economy between 1914 and 1918, and the neo-socialists envisaged the integration of trade-union structures in their state-regulated 'St Simonian' technocracy. The ex-SFIO politician, Joseph Paul-Boncour, leader of a short-lived Government in January 1933, made his central policy the offer of regular consultation and collaboration with trade-union leaders.

23   Many of these writers remained faithful to the Maurrassian version of the monarchy. Some were later to support the Fascist proposals of Doriot's PPF. Their corporatist ideas were thus set within a fundamentally elitist perspective, and their social implications were at best paternalistic and at worst thoroughly authoritarian, *L'Ordre Nouveau's* recommendations were more radical, including as they did schemes for profit-sharing and for the sharing of tedious manual tasks through an eighteen-month draft of men from all walks of life into factory labour. These utopian formulae were, however, still derived from the sentimental belief that class antagonisms could be dissipated without fundamental changes in existing property relations. *Esprit* was more conscious of the reactionary implications of 'corporatism' within the framework of capitalism. It recommended new forms of common ownership within the firm and the development of a flexible planning process, and deferred the introduction of the 'corporatist' structures to a 'post-revolutionary' period by which time the balance of social forces would have been profoundly modified.

24   The Solidarité Française was formed in 1933 by the war veteran, Jean Renaud, and enjoyed the support of the industrialist, François Coty, and his newspaper, *L'Ami du Peuple*. It was never much more than an organised street-fighting force with crude slogans imported from Nazi Germany and Fascist Italy. Maxence later explained that it was this absence of doctrine which led him to see Solidarité Française as a potential platform for his ideas (Loubet del Bayle, op. cit., p. 60).

25   Jean Coutrot, an economist and *polytechnicien*, is credited with having formed a group called 'Synarchie', composed largely of graduates of the Grand Ecoles and seeking to replace parliamentary democracy by a system of government by professional technocrats.

26   Hence the coining of the aphorism 'Rocard d'Estaing' by sections of the left-wing CERES group in the PS.

27   This concept has entered the discourse of the established political parties. Socialist party spokesmen frequently talk of *une autre croissance* and of *une nouvelle croissance sociale*. See also *Energie: l'autre politique* (Club Socialiste du Livre, 1981), p. 35.

28   By the late sixties the membership of the SFIO was down to 60,000, and at the presidential elections of 1969 the Socialist candidate, Gaston Defferre, won only 5 per cent of the vote. The process which saw the disbanding of the SFIO and the formation of the new PS between 1969 and 1971 involved not only an organisational but also an ideological transformation. The adoption of many of the themes of May 1968 and the new strategy of political collaboration with the Communists marked a radical departure from the centrist social-democratic image displayed by the party in the fifties and sixties.

29   The 1975 occupation and work-in at the Besançon watch factory of *Lip*, and the struggle of the Larzac farming community against the use of their land for military purposes acquired considerable mythical importance in the 1970s as symbols of the *autogestionnaire* ideal.

30   For a consideration of the problem of class alliances in relation to the recent evolution of the French Communist Party, see the chapter by Jolyon Howorth in *Contemporary French Political Parties* (D. S. Bell (ed.), Croom Helm 1982).

PART II   WRITERS AND INTELLECTUALS

5   Nizan: a matter of death and life

WALTER REDFERN
University of Reading

I start with an apology (a false one). My approach, my preferences, my professional formation (and deformation) are mainly literary. But I want to argue that literature, and in this instance one haunted by death, can still contribute something of value to political reflection. To dwell on death is no doubt to begin with the end. Yet some centuries ago Pascal found that this was an efficient intellectual and rhetorical strategy. In our own time, writers of the broadly 'Existentialist' persuasion – Malraux, Sartre, Camus – have given a lay extension to Pascal's theological terrorism. Instead of the fear of God, they have sought to instil in us the dread of the unlived life. Nizan belongs with this tradition.

In the late 1920s, Nizan bolted from Paris and the Ecole dite Normale et prétendue Supérieure to Aden. He was suffering from intimations of asphyxia. As a *Normalien*, he experienced the very special world of that select establishment as a hothouse severed from and insulated against reality, a buffer-state against the facts of life. Like most well educated (indeed over educated) young Frenchmen, until the recently erupting counter-culture began to devalue literature and to promote optical effects, rhythms and noise, Nizan was a very literary youth. (The question of bookishness is almost always crucial in any consideration of French writers, who could nearly all say, like Camus's clamence: 'au-je lu cela ou l'ai-je pensé?' Did I read that somewhere, or was it my own idea? This is why *Madame Bovary* is so central a text in the French tradition). Nizan exploited this bookishness against the ruling class that he had begun to hate. His essay, *Aden Arabie,* focuses on the twin targets of the *Université* and colonialism: the parochial and the universal. (Though some Frenchmen are notoriously given to mistaking their *alma mater,* or Paris, for the whole world. This has been called umbilicism.) The connection between the two targets is that the spurious values inculcated by the first agent (the *Université*) – the cult of impersonal reason, which leads to a-historical stances and to political absentionism (i.e. conservatism) – permit and indeed encourage the practice of the second: colonial exploitation. Aden itself lies in the centre of an extinct volcano, like a huge shell-crater, and ecologically it is largely sterile. It must be an apocalyptic landscape, and Nizan's figurative description of it as 'the mouth of hell' hardly an exaggeration. Spotting fishbones exposed on the beach led him to see Aden as a skeletal image of Europe. The sign-language of capitalism, its obsession with ciphers on paper, create an abstract drama with two-dimensional supernumeraries. Yet these phantoms, these superior sub-men, exercise real powers of life and death over their employees. Seeking to do the dirty on his class of origin as a small blow of solidarity for the oppressed workers, Nizan, in line with Lenin's instruction to steal back and to use against the bourgeoisie what it had stolen from others, exploits capitalist imagery and expropriates a lordly register, in order to indict the bosses on behalf of the bossed. But his critique is not all turned outwards. Having seen Western man resumed in an Eastern context, he felt he was receiving a terrible warning of his own imminent collapse into death-in-life. *Aden Arabie* is the account of a near-miss. Nizan treats sardonically his own foolish need to travel abroad in order to discover some home truths. His cerebral vertigo would begin to abate only when he could find a precise direction for his hatred and his energy. He was always pregnable. His work is built on the tensions of the narrow escape, last-ditch salvage, precarious survival. The movement of *Aden Arabie* goes not so much from dilemma to solution (Nizan was caustic, a long time before Sartre's *Les Mots*, towards the whole concept of the writer-as-saviour: no man can be a St. Bernard dog), as from a nameless fear to an identifiable opponent.

His first novel, *Antoine Bloyé*, brooded more comprehensively on the question of death-in-life. It starts and ends with the death of its hero. In between, his life-curve is pictured as a treadmill. He is a brighter than average lad of peasant stock, directed by his 'betters' to a technical education designed to provide the middle management for the railway-boom of the late-nineteenth century. He moves steadily through the stages of driver, engineer, depot manager, in the course of a life which is outwardly successful but inwardly frustrated. At intervals, this inarticulate good worker senses that much of his being lies fallow, but he does nothing to get himself off the rails of his seemingly preordained life. He never integrates his spasmodic anger into political action. Though written by a Communist, this novel deals with a pre-Communist man. This is Marxism with a strong emphasis on personal responsibility as well as on economic determinism. Antoine, besides, is caught not only in the spider's web of capitalist industrialism, but also in the 'saccharine slavery' of a respectable bourgeois marriage. Nizan makes full room for psychology, for the role of dreams, for the private self. Indeed, the most impressive section of this powerful novel describes the aging of Antoine: his impotent sex-furies, his naked terror of dying before he has truly lived. He has been living what Céline would later call *la mort à crédit*, — death on the instalment plan.

This novel accommodates not only Marx and Freud, but also Pascal. Bloyé's life is one long *divertissement*. In a rare moment of awareness, Antoine telescopes a lifespan of seventy years into one day. The idea of dying 'at midnight' instead of in some vague 'thirty years from now' has a real Pascalian flavour and punch. Shortly before his actual death, Antoine sees a 'defeated image of himself, that headless being that walked in the ashes of time with hurrying steps, aimlessly'. Disciples of F. R. Leavis might well judge this novel's death-motif life-denying, but I myself find here not gratuitous morbidity but a generous concern for what men do, or sadly fail to do, to counteract their imposed fates. Besides, as well as the convincing account of alienated labour, this novel includes, by way of counter-balance, an equally persuasive picture of fulfilling and exciting work (in Antoine's youth). Nizan's first novel clearly accentuates the negative, but as a way of building an honest foundation for the positive. Its protagonist, or rather agonist, submits to the 'call of the tame', but his son's growing anger foretells different options for the next generation. *Antoine Bloyé* says, in effect: here are the facts. Now, what are we to do with what is done to us?

Nizan's second novel, *Le Cheval de Troie*, switches from the helpless solitary to the militant group: Communist workers and intellectuals in the French provinces. It is the time (the early 1930s) of the physical confrontation between Fascist and anti-Fascist groups. In a climactic street-battle, the latter are eventually routed by the riot police after putting the Fascists to flight. Their losses mean that any sense of victory is reduced and tempered, but at least they have learnt in their bones the value of solidarity in action. Any propagandist element in this novel is likewise muted, or diversified, by Nizan's awareness that political commitment does little to abolish private anguish. While the workers are winning their dubious battle on the streets, the wife of one of them dies agonisingly and alone after an abortion. In Nizan's non-miraculous world, everything has to be paid for. Real death, then, confronts combatants and non-combatants alike. A more metaphysical, cerebral variety obsesses an intellectual, Lange, who ends up siding with the Fascists, when his speculations, spinning around in a void of scepticism and indeed nihilism, propel him to grab a gun and to fire on the crowd of workers. Abstract, unattached thought, for Nizan (and he probably had in mind figures like Drieu la Rochelle) can easily veer into lethal options. *Le Cheval de Troie* can no more be summed up as 'edifying' than *Antoine Bloyé* could be as 'negative'.

Nizan's true domain is the problematical, and this is quintessentially that of the genuine writer.

While writing his novels and essays, Nizan was also functioning as a party hack, or at least journeyman, penning foreign affairs commentaries, book reviews and polemical cultural articles for a wide range of Communist or fellow-travelling journals. Within the Communist Party, his position was one of animation, but perhaps of the suspended variety. I think Pascal Ory is right to stress how much Nizan refused to say or to think in such circumstances. As a boxer can pull his punches, so Nizan increasingly 'pulled' his initial sectarianism. Although on his ritual tour of Soviet Russia Nizan was sincerely impressed by some of the improving metamorphoses he witnessed, he never forgot to ask the sixty-four dollar question: does Communism help you to face death with any more equanimity?

In *La Conspiration,* he provided the most achieved and balanced of his three novels. In it, he states: 'a young man is the only one with guts enough to demand all-or-nothing, and to feel robbed if he does not get it'. But simultaneously he was offering the counter-proposition: 'I will not allow anyone to tell me that youth is the best years of our lives'. It is this coexistence of passion and cold-eyed judgment that gives Nizan's prose its characteristic tone.

The young men in question are university students in Paris in the mid-1920s. But beyond this particularised area, it is general French intellectual life in one of its habitual postures that is being scrutinised here: the readiness to believe that a thought is an action, that the mere fact of verbalisation actually influences situations. Nizan's young rebels indict their society which they persist in seeing mainly in terms of their families. The periodical that they launch is directed much more against the idealist philosophy of the Sorbonne than towards concrete militant action. The first issues provoke that response intolerable to rebels: impunity (or, in a later term, 'repressive tolerance'); they find they can say, if not do, what they feel like. For all his cloak-and-dagger intellectual bravado, the peer group's leader, Rosenthal, frets over what Nizan calls 'the family poisons which his liver and kidneys would never be able to evacuate'. When he embarks on an adulterous love affair, he keeps it within the family: his sister-in-law. Summoned before a family tribunal after the affair has been discovered, and having already lost interest in his would be seditious plans for military and industrial espionage on behalf of Soviet Russia, Rosenthal concludes precociously that the only irrevocable option left open to him is the will to die, and he commits suicide. After taking poison, he as last sees clearly that he is the victim of a robbery, though not clearly enough that he himself connived at the robbery by not asserting his independence forcefully. I think it is a measure of Nizan's imaginative powers that he can persuade us both that Rosenthal is a fake, a *poseur*, and that his premature death is a waste of someone who could have made of his life something more useful to others and hence to himself. He is something of a luxury victim, but luxuries are important in the general economy of Nizan's world view.

Another young man, Laforgue, altogether more serious than Rosenthal, borrows from his readings in anthropology the notion of the puberty rites of primitive tribes. Whereas young tribesmen accept physical testing and educative punishment, Western youths are left to wallow in their psychic malaise. When Laforgue falls gravely ill, his illness acts as his initiator, his 'medicine-man'. For the first time, he is obliged to immerse himself totally in an experience. When the coma eventually relents, he is bowled over by the sheer and simple joy of survival. His second go at life begins, but the price he pays is the knowledge that, after twenty years of marking time, he is now living towards death. And the lucid, but not paralysing, consciousness of death is essential to Nizan's conception of how to life authentically. Although the idealistic Rosenthal kills himself; and another young man, the absolutist turncoat Pluvinage, ends up in moral suicide, *La Conspiration* finishes with Laforgue's symbolic death and rebirth, his change of life in an initiation rite. Nizan always insisted on the painfulness of all transitions.

This novel features two Communist Party members: the veteran Carré, sure of his choice and its meaningfulness, and young Pluvinage, a misfit. Anticipating the Sartrean motif of *le regard,* Nizan stresses that it was the condemning gaze of his family that first induced in the as yet guiltless adolescent a sense of guilt. Indeed, so full of empathy is Nizan's motivation of Pluvinage, this novel's chief betrayer (he eventually consents to becoming a police informer), that when Nizan left the Party at the time of the Hiter–Stalin Pact in 1939, his erstwhile comrades claimed hysterically that he was a twenty-four carat traitor and that his understanding of Pluvinage proved it. This is rather like saying that Walt Disney must have been a rodent to conceive Mickey Mouse. To me, all that Nizan's close attention to the young man's act of betrayal proves is that Nizan knew his duty as a novelist (and indeed as a student of politics): know your enemy, think his thoughts.

The father of Pluvinage was the director of the Paris registry of deaths. The boy was conditioned by the mortuary world from early childhood, to the extent that his juvenile collection was of catalogue pictures of coffins and tombstones. Nizan gives him all the trappings of the Dostoevskyan

morbid intellectual, a marginal being terrified of becoming totally superfluous. He has an early intuition of the complex structure of social organisation, and is much preoccupied with the contrast of underworlds and
overworlds. He is clearly already ripe both for joining the Communist
Party and then later deserting it for the secret police. Just as Rosenthal
takes his own life, Pluvinage hands over his: two forms of self-destruction
after two abortive existences. (If you think that, in his treatment of
Pluvinage's death-haunted environment and his hapless life, Nizan is
piling it on thick, then you are dead right. But medical opinion accepts the
condition known as accident proneness. Should we not also allow for the
state of misery-proneness, a natural or induced affinity with the lugubrious?)
Through Pluvinage, Nizan warns that Communism may be the salvation
only of those who devote themselves to its aims generously, and that it
cannot afford to be a foster home for the neglected children of the bourgeoisie who refuse to grow up. *La Conspiration* finishes, not with Pluvinage's
end-stopped position, but with Laforgue's as yet shapeless and incipient
transformation (which was due to be developed in a later novel, lost when
Nizan was killed in 1940). Some of the elements of Nietzsche's recipe
for rebels in an unrebellious age are already present and active within
Laforgue: 'objection, joyous distrust and love of irony are signs of health:
everything absolute belongs to pathology'.

I want to stress that Nizan's own sense of humour, of fun, was as deep
rooted, as visceral, as his nightmares and his frequent gloom. His photos
make him look disconcertingly like Harold Lloyd, one of his culture
heroes. Like Harold Lloyd, Nizan was as obsessed with the death-defying
(what Malraux would more pompously call *'l'anti-destin'*) as he was with
death itself. Acrobatically, Nizan survived being a member of the Communist Party all those years, a *funambule* to Louis Aragon's *fumiste*. He
never went in for what linguisticians call 'the mucker-pose' (i.e. the
affectation of sub-standard speech), and indeed was always something of
a dandy, like another of his heroes, the poet Jules Laforgue, who also
died young and who also sported a mask of insolent nonchalance over
deep-seated anxieties. Nizan's fixation on death never made him limp or
fatalistic. It always seemed to act as a spur, because it was teamed with
anger. Like Dylan Thomas, he could urge: 'do not go gentle into that good
night'.

Nizan was murdered, posthumously, by the hatchet-men of the French
C.P. It has of recent years become possible for a few party intellectuals to
admit, and to regret, this attempted liquidation. But Nizan has been since
his death, as his loyal friend Sartre put it, 'a vigorous corpse'. (This was
the projected title of my book on Nizan, but the publishers thought it

would flummox booksellers, who might shelve it alongside *Dracula* books.) Nizan's splendidly vital widow, Henriette, commented recently that Nizan, in each of his novels, tries on different forms of death, as a means of exorcising his own fixation on dying. Perhaps *memento mori* has always been a more usable motto than *dulce et decorum est pro patria mori*. I think Nizan himself put it best, in *Le Cheval de Troie*: 'on ne change rien qu'au risque de la mort, on ne transforme rien qu'en pensant à la mort'. He uses death to measure life, to ask all the awkward questions: who does our thinking for us, and why do we allow it? Why do we let ourselves live so badly? No doubt the reader will add his own awkward questions.

6   Political perspectives in Resistance fiction

MARGARET ATACK
University of Leeds

Resistance literature was never meant to be read or judged in purely literary terms, never saw itself as detached commentary on a particularly difficult situation. The *Manifeste du Comité National des Ecrivains*, published in the first issue of its journal, *Les Lettres françaises,* in September 1942, makes it perfectly clear that Resistance writing is part of a wider context, that of the fight for the liberation of the country. Only once the imprtance of the Resistance and the role of the Front National, the broad alliance organisation of the Parti Communiste, have been affirmed does it present the specific attack on French literature and culture and the particular role of the writers. But this is not to say that cultural activity was considered to be of secondary importance — on the contrary, it is one of the commonplaces of Resistance writing that the war was being fought as much in defence of the ideas and beliefs broadly defined as humanist as for the liberation of the national territory. Equally important to the definition of the social value of culture under the occupation is the fact that this was a time when the material conditions of the production of literature and the nature of what was being said are seen to be explicitly linked, since public speech was subject to the approval of the German propaganda bureau:

> Le régime qui nous est imposé, où toute liberté de pensée et d'expression est supprimée, où seuls ont le droit d'écrire et de parler ceux qui chantent les louanges de l'ennemi, préfigure ce que serait dans l'Ordre Nouveau le sort de notre culture.[1]

Many writers refused to publish in the press, for to accept German censorship was ultimately to accept the presence of the German army from which it drew its power, and to give an impression of approval, or at least normality, to an unacceptable situation. To write and speak within officially sanctioned limits was necessarily to remain quiet about a range of issues and events whose suppression was essential to the maintenance of official discourse. The first issue of *La Pensée libre* proclaimed in February 1941: 'aujourd'hui, en France, littérature légale veut dire: littérature de trahison'.[2] And so that which cannot be said officially has to be said unofficially. The first and most obvious thing to remember about most of the literary production of the Resistance is that it was clandestine. No literature of the period could avoid being placed across the great public/clandestine divide, at no time could the arguments for the neutrality and autonomy of the literary sphere have been weaker. Indeed, the championing of the values of 'pure literature' was derided in the pages of *Les Lettres françaises* as a transparent means of silencing uncomfortable references to the real situation. That awareness of a political context determining what could or could not be said was a crucial factor in the constitution of clandestine literature as a Resistance *activity*. To read the fiction, or indeed the tracts and newspapers, as documents reacting to and reflecting the events is really to miss the point. Those words were not reflecting the struggle, they were deliberately and overtly part of it. The second issue of *Les Lettres françaises* published an 'Appel aux écrivains français', which included the following exhortation: 'passez à la résistance active en publiant des oeuvres exaltant l'amour de la patrie et de la liberté, rendant hommages aux Francs-Tireurs et Partisans qui luttent courageusement pour bouter hors de France les hordes nazies et leurs valets Kollaborateurs'.[3]

However, to emphasise the social and political function of clandestine literature is not to suggest that it was informed by a homogeneous vision of the nature of the war which was being waged. If we turn to the structures of writing, a clear distinction can be established between a national and a political perception of the situation, which can be seen most clearly in the changing nature of the enemy to be faced.

The national discourse opposed the two nations, France and Germany, and was characterised by an insistence on national identity and psychology. It therefore inevitably drew on the long-established cultural differences opposing either France and *l'éternelle Allemagne,* the dangerous neighbour constituted by Germanic hordes of the distant past, Prussian militarism and nationalism, a lack of individuality and a culture characterised by dark irrational passions in pursuit of the absolute; or, on the other hand, France and *les deux Allemagnes,* where Germany's cultural achievements were continually menaced by the Prussian element in the German nature. The discourse of anti-facism opposed the political forces of the oppressor, the fascist invader, to the people of France, who, in alliance with the peoples of Germany, Russia and England, was struggling against them. These two discourses were therefore formally heteregeneous — there was no possibility for the national configuration opposing the German to perceive any group of Germans as not being the enemy. Henri Michel considers that this position was typical of the Resistance movements as a whole. He argues 'Les Mouvements de résistance ne croient pas, ou ne disent pas, comme les Communistes, que le peuple allemand lutte, lui aussi, contre ses oppresseurs, et qu'il recèle des trésors de bonté'[4] and sums up their position as 'Nazisme et Allemagne, c'est tout un'.[5] He was right to exclude the Parti Communiste, whose strategy, as exemplified in the constitution of the Front National pour la libération et l'indépendance de la France, is essentially a continuation of its policies under the Popular Front, a broad alliance against fascism in combination with a patriotic defence of the Republican and revolutionary traditions. The Comité National des Ecrivains therefore grouped intellectuals of all political persuasions, many of whom were already active in the anti-fascist movement of the thirties, axiomatic to which was solidarity with the victims of fascism everywhere, in Spain, Italy or Germany. This distinction between political and national attitudes and themes was further compounded by the division between the occupied and unoccupied zones. In the absence of the Germans in the south until November 1942, there developed a strongly ideological and political movement in opposition to Vichy.

There are none the less definite overlaps in the two discourses, however different the logic behind them may have been. This is due primarily to the fact that they both relied on the terms of humanism to mediate the opposition. To the France of reason, of individual freedom and tolerance, the national configuration opposed a militarist, barbarian Germany. But the anti-fascist movement also defined Nazism as anti-humanist, monstrous and barbarous, as committed to the destruction of German culture as it was to that of the French, which means that the defence of culture, and specifically French culture, was *de facto* ideological opposition to Nazism. To this must be added the political analysis of the Nazi use of culture, imposing German culture on the French as part of the process of subordination, a German culture which the Nazis have no compunction in distorting to serve their own ends. *Les Lettres françaises* denounced their control of the media, theatre and cinema, the transformation of the Opéra de Paris into a *succursale de Berlin*, the Comédie Française into a *troupe allemande*. Rejection of public performance of German culture was therefore necessary as part of the struggle against the Nazis: 'assez de célébration d'Allemagne, de jubilés allemands. Assez de commémoration de gloires allemandes volées par les nazis! Vive le génie français!'[6] This patriotic defence of French land, French culture, tradition and history was so close to the purely national defence of France as to merge with it at times. Longer expositions especially tended to slide into a patriotic fervour where the unique quality of 'Frenchness' is indistinguishable, on its own, from the qualitative definition proper to nationalism.

More importantly perhaps, it was difficult to avoid a specifically national element in Nazism when the terms of the debate were those of the opposition essential to humanism, between the particular and the general. Humanism posits a common universal humanity in which each unique individual partakes, and respect for the individual is a recognition of the value of this human quality. By the logic of the oppositional structure, to criticise Nazism in humanist terms was therefore to present it as humanism's negative image, as a force which rejected the notion of the individual in the name of the collective, outside which the individual had no value, and rejected the universal in the name of the purely national. But these were also elements in the traditional images of Germany. The humanist denunciation, an integral part of political opposition to Fascism from the thirties on, tended therefore to continue the dichotomy of *les deux Allemagnes* even when it was insisting on a specifically dated opposition rather than a general national one. But what is interesting about the fiction of the Resistance is that it was formally impossible, within the oppositional structure of the narrative, for the two positions to overlap.

Resistance fiction is defined by its very name: it is fiction which sought to promote a pro-Resistance interpretation and to exalt the values which it considered were officially silenced. It is literally a *littérature de combat* and as such is very different from most of the postwar novels which took the Resistance or the occupation as their subject. Essential to the structures of this writing was the figure of the enemy who, either as function or subject of the text, constituted the negative element which was to be fought against. Both the identity of the enemy and the nature of the opposing group were determined by the overall perspective of the narrative, be it national or political, since there was a formal necessity for a certain homogeneity between the two terms to maintain the structural coherence of the narrative. The clearest example of these two different orders operating within the narrative lies in a comparison between Vercors' famous story, *Le Silence de la mer*, and 'Le Tilleul', one of the *Contes d'Auxois*, which were written by Edith Thomas, an important member of the *Comité National des Ecrivains,* and also published clandestinely by the Editions de Minuit.

Both stories are concerned with the process of identification of the enemy. The basic narrative enigma of *Le Silence de la mer* is similar to that of many pre-war novels about the German: is he friend or foe? It was written against the official policy of collaboration, against what Sartre calls the *courtoisie apprise de l'occupant*[7] and seeks to prove to the reader that whatever his personal virtues, the individual German soldier is still the enemy, as representative of a military occupying power which is bent on the destruction of France. These relations of hostility and friendship between France and Germany are devolved onto individual characters who are virtually reducible, in this very short story, to functions of that opposition. To take the elements of the German first: this is constituted by the military invader (the soldiers who approach the house to see if it is suitable to billet an officer there, and Werner von Ebrennac, the officer himself); by German culture, and especially music (von Ebrennac is a composer); by the brutality of the German nature (von Ebrennac's fiancée tears off a mosquito's legs one by one — he ends the engagement); and by Nazi oppression (von Ebrennac's German friends in Paris who tell him they are pretending to want an alliance with France the better to destroy her). These are the terms of the pre-existing structure opposing France and *les deux Allemagnes* and to which individual psychology is subordinated. The French is the homogenous other term, constituted by an old man and his niece, who just *are* and are French, with no particular qualifying attributes. They maintain their dignified silence of protest, while von Ebrennac, his dreams of a complementary union between the two countries destroyed by contact with the realities of Nazism, displays the virtues of German obedience and departs for the Eastern front, effectively being reclaimed by the military machine which first deposited him on the French people's doorstep.

Unlike *Le Silence de la mer*, *Le Tilleul* is written from an overtly political perspective, but its narrative structure is not dissimilar. From an undifferentiated group of German soldiers, one, Hans, will be singled out for special attention. He makes friends with a French woman, La Renaude, in the village where he is staying — he does errands for her, she mends his socks and makes him drinks of *tilleul* in the evening. Her positive evaluation of him is to be confirmed as he relates the situation in Germany and his own family history of hostility to the Nazis. It is shown that Hitler's first victory was over fellow Germans:

Mais vous êtes vainqueurs, vous, dit la Renaude.
Nous sommes vaincus, dit Hans. Nous sommes vaincus depuis le 30 janvier 1933.[8]

Opposition to the Nazis came from the factory workers, the unemployed and the communists. Hitler was on the side of the rulers: 'C'est Hitler qui

a sauvé le capitalisme chez nous. Et c'est nous qui le sauvons chez vous.'[9]
Those hostile to Hitler, like Hans' father, who is finally arrested and shot,
hold meetings after dark, have to be careful of those who were known to
be Nazis. The parallel with the Resistance is obvious: the arrests, the
tortures, the trust that those caught would not give the names of the
others — everything recalls the life of those opposed to the occupation
in France. The distinction was thus firmly established between the Nazis
and the German people. Elimination of their opponents allowed the
Nazis to claim they were speaking in the name of the whole German
nation and to trick people into believing they were free. They had been
duped, and one of the major ways in which this was achieved was by
the suppression of certain books. Hans comments: 'Moi je me souvenais
de la mort de mon père. J'avais réussi à me procurer les livres interdits
qu'il lisait. J'apprenais à comprendre la mort de mon père. C'est le seul
espoir qui nous reste d'être sauvés. Et à vous aussi, peut-être.'[10] There is
no contradiction between Hans' criticism and the reality of the Nazis for,
unlike von Ebrennac, he is formed within an historical and political
perspective.

This historical perspective to the narrative is essential to the identification of a political enemy for it constitutes the Resistance as the culmina-
tion of a long struggle against Fascism. In both Simone de Beauvoir's
Le Sang des autres and Aragon's *Les Rencontres,* the main characters pass
through the experiences of the Popular Front, the Spanish civil war and
Munich, until the presence of the foreign invaders in France clarifies the
narrative conflicts and allows the characters to pass into action. This
history can also be indexed by brief references, such as the following
comment from Elsa Triolet's *Les Amants d'Avignon*: 'Dans le patelin . . .
ils avaient tous voté pour les communistes, en 36, c'est dire combien ils
les aiment, les Boches!'[11] *Le Puits des miracles,* by André Chamson, is
concerned with the identification of the internal enemy, Vichy and its
supporters, presented as the exploiters of the people. It is set in a town in
the southern zone, and ends with the arrival of the Germans on Armistice
Day 1942. But the rich and powerful group in the town have already been
identified as the enemy: the novel is devoted to accounts of the financial
profiteering accompanied by denunciations of materialism, of the rich,
and the suffering of the poor. The narrator is completely confused by all
this until the occasion of a great banquet, set for 200 places, to celebrate
the new order, at which the main speaker declares: 'cette France abattue,
écrasée par le malheur, je la préfère à l'autre!'[12] Together with the diatribes
from the narrator against the 200 guests, the direct descendants of the 200
families denounced in the thirties, this inevitable recall of the famous

phrase 'plutôt Hitler que le Front Populaire' again establishes the historical continuity with a political past.

It is interesting to consider for a moment the postwar destiny of these political stories which, unless they are still read because of the importance of their author, have by and large been forgotten. Compare this to *Le Silence de la mer*, probably the single most famous Resistance story, though its function has significantly changed since 1942. The precise circumstances in which it was written, the policy of collaboration, the meeting of Hitler and Pétain at Montoire, have virtually been forgotten, and it is read above all as a paradigm of what resistance was. In this text, defence of humanism is elided with the defence of the spiritual and cultural soul of France, which was fully present in the two French people. This is typical of the national configuration, and is illustrated quite clearly by R. P. Chaillet, in the context here of Christian resistance: 'Il a suffi d'aimer la France pour ne pas la trahir . . . Les Français n'ont fait qu'obéir à la loi de leur être et rien n'a pu les détourner de cette fidélité essentielle.'[13] The figure of the German in *Le Silence de la mer* is a composite one, and necessarily so in a narrative structure which uses it as the focus for the articulation of the military, the cultural and the individual. France and the French, however, are homogenous and inseparable; the atmosphere in the room, the dignity of the individuals constituted the tangible embodiment of the spiritual essence of France. All they have to do is to *be,* in order to coincide with the values of honour and humanism, for that is their being. It is so difficult not to see here one of the reasons for the postwar popularity of this story, as all the complexities, and indeed the nastiness of the period disappear in favour of a confrontation between two national entities, where resistance is equated with a dignified refusal, both noble and poignant, which is innate in the French character.

I would argue that this is partly because, after the event, it is no longer functioning as an argument but as a statement; but also that its success may provide literary evidence of the postwar devaluing of the political aspects of the Resistance in favour of a purely national confrontation involving a conception of an essential, ideal France in which all French people necessarily partake. As the political fiction shows, there were other forces behind the opposition to Germany and Vichy. It is a regrettable impoverishment of the literary production of the Resistance that these stories are so often overlooked.

Notes

1.   *Les Lettre françaises* no. 1 (September 1942), p. 1. 'The regime imposed upon

us in which all freedom of thought and expression is suppressed and where the right to write and speak is only allowed to those who sing the praises of the enemy, prefigures the fate of our culture in the New Order'.

2. Quoted in Pierre Seghers, *La Résistance et ses poètes*, Paris, Seghers, 1974, p. 105. 'Today in France legal literature means literature of betrayal'.

3. *Les Lettres françaises* no. 2 (October 1942), p. 4. 'Go over to active resistance by publishing works exalting love of the homeland and freedom and rendering hommage to the irregulars and partisans fighting courageously to boot out the Nazi hordes and their collaborating lackeys'.

4. Henri Michel, *Les Courants de pensée de la résistance*, Paris, P.U.F., 1962. 'The resistance movements do not believe or do not say, as the Communists do, that the German people is also struggling against its oppressors and that it contains great goodness'.

5. Ibid, p. 209, 'Nazism and Germany, it's all one'.

6. The failure of cultural propaganda, *La scène française* in *Les Lettres françaises*. 'Enough of German celebrations and German jubilees. Enough of commemorating German glories stolen by the Nazis. Long live French genius'.

7. Jean-Paul Sartre, *Situations II*, Paris, Gallimard, 1948, p. 122.

8. 'Le Tilleul' in *Contes d'Auxois*, Paris, Ed. de Minuit. First public edition 1945, p. 33. 'But you are conquerors, said La Renaude. We are vanquished ourselves, said Hans. We were vanquished on the 30th January 1933'.

9. Ibid, p. 33. 'Hitler saved capitalism in Germany and we are saving it in France'.

10. Ibid, p. 36. 'I remembered my father's death. I had managed to get hold of the forbidden books that he read. I was learning to understand my father's death. It's our only hope if we are to be saved, and perhaps yours too'.

11. Elsa Triolet, *Les Amants d'Avignon* in *Le Premier Accroc coûte deux cents francs*, Paris, Denoël, 1945, pp. 38-9. 'In the village they'd all voted for the communists. That's how much they liked the Boches!'

12. André Chamson, *Le Puits des miracles*, Paris, Gallimard, 1945, p. 207. 'This France, beaten, crushed by misfortune — I prefer this France to the other'.

13. Quoted in Louis Parrot, *L'Intelligence en guerre*, Paris, La Jeune Parque, 1945, p. 190. 'It was sufficient to love France not to betray her . . . The French merely obeyed the law of their being and nothing could distract them from that essential faithfulness'.

7 'Que reste-t-il de nos amours?'
Intellectuals and the Left in post-1968 France

KEITH READER
Kingston Polytechnic

Developments on the French intellectual Left since the events of 1968 cannot be considered in isolation from what has gone before, however hard certain sections of that same Left may have tried to hypostatise superstructure and theory. That intellectuals have long since occupied an important and privileged place in the French social and political formation is a widely accepted fact, on which a good deal of work has recently been done. The sociologist Raymond Boudon, in his article 'L'Intellectuel et ses publics: les singularités françaises',[1] has detected a tendency in recent years away from specialist evaluation of an intellectual product by the producer's peer-group towards a more diffuse and general market, in which press, radio, and television journalism play a crucial part — in Boudon's perspective a move towards vulgarisation in the English sense as well as *vulgarisation à la française,* and one which will clearly place intellectuals very much more in the centre of the national consciousness. For Régis Debray in *Le Scribe,* the intellectual's central importance in French political life goes back much further, to France's emergence in 1789 as the first bourgeois nation-state, which in some manner 'patented' the modern idea of a nation that had been prefigured by such writers as Montesquieu and Rousseau. Hervé Hamon and Patrick Rotman, in their entertainingly scurrilous *Les Intellocrates,* placed great stress on the concentration of French intellectual life on Paris and of Parisian intellectual life on a relatively small area of the Left Bank — a world geographically barely larger than the cut-throat publishing microcosm of Balzac's *Illusions perdues,* but one whose repercussions are amplified by the media throughout France and beyond. Debray in his earlier *Le Pouvoir intellectuel en France* had spoken of the close connection between intellectual — particularly academic — life and the power and apparatuses of the state, evidenced by such institutions as the academic *concours* and the automatic publication of a successful *doctorat d'état* thesis (until recently at any rate). My own article in *Media, Culture and Society* (July 1982), comparing the role of the intellectual in the French and British social formations, attempts to draw out the implications of these diverse factors for the possibilities intellectuals have for political intervention. Debray's co-optation as one of President Mitterrand's political advisers is the best possible proof that this situation is widely recognised in the France of today.

It remains to be explained why I have chosen to address myself to the role played by French intellectuals on the Left after 1968. The events of May 1968, after all, though they started in the universities and can be said also to have finished there (where they yielded the most palpable and enduring results — *les acquis de mai*), were hardly an 'intellectual' pheno-menon, or not primarily one. The whole package of sexual 'liberation', *l'imagination au pouvoir,* the would-be opening of the universities to workers and peasants, and the exotic 'political armchair tourism' inspired by the examples of Cuba and China, while it could have sprung only from an educated milieu, could not best be described as intellectual, and the pressure to abolish or amend outmoded structures of university centrali-sation, curriculum and assessment often smacked as much of hedonistic anti-intellectualism as of a genuine desire for radical change. Yet the changes in the university world secured as a result of May did have a real impact on the pattern of French intellectual life. Boudon, sounding not unlike a French equivalent of Rhodes Boyson, goes so far as to blame the 'anything-goes' anarchism of May for rubbing off on intellectual life and eroding its rigour, and ascribes the decline in specialised research for a limited market to the greater equality and more automatic promotion that the teachers' unions were able to secure after 1968. Furthermore, the 'tenth-anniversary celebrations' and analyses produced in 1978, and then the election of a Socialist President in 1981, have contributed to the con-secration of May 1968 as a watershed or 'moment' in French intellectual and cultural history.

It seems most convenient and logical to look first at the evolution of the *gauchistes* of 1968 before examining the repercussions of the events upon the parties of the established Left (above all the PCF) and their attitudes towards the intellectuals in their midst. The term *gauchiste* seems now even more nebulous of definition than the political positions of some of those to whom it applies, but the category most interesting from our point of view is probably the Maoists, whether *maos-staliniens* or what came to be known as *maos-Spontex*. The latter term (based upon a well known make of domestic sponge) refers ironically on one hand to the Maoists' purist contempt for established French political institutions and obsession with spontaneous guerrilla-based insurrection; on the other to the blithe eclecticism with which they imbibed notions about the con-

junction of cultural and worker-peasant struggles. It involved a romanti-
cised view of China as the 'socialist paradise' the USSR had signally failed
to be, a concomitant belief that popular pressure for an end to the war in
Vietnam would somehow open up a revolutionary pathway between East
and West, and a Marcusean faith in the revolutionary potential of sexual
liberation; with hindsight the latter appears ironically incompatible with
the extreme puritanism of Chinese society. (I should perhaps make it clear
that it is not to any of the individual points of view itemised here that the
pejorative suffix *Spontex* applies so much as to their uncritical harnessing
to the same, largely non-existent revolutionary chariot.) The *maos-
staliniens* were to aridity and rigour what the *maos-spontex* were to
impulsiveness, tracing the onward path of Marxist-Leninist revolution
through Stalin to Mao and Enver Hoxha.

It was from the *mao-spontex* milieu that many of the so-called *nouveaux
philosophes* sprang — such names as Bernard-Henri Lévy, Philippe Némo
and their close associate Philippe Sollers, self-proclaimed 'Maoists' in 1968
but at best textual socialists. By this I mean that there was a tendency in
the France of the late sixties and early seventies, accentuated if not
actually sparked off by the 1968 stress on cultural struggle, to suppose
that the free floating of desire in and across the texts of such writers as
Nietzsche, Mallarmé, Joyce, Raymond Roussel, or Georges Bataille had a
revolutionary potential that went far beyond its impact on the censorious
worlds of criticism and academia. The extraordinary work of Jacques
Derrida demonstrates how rewarding and at the same time disturbing
such an approach can be at its best, yet all too often the link between
a style of textual (psycho-) analysis and a political stance was taken for
granted. What this often meant was that there was so to speak a lack of
analytical 'connecting-tissue' between the text(s) and the various forms of
Maoism or Socialism, so that the revelations of Solzhenitsyn about the
Gulag provoked even in so prominent a figure as Philippe Sollers, editor of
Tel Quel and sometime Maoist petition-signer extraordinary, a reaction
more evocative of Bernard Levin at his most vaporously philosophical
than of a writer supposed to have a high degree of political awareness.
The *nouveaux philosophes* salvaged what they could from the vocabulary
of Althusserian Marxism and Lacanian Freudianism in the interests of a
spiritualised humanism that, as John Ardagh suggests in his *France in the
1980s*, is reminiscent of a warmed-over version of the Camus of *L'Homme
Révolté*.[2] The effect is a little like meeting an ardent British 'sexual
revolutionary' of the late sixties, now married with 2.4 children and
solemnly extolling the liberating benefits of suburban life and the dangers
of promiscuity.

Psychoanalysis, thanks to the conjunction of the late-sixties concern with sexual liberation and the seminal work of Jacques Lacan at the École Freudienne de Paris, played a prominent part in the work of *Tel Quel* and of the *nouveaux philosophes*, often as the complement of Marxism. Its role in French intellectual life of recent years has arguably been more important than that of Marxism, if only because a great many former Maoists have tended to turn aside from politics altogether and find their way onto the psychoanalyst's couch. I would not care even to speculate on the reasons for this, having nowhere near sufficient evidence to go on. The explanations generally advanced seem to me either perilously neat (variants of the 'God-that-failed' approach with its implication that a commitment to revolution in the external world is but a symptom of discord and unhappiness within), or unpleasantly flip (psychoanalysis is the mode of the 1980s as revolution was of the 1960s and 1970s). This is not, of course, to deny that they undoubtedly contain elements of the truth; but more research and *recul* will be required if we are to go beyond them.

The most striking and tragic case of psychoanalysis impinging upon intellectuals on the French Left, however, was within the Communist Party — that of Louis Althusser. Always marginal to the mainstream of the Party's activities, and frequently in conflict with its leadership (from the time of his public debate with fellow-'dissident' Roger Garaudy in 1966 through to that of his continued defence of the concept of the dictatorship of the proletariat after the Central Committee had abandoned it), Althusser was the major advocate of Mao's philosophical ideas within the French intellectual world. His work on the concepts of contradiction, overdetermination, and the material specificity of the Marxist dialectic (in the collection of essays *Pour Marx*) secured him a considerable following, among students at the École Normale Supérieure (who worked on the publication *Cahiers pour l'analyse*) and an important faction of the PCF intelligentsia. It also led to the sacking of his office at the height of the May events, by self-styled 'Maoists' irate at Althusser's continued membership of and support for the Communist Party. That it was an essay by Althusser (published in an English translation as 'Freud and Lacan', as part of the collection *Lenin and Philosophy*) that brought to the fore possible connections between the decentring activity of Marxism and that of psychoanalysis appears in retrospect ironically prophetic. Althusser was in analysis for a long time and is at the time of writing interned in a psychoanalytic clinic after strangling his wife — an action interpreted by many as a kind of philosophical suicide *par personne interposée*, consequent upon the hostility his work had begun to attract from a variety of quarters. As well as the controversy he had aroused within the PCF (where his 'line' on the dictatorship of the proletariat was defeated), Althusser had been increasingly criticised by others on the Left. The 'Far Left' (Maoists, Trotskyists, and non-aligned left-wingers) had long been opposed to his support of the PCF, and in more academic and philosophical circles the tendency of much 'Althusserian' thought to bypass or minimise the importance of history and sociology, in favour of the construction of what appeared increasingly more remote theoretical models, had been strongly attacked. If one is to pursue the analogy of philosophical suicide, it is interesting in this connection to note that Madame Althusser was in fact a sociologist.

The other leading PCF intellectuals of the period — Henri Lefebvre, Roger Garaudy, Jean Elleinstein — all finally left the party, whether through expulsion, resignation or being adjudged to have 'excluded themselves'. The party undoubtedly wanted to regain as much as possible of the intellectual credibility it had lost as a result of its attitude to the May events, and this combined with the failure of most of the *gauchiste* movements to sustain their momentum after the June 1968 elections to boost the party's stock — at least temporarily — in the intellectual and academic world. (Elleinstein's little manual *Le P.C.* is a fairly representative distillation of the kind of discourse dominant among PCF intellectuals in the seventies.) But the *renouveau* was a relatively short-lived one. The leadership's attitudes towards first Afghanistan, then Poland; the rise of the *Parti Socialiste* as a more congenial alternative for those intellectuals hostile even to the suspicion of Stalinism; the marginalisation of successive oppositional intellectual currents, even to their forcible exclusion from the Party — all combined to see to that. Only a few years after producing *Le P.C.*, Elleinstein was writing for *Le Figaro-Magazine*, most widely read mouthpiece for the *nouvelle droite*, amid accusations of having sold himself to them as the 'token Jew'.

Que reste-t-il, then, *de nos amours?* — to reprise the Charles Trenet song cited in my title: of the libertarian *amours* supposedly unleashed by the sexual and hedonistic side of May (and in fact owing more to an affluent society's updating of surrealism than to any left-wing intellectualism in the true sense of the expression), and of 'those we have loved', the gurus of the May and post-May period of cultural and intellectual stirring? Derrida apart, the remainder of the hagiography is a rather mournful litany: Barthes killed in a road-accident, Lacan dead and heavily under fire for phallocracy both intellectual and personal, Foucault having produced hardly anything since the rather unsatisfying first volume of his projected *Histoire de la Sexualité* in 1977, Althusser seemingly destined to spend the rest of his life in a mental institution. Yet the picture is not so jaundiced as this might lead us to suspect. Debray's co-optation indicates how seriously the *nouveau régime* is prepared at least to appear to take the intellectual world. The mandarin exclusiveness and cultishness of much Left Bank post-structuralism is being offset in many areas — by feminist reappraisals and critiques of Lacan, by the important and detailed socio-logical research going on at the Maison des Sciences de l'Homme and influenced by the ideas of Pierre Bourdieu (himself an embryonic mandarin?), by a general feeling that the sixties' and seventies' stress on the importance of theory, will require constant scrutiny and an attention to practicality and practice as well as to praxis if it is not to get out of hand and lead left-wing intellectuals, by a route of elegant circularity, back into the ghetto from which they have been trying to emerge. It is as difficult to predict what will have become of the intellectual Left by the end of the Mitterrand presidency but the signs are not all unpromising.

Postscript

This chapter reproduces the paper given at the 1982 ASMCF Conference. However, it was felt necessary to give some account of the adverse com-ments it aroused there and of the author's response to them — both because the paper represents 'work in progress' towards a book-length study of the subject and because the criticism stemmed from two French participants (Madeleine Rebérioux of the University of Paris-VIII — formerly Vincennes — and François Hincker of the University of Paris-I).

These criticisms were of two kinds: factual and ideological. Thus, Hincker pointed out that Althusser's work was spoken of as though it had made its primary impact in France in the mid- and late sixties, whereas many of the essays grouped together in the collection *Pour Marx* (notably *Contradiction et surdétermination*) had first appeared in the earlier part of the decade, and had an immediate influence on left-wing thought. Mme Rebérioux pointed out the absence of any reference to the University of Vincennes, the major testing-ground for many of the anti-elitist ideas of 1968 until its (literal) des-truction and removal in a much more convenient form to Saint-Denis. Inevi-table constraints of time and space, given the condensed format of a con-ference paper, primarily accounted for this; but there was also the whole question of the 'British perspective' on 1968, which meant that many of the key ideas and developments on the Left in 1960s' France percolated through into British intellectual life with a delay of several years, and that it took the 'explosion' of the May events to bring to a wider intellectual audience work that had been influential in France for many years previously.

The discrepancy between French and British perspectives likewise underlay the two main ideological criticisms.[3] The first of these was the anecdotal treatment of the period, focusing on individuals and their death or decline rather than on ideas, institutions (such as Vincennes), and the general change in perspective on the Left wrought by the May events, and characterised by Mme Rebérioux as the 'rejection of economism'. The second, so closely allied with the first as to be almost indissociable from it, was rooted in the denigration of 1968 that (especially since the 'tenth-anniversary celebrations') has become fashionable in certain Parisian intellectual circles. The reasons for this are complex: the trough in left-wing political fortunes between the breakdown of the original *Programme Commun* and the Socialist presidential victory, the failure of most of the 'far-Left' groups to consolidate or build upon the gains they made as a result of May, and disillusionment with the Communist Party because of its increasingly pro-Soviet stance are among the most important. But there is another important point, alluded to by Mme Rebérioux in correspondence with the author when she spoke of 'those who spit upon what they once loved and thus make a double career'.[4] Many of the most ardent *gauchistes* of 1968 (notably the Maoists) have since turned to a radical individualism, which would doubtless describe itself as 'apolitical', and precisely in so doing would reveal its fundamental social conservatism. The movement towards psychoanalysis alluded to in the paper is one aspect of this, though the relations between Marxism and psychoanalysis are far more complex and ambiguous than that might suggest. The 'nine-days' wonder of the 'new philosophy', much of which was based upon a de-politicised, mysticalised deployment of Lacanian and Althusserian concepts,[5] was the most notorious example. Many of the 'new philosophers' and their adherents overtly favoured a right-wing stance, generally in the name of revolt against the so-called 'tyranny of ideology'. Thus, Philippe Némo became a committed Giscardian, and Philippe Sollers (erstwhile Maoist) went on record as saying that only with Solzhenitsyn's revelations about the Gulag did he understand what Marxism really meant. (Developments such as these are alluded to in the paper, but it seems necessary to spell them out at slightly greater length if the full force of Mme Rebérioux's criticism is to be appreciated.)

The concept of an intellectual 'career' — a vestigial one by and large in Thatcherite Britain — is also an important contributory factor in Mme Rebérioux's remark. The 'new philosophers', notably their guru Bernard-Henri Lévy (a series director for the publishing house Grasset), made a great deal of money in a very short time, and set in motion a bandwagon of lectures, television appearances, and publications that was often criticised as much for its mercenary qualities as for the ideological treachery that was felt to inspire it. And it is, paradoxically, the increased sociological and even economic emphasis of much left-wing writing in France (Pierre Bourdieu and Régis Debray are perhaps the best-known examples) that, as the paper suggests in its conclusion, offers the most stimulating perspectives for the intellectual Left today. The dismantling (one might almost speak of 'deconstruction') of the market edifice of the 'new philosophy'; the debate that has gone on around the 'mediatisation' of intellectual life, particularly via the television programme *Apostrophes*; the increasing importance attached to empirical and sociological data — these are central to a left-wing intellectual life in the France of today that (as I stated in my conclusion but welcome the opportunity of emphasising once again here) has profited, and continues to profit, by the *acquis de mai* at the same time as it denounces May's backsliders. Even — or especially — under a Socialist regime, *la lutte continue.*

Notes

1   In *Français, qui Êtes-Vous?*, published by La Documentation Française in 1981.

2   François Aubral and Xavier Delcourt tackle the question of this 'reappropriation' of Althusserian and Lacanian terminology trenchantly in their *Contre la nouvelle philosophie*, Idées, 1977.

3   I use the word 'ideological' here in a general, even nebulous, sense rather than in its narrower 'Althusserian' definition.

4   Mme Rebérioux was at pains to stress that her criticism was directed at intellectuals in France, rather than at the present writer.

5   François Aubral and Xavier Delcourt, op. cit., illustrate this well.

PART III   ECONOMICS

8   Defining the new French industrial policy: the burden of the past *

PASCAL PETIT
CNRS, Paris.

On 12 June 1982, the French government announced a new devaluation of the franc and the setting up of a new plan to combat inflation. At this time of assessment of the first year of Socialist government, harsh economic realities demanded a policy of austerity in contrast with the aim of stimulating the economy affirmed only a year before. This change of course, though temporary, was largely motivated by the alarming results of foreign trade. The overall trade deficit since January 1982 had more than doubled since the previous year (43 billion fr. against 21 billion from January to June 1981). The stimulation of domestic demand had resulted in a sustained growth in the volume of imports, while the volume of exports fell.[1]

Furthermore, the rate of price rises had remained about the same as in previous years (13 per cent), while inflation had noticeably fallen among France's principal trading partners. Also, investment by companies continued to fall and was expected to be 6 per cent down in 1982. So that the change of policy announced in June recalled the stop-go experiences of the British economy in the 1960s. However, the Mauroy Government, aware of the dangers, had only undertaken, in July 1981, a fairly moderate stimulation of demand, although it did provide a contrast with the austerity policies of all other countries.

Looking beyond the short-term aim, the French government aimed to set up an industrial policy which would restore the foundations of a competitive economy and which would ensure a durable economic revival. In the present climate there are many question marks against the nature and feasibility of this industrial policy, which for the most part is still undefined. (Some people criticise the harmful delay in setting it up.) However, if one considers the placing and timing of the different aspects of what will be France's industrial policy of the 1980s, one is encouraged to believe that its main characteristics may already be apparent. On the other hand, the various gaps that exist indicate that it is still not complete. This chapter seeks to draw up an initial balance of the apparent orienta-

* Translated by Stuart Williams

tions of French industrial policy. However, its results concern us less than the current difficulties caused in setting it up. The stakes are high. Also, one notes the government's limited freedom of action since the country is considerably involved in a network of international trade.[2]

The elements of the industrial policy

In the first stage following the elections of June 1981, the government sought to acquire the means to carry out an industrial policy of wider scope. The means in question are of three types: an increased nationalised industrial sector constitutes the main element of the policy; the complete nationalisation of the banking sector (and in particular the commercial banks) should provide the financing desired by public and private firms; finally, a set of sectoral plans to ensure the coherent development of competititve production units in a given sector forms the third section of a range of governmental interventions.

This is an impressive basis. The industrial sector has tripled in size. Apart from the two biggest producers of steel (USINOR, SACILOR) and the two groups principally engaged in military manufactures (Dassault, Matra), five large groups dominating the sectors of chemicals, pharmaceuticals, electronics and electrical construction have been nationalised (see Table 8.1).[3]

These groups, whose productivity is above average (they produce 22.5 per cent of added value using 19 per cent of the labour), also produce a third of exports. The high technology that they use necessitates a high investment input to maintain their competitiveness. This involves the downgrading of older equipment and so the government intends to invest 30 billion fr. in these new nationalised groups over five years.

A considerable involvement in exporting means these new public industrial groups are in the business of defending and enlarging their share of foreign markets. By contrast, the sectoral plans seem much more defensive. In this respect, they follow on from the support measures that were not very successfully carried out by previous governments (e.g. in machine tools). The objective is to reconquer a domestic market in which imports have captured a rapidly increasing share over ten years.

These sectoral plans are wider in scope than hitherto and regularly call on all possible state aids (training, research, public contracts) and call also for the creation of co-ordinating and harmonising bodies that are not explicitly banned by commercial agreements entered into by France (Rome Treaty, GATT, etc). Five sectoral plans have already been created affecting textiles and clothing, leather and shoes, machine tools, furniture

Table 8.1: *Share of industrial activity of foreign subsidiaries and nationaised sector before and after recent nationalisations (percentages, energy sector omitted)*

Industrial Activity	Employment	Production	Exports	Added value	Investment
Present nation-alised sector	18.9	24.4	32.1	22.5	24
Former nation-alised sector	6.4	8.9	12.2	8	9.3
Foreign subsid-iaries	12.8	15.2	18.2	—	—

Source: STISI publication no. 25, Ministry of Research and Industry, 1982).
Notes:
The above estimates are based on 1979. The former public industrial sector (including energy) comprised the following groups: CDF, EDF, EMC, GDF, Renault, SNIA, SNECMA, CEA (subsidiaries), BRGM (subsidiaries), ELP. The newly nationalised groups include: CGE, Dassault, Matra, PUK, Rhône-Poulenc, SACILOR, St. Gobain, Thomson, USINOR. The 'foreign' groups which may be nationalised, Roussel-UCLAF, ITT, CII, Honeywell-Bull, are nowhere included in Table 8.1, their status being unclear. Only industrial groups have been considered, so that subsidiaries of RATP, SNCF, Air France, banks and insurance companies, as well as industrial subsidiaries of the Caisse des Dépôts or the Industiral Development Institute are not included.

and toy-making. Four types of measures are proposed, taking forms specific to each sector: market organisation involving improved promotion and distribution circuits are common to all the plans; public contracts (e.g. machine tools); training and research promotion (textiles, machine tools and toys);[4] investment aids (textiles, machine tools, furniture). The direct costs to the public purse vary according to the participation of the industrialists concerned in the different plans. The costs of the Textile Plan (involving 500,000 jobs) and of the Machine Tool Plan (considered to be an area of strategic importance) are around 5 billion fr. each, while the other plans would require less than a billion from public finance. Other sectoral plans are in preparation, in particular for shipbuilding[5] and paper and cardboard. The development of these plans involves joint co-operation of public authorities and industrialists in the sector concerned. Financing can involve public funds, funds raised by the sale of services or by special taxes or funds raised through the banking system. The nationalisation of the entire banking sector was particularly aimed at facilitating the financing of industrial projects at a decentralised level. The banking sector should certainly still be involved in financing the investments of the big industrial groups. But one of its principal functions should be to finance projects at a local level[6] such as those occurring within the sectoral plans. The retention of thirty-nine competing nationalised banks is supposed to facilitate these decentralised measures. Governmental action in industrial policy therefore has three modes of intervention: public industrial groups, sectoral plans and financial control.

Transition-phase options

In the world recession prevailing since the beginning of 1980, the French economy could not take a year or two to define its industrial policy. The groups which might be nationalised had to take decisions regarding policies and investments. This necessity to act and the impossibility of standing aside mean that there is a risk, in the transition phase, of a too hasty definition of the main features of a future industrial policy.

After a six-month political debate, the nationalisation law was voted in February 1982. This law did not however settle all the problems. The status of the groups with foreign involvement remained to be defined as did the future of subsidiaries. In fact, the new managements of the public groups found themselves called upon to define the effective sphere of public sector intervention.

The complexity of the financial relations within the nationalised groups made an initial inventory necessary. Apart from majority holdings, the power structure of these groups rested on controlling minorities, reciprocal holdings or autonomously controlled firms. Such products of multiple mergers, take-overs and company creations were particularly numerous in the portfolio of the two finance companies: Suez and Paribas.[7] In the absence of any precise framework regulating the hiving off to the private sector of subsidiary interests of nationalised groups, the new managements had to define the exact limits of their own domain. Drawing up this inventory was made difficult by the various systems of control operated by the industrial groups and went hand in hand with the need to establish links between the nationalised groups. Also, the need to maintain competitive positions as well as the desire not to depress the economic climate required the rapid commitment of initial investment finds.

The stakes were high. In the period 1970–80, competition had become much more lively but these groups had succeeded in retaining their share of export markets.[8] These initial options indicated a desire for a degree of coherence involving the reorganisation and share-out of markets among the newly nationalised groups.

Moreover, the former public sector (in particular the energy sector) and national agencies (especially the postal service and defence) had already agreed on some sharing of functions and markets with the newly nationalised groups. These agreements are undergoing revision. The new situation favours seeking economies of scale and merging less profitable units. Such reorganisation is particularly sensitive in electronics and chemicals.[9] The contours of the public groups are thus redefined on the basis of certain principles of industrial policy, but there is still no rational framework at the national level for the principle options chosen.

The Interim Plan covering the transition period up to the enactment of the 9th Plan (1984–9) scarcely went beyond the statement of general management principles. It re-stated the relative autonomy of the nationalised industrial sector in the framework of five-year plans. Planning contracts indicating production, investment and recruitment goals are to be negotiated with the economic authorities following the guidelines laid down by the national plan. For the transition phase, the public groups must have, by the end of 1982, presented company agreements covering a three-year period. This would put an end to uncertainty and also show clearly the financial requirements of the groups once restructured.

In parallel with this, but more slowly, the institutional framework charged with defining and motivating a national industrial strategy is being set up. In the present phase, decisions on industrial policy are taken in various quarters: ministries, the presidency, the Planning Commission, the Institute for Industrial Development, the Caisse des Dépôts, finance companies. The new dimension of the industrial public sector and the financial possibilities afforded by the banking sector have modified the distribution of powers concerning industrial policy among the different public authorities. On the one hand, the Finance Ministry is no longer the only source of finance for public operations; on the other hand, the Ministry for Industry has acquired greater autonomy to carry out the industrial projects that it defines. This redistribution of responsibilities among ministries recalls the power struggles provoked by the Gaullist plans (information technology, nuclear, aviation). Within the existing structure, new decision-making bodies have to be created to further the revitalisation of national planning with the participation of all social groups and in a less centralised framework than hitherto.

The aim has been stated: an outline law for industrial development in the period 1984–9. This corresponds to a commitment by the state more demanding that the indicative proposals of the 9th Plan. We are witnessing in this connection a general mobilisation of public and private institutions to debate industrial policy.[10] The debate will judge the rightness of the initial options made in 1982. The feasibility of a new industrial policy will depend in effect on the rightness of the initial measures.

The first stages of an industrial policy

The first options concerning the reorganisation of the public groups, investments and sectoral support plans were guided by three criteria: the trade balance, technological development and employment.[11] These criteria can lead to indecision and contradiction in the short term: reducing the numbers employed can lower production costs and improve competitiveness. A national industrial strategy makes it possible to arbitrate between different projects. In the absence of such a strategy, these criteria are drawn into the definition of three main lines of policy, forming the basis for the initial measures: the reconquest of the domestic market, the reconstitution of production networks and technological independence.

The reconquest of the domestic market is an ambiguous term applied to directly protectionist measures (import controls) and to a longer-term aim of restoring the competitiveness of companies. The rapid penetration of the domestic market by imports is the first cause of the relative decline of industry. To restore the competitiveness of the sectors concerned, it is necessary to reorganise every stage from product conception to product distribution and all the stages of production in between. The sectoral plans are particularly appropriate to this notion of reconquering the domestic market. Some of the types of market organisation contained in the plans are in opposition to the principle of free competition enshrined in the Rome Treaty. Some actions being taken on this point may result in the suspension of the plans.

Since France is considerably integrated in the network of EEC trade, it might be more appropriate to interpret the domestic market as the European market. However, the measures taken at this level have been more concerned with disengagement through the imposition of quotas (in textiles and steel for example) than with restoring the competitiveness of threatened industries. The reconquest of the domestic market is linked, in fact, with two additional operational notions. The first considers that any action aimed at restoring the competitiveness of a sector must be applied to the whole of the production network. The other emphasises that international specialisation encourages developed countries to concentrate on products requiring a high level of technology.

The strategy of creating production networks considers the whole of the production chain. Such thinking led in the 1950s to the development of the energy and steel sectors as the basis of the whole engineering sector. One also finds traces of such thinking in the big projects of the 1960s: the *Plan Calcul*, the nuclear project, etc. In its recent version, the production network strategy aims to reduce uncertainties regarding supply quantities and costs as well as to avoid detachment from the final markets. It tends towards vertical integration of the production process by controlling all the intermediate stages from the raw material to the market place. Thus one refers to the wood, leather, glass networks, but also by extension to the electronics network, including all the productions using micro-conductors. The desire to integrate the distribution circuits, in the manner adopted by Japanese industries, appears to be a new element. It has not however produced any important achievements so far.

All the sectoral plans are based on this network strategy and seek to reduce dependence over the whole production chain. Yet this strategy does not inhibit the selection of market opportunities (*créneaux*), that is, openings for products whose conception or production use qualities particular to a developed country like France (intelligence, technology, design, etc.). Thus integrated, the production chain offers little opportunity for import penetration. This strategy is not uniquely defensive. Thus the electronics network aims to become the third in the world and capture foreign markets.[12] But to attain this goal it will first of all develop on the basis of an internal market in large-scale equipment (postal service, defence). It is also significant that this industry is making a particular effort to acquire new technology by research and investment (plus 140 billion fr. in five years). This 'grand technological design of the Mitterrand administration' is somewhat similar to the nuclear programme of twenty years ago.

The desire for technological independence is the logical complement of the independence aim of the production network strategy. Technological dependence is in conflict with the view France has of its place in the international division of labour, that of a developed country seeking mastery over high technology.[13] In the second place this dependence results in patent and licence (*brevets*) imports which are double the exports in this field.[14] Finally, the mastery of advanced technology is the only way towards the new products that will bring about the recovery of the world economy in the long run.

This strategy of technological independence involves giving priority to research expenditure. Since 1973, France has devoted 1.8 per cent of its gross domestic product to research and development, which places it among the lowest ranks of major developed countries (USA, 2.4 per cent; U.K. and West Germany 2.2 per cent; Japan 2 per cent). A programme law aims to bring this percentage up to 2.5 per cent by 1985. It will be noted that the low research expenditure up to 1981 was mainly due to the low expenditure in this area by private firms.

Apart from the main lines of industrial development revealed by the plans to reconquer the domestic market, the production network strategies and plans for technological independence, two series of measures aim to transform the environment of industrial development. The one aims to improve social relations in companies by institutionalising joint consultation practices between employers and employees. The other seeks to develop a national savings scheme to finance industrial growth.

It will be recalled that in the energy field the nuclear programme, laid down in 1974, is being pursued at the rate originally intended (70 per cent of electricity consumed in 1990 will be nuclear in origin).

At this stage, the burden of the past in this process of defining industrial policy seems to have been a double one. On the one hand, the crisis situation in industrial structures necessitated rapid decisions concerning finance and reorganisation. On the other hand, a certain French tradition of state intervention has influenced both the balance of centres of power and the industrial policies underlying decisions taken since 1981.

Conclusions

If one notes the relationship between the government's actions in the sphere of industrial policy and those of the de Gaulle Government of the 1960s, this is not done to diminish them: there is the same desire to develop national networks, the same decision-making centres, the same wish to promote technological independence. Of course, the scope of these policies is different because of the considerably increased size of the public sector. But above all the international environment has changed. The world economic recession and the penetration of the domestic market have not only encouraged policies to reconquer the market but have also altered the stakes. It is now vital for the French economy that these projects are commercial successes. The Gaullist projects had positive external effects on economic growth but they were not its direct driving force.

In fact, the Gaullist projects in information science, nuclear development and aviation (Concorde) came up against the difficulties for a medium-sized country of developing complex technology without a vast internal market to support it. Because of a similar fear, it has been emphasised that the French industrial projects are strictly national in character. Can an industrial policy do without the co-operation of other developed countries which are faced with identical problems?

The preceding government left industrial groups to develop network strategies in co-operation with foreign groups.[15] This international collaboration is all the more necessary since foreign subsidiaries represent one-fifth of industry (see Table 8.1) and multinational firms define their own international division of labour within developed countries. This division of roles between developed countries is as important as that which divides the world on the basis of high or low wage costs. So the joint private and public development impetus that the new French industrial policy is seeking to promote runs the risk of being less effective if it takes no account of tendencies within other developed countries. The development of international collaboration in industrial projects does not merely seek to counter the autonomy of foreign subsidiaries in relation to national policy; it also corresponds to a necessity for a medium-sized country at a time when competitors in vast units like the USA are themselves experiencing the need to co-operate.

The conception of a mode of international co-operation in industrial policy not solely dependent on support from money markets remains an essential component of the policy still to be defined. It is not the only one. One of the novelties awaited after the change of government in France concerned the aim to revitalise the planning process by opening it up to social and regional forces. This is a necessary condition if a national plan is to have overall coherence and respect social and regional aspirations. It is also one of the only ways of ensuring that, before industrial policies are fixed, a debate occurs about the nature of the country's needs.

The electronics industry is particularly rich in network projects of all kinds. Can one choose? It is true that the relation between production and demand is sufficiently 'dialectical' for any product brought to the market to find buyers. However, it then becomes important to consider modes of operation and norms designed to prevent unwanted results. In this connection, the history of the automobile is revealing and the next decade will no doubt be marked by the extension of safety, energy conservation, and anti-pollution norms. It is no surprise that the three countries with the most advanced industries (USA, West Germany and Japan) are also those in which such norms are most widespread. One could see this as an aspect of a network strategy to the extent that such norms protect the domestic market. One could be more ambitious and see in this the first stage in a wider consideration of the quality of life and the goods we produce.

Notes

1   From May 1981 to May 1982 imports rose by 5 per cent in volume and exports fell by 4 per cent. The worsening of trade with EEC countries is particularly clear: minus 28 billion fr. against minus 10 billion for the same six months of 1981.

2.   In 1981, 42 per cent of French industrial production was exported while imports represented 38 per cent of domestic demand for manufactured goods.

3   The size of the public industrial sector would be considerably greater if one included the industrial subsidiaries of all public establishments. However, the exact extent of public sector control is difficult to measure since in some cases the holding of a minimum share of capital is enough to ensure control of a firm.

4   In the form of a semi-public company making prototypes of electronic toys.

5   In this sector it is less a matter of resisting foreign imports (8 per cent) than of planning the reorganisation of a sector with excess production capacity.

6   In various ways, for example participatory loans by which the financing agency shares the risks and the gains of the projects it finances.

7   The fluidity of control within the Suez group explains why the new chairman is still trying to regain control of the insurance subsidiaries of the group. See J. M. Quatrepoint in *Le Monde*, 24 August 1982.

8   As in most European countries, exports are mainly produced by big companies and multinationals. About 100 firms realise half the exports. This competitiveness in exporting contrasts with losses of internal markets in other products. Between 1970 and 1980 the rate of import penetration rose from 100 to 180.

9   The authorities had overseen the market share-out in 1969 between GCE and Thomson. Now the evolution of technology calls this share-out into question to the extent that specialisation by product is no longer justified. The common public status of the two groups calls for developing co-operation. The nationalisation of the French subsidiaries of ITT necessitates reorganisation in order to reintegrate them into national groups. At the same time, an important client like the postal service (PTT) wants a certain level of competition between the groups to be maintained. In the chemicals field, Charbonnages de France (coal) and Rhône-Poulenc are redefining their production spheres.

10   The Ministry of Industry, via various committees, prepared a National Industrial Assizes to be held from November 1982 to June 1983. Echoing this, the Estates General organised for December 1982 by the CNPF (Employers' Federation) will have produced concrete proposals to improve the competitiveness of firms. Also, the engineers and executives in the CGT (union) launched 'a great campaing of concrete proposals and initiatives in respect of industry, technology and management at the level of the firm'.

11   The Ministry of Industry recalled these criteria to the directors of the nationalised sector on 31 August 1982.

12   The nationalised groups GCE, Thomson, Matra, CII, Honeywell Bull, are responsible for half of the production in the electronics field.

13   The subordinate status revealed by American opposition to the European agreement to construct the Siberian pipeline strengthened the desire to escape from all technological dependence.

14   The deficit in patents and licences reached 2.6 billion fr. in 1981. The rates

of cover of the patents and licence fee balance are low in information technology (1.35 per cent), food processing (2.8 per cent), electronics (8.7 per cent)
and basic chemicals (26 per cent). Report of M. Saint Cricq to the Economic
and Social Council, 'The Place and Size of Technical Transfers in External
Trade', (18 May 1982).

15   According to the doctrine of 'orderly growth of foreign trade' of R. Barre,
only sectoral support plans were the concern of the government (steel, textiles, machine tools).

9 Economic policy: crisis management, structural reform and Socialist politics*

PHILIP G. CERNY
University of York

Economic policy is the centrepiece of the action of the Socialist government in France as it is in most governments most of the time in advanced capitalist society, especially in the context of recession and economic crisis. That crisis, however, is merely an urgent reminder of the fact that, despite the formal internal political sovereignty of nation-states — the framework that legitimates regimes and comprises the precinct in which political parties and other forces identify and constitute themselves — their political economies have always been inextricably intertwined with each other. They are criss-crossed by a range of relationships which may be seen as both lateral, cross-cutting the state and international structures at several interacting levels, and interstitial, operating in spaces only partially controlled by states, if at all. This quasi-autonomous, interpenetrative structure constitutes a series of constraints upon the actions of states, actions which are conceived within the ideological and cultural context of pursuing the 'national interests' of discrete political units with particular histories, socio-economic structures, and relationships of power.

Within this context, states too have resources — bureaucracies, hierarchies of power, status and representation, taxation and expenditure, and legal structures of sovereignty — which embody a continuous process of attempting to control or liberate, utilise or adapt to, this interpenetrative structure. War has most often provided the cauldron of this construct, while the complex interaction of economic problems and the development of state responses in the capitalist era has shaped the set of problematics which lie at the heart of contemporary politics, especially in the liberal-democratic advanced capitalist states, which form the core of the world

* The research for this chapter forms part of a larger project which has benefited from financial assistance provided by the Nuffield Foundation, the Social Science Research Council and the Centre National de Recherche Scientifique. The Center for European Studies, Harvard University, and the Institut d'Études Politiques, Paris, generously provided research facilities. I should like to thank the numerous people whose comments have been so helpful, particularly Martin Schain, Stanley Hoffmann, Jolyon Howorth, George Ross, Jane Jenson, Peter Hall and Douglas Ashford.

system. These problematics can be represented as arenas of tension between the state and the interpenetrative structure I have described, as interrelated levels where the contradictions inherent in the system itself are played out in conjunctural terms — in specific situational contexts wherein the tenuous stability of the overall system (especially in the wake of the intense expansionary cycle after world War II) may be threatened by new power struggles and/or economic decline.

Four of these problematics, or arenas of tension, form the context in which the argument of this chapter develops; they will appear in different guises, and we shall return to them in the conclusions. They are central, in different ways, to a variety of approaches to political analysis. They are, firstly, the parameters of public choice in liberal-democratic, advanced capitalist polities; secondly, the parameters of state action in capitalist society; thirdly, the problem of social democracy, or democratic socialism and, finally, the debate about policies designed to meet the current crisis, and the various models which have emerged. These will be viewed within the perspective of the particular heritage of the French state tradition, and of the modern version of that tradition, the Fifth Republic,[1] which provides the political-structural framework for the current government's economic strategy, as well as within those of party politics, French socialism, and, of course, domestic and international economic factors.

The main theme running through the chapter will be the structural and conjunctural pressures and constraints which led to the first formulations of Socialist economic strategy, highlighted the tensions within that strategy in practice and forced a refining and reconsideration of that strategy — leading to a shaking out of priorities, which stands in contrast with certain of the original conditions and objectives of the overall strategy itself. In particular, we shall focus on the relation between conjunctural crisis management, long-range objectives of structural reform within the French economy (and, indeed, within the world economy) and the problems of Socialist coalition-building and of political stability in general. We shall first look at contextual factors both political and economic; then we shall broadly trace the path of changing French economic policies after the Socialist Party came to power in May–June 1981 and finally we shall attempt to set out the main features of the more austere economic strategy that emerged in the latter half of 1982. It will be suggested that although there is clear evidence of limits to the autonomy of state action — and therefore to public choice, to democratic-socialist goals, and to the range of responses available in recessionary conditions — the Mitterrand/Mauroy Government is constructing an ambitious 'state capitalist' approach that reflects not only the limits of, but also the scope and flexibility of action within, the capitalist world system.

Background and problems

In general, socialist, democratic-socialist or social-democratic parties, when voted into office in advanced capitalist liberal-democratic political systems, face particular problems in attempting to pursue the goals on the basis of which they formed their appeal to the electorate.[2] These goals generally involve not only innovation and change but also the need to use governmental power as the main instrument of change. But the range of potential specific objectives is vast, reflecting the complex changes in capitalist societies themselves (and in the capitalist world system) and the historical experiences of socialist movements and parties which have accepted, for a wide variety of reasons, to work within the existing political and economic 'rules of the game'. Among the main factors influencing the specific choice of goals in particular countries are the historical development and institutional capacities of the state itself, the requirements of building and maintaining a winning coalition, the long-term structural features of the national economy and its position in the international economy, and the issues and trends dominating the economic conjuncture.

In France, the particular combination of factors led to the development of a strategy which sought to make use of the institutional resources of the French state on a wide range of fronts in order to reconcile the contrasting demands of different factions within the Socialist Party (not to mention its coalition partners, the moderate Mouvement des Radicaux de Gauche, on the one hand, and the Communist Party, on the other) and to bring together in a complementary fashion policy proposals both of a traditional social-democratic kind, aimed at counteracting social inequality by redistributive and 'demand side' measures, and of a more far-reaching structural or 'supply side' kind, aimed at reorienting the French economy to longer-term changes in the international economy. It was thus hoped simultaneously to meet both the structural and conjunctural problems of the economy while protecting the government's political base. But the risks inherent in such a project are great. Failure along any one of the dimensions would carry with it the danger that latent tensions in other dimensions would be revealed and exacerbated.

The dimension which throughout the 1960s and 1970s, was regarded as the most problematic for a Socialist government, the political institutions of the Fifth Republic, has in fact turned out to be the least. Despite the identification of the founding and consolidation of the institutions with a long period of right-wing dominance, twenty-three years, with all of its attendant electoral and administrative frustrations for the Left, a number of features of the state made the transfer of power and Socialist control relatively smooth. In the first place, the French administrative tradition had, since the seventeenth century, always involved a strong element of 'relative autonomy', a close, corporatist relationship with the major economic forces in society, and a *dirigiste*, interventionist role in the process of economic development – the *colbertiste* tradition. Further- more, this tradition was harnessed during the 1960s and early 1970s, when the Fifth Republic was controlled by the Gaullists, to an earlier wave of economic modernisation which had begun after World War II.[3] Indeed, this tradition, far from being based on a simple and rigid centralisation, struck deep roots in the system of local government and politics.[4] In the second place, the manner of the Socialist victory in 1981 – the capture of the presidency, followed by the winning of a large parliamentary majority – has avoided the pitfalls of the 'new rules of the game' in the Fifth Republic and maximised the institutional resources of Socialist office- holders, particularly in the executive branch.[5] Indeed, this has reinforced and extended the legitimacy of the regime itself.[6] The only hitch has been the intervention of the Constitutional Council in the nationalisation process, which we shall come to again later.

The building of a winning electoral and social coalition prior to the 1981 elections was a long and difficult process. It was essentially carried out on three fronts, sometimes simultaneously, sometimes separately. In order to build a winning majority, the Socialist Party had to broaden its alliances and its electoral appeal on both flanks – towards the Centre parties, and towards the Communists. However, in order to be able effectively to move in both of these directions at once, the PS itself had to go through a long process of restructuring and renewal. Attempts first to marginalise the PCF, in 1963–4, followed in 1965–8 by attempts to marginalise the Centre, merely emphasised the splits within the SFIO (as it was known until 1969) and seemed to reinforce the electoral dominance of the Right. After 1971, however, when François Mitterrand became First Secretary of a restructured PS, the internal factions were gradually reconciled amd manipulated, pushed by Mitterrand and pulled by the prospect of more effective electoral mobilisation, into a strategy with a seemingly radical economic content, embodied in the Common Pro- gramme of Government, signed by the PS, the PCF and the MRG in 1972. The essence of this programme, formulated as it was during a period of great prosperity, when France had the fastest growing economy in the

West, except for Japan, and was regarded by American economic fore-casters like Herman Kahn as an emerging economic giant, was the notion that the nation could afford a wide range of economic measures, from redistributive social policy to extensive nationalisation, which would please all left-wing factions and attract floating voters.

This programme suffered two major setbacks. The first was the first large rise in the international price of oil in 1973-4, which exposed certain weaknesses in the world capitalist system — in particular its vulnerability to simultaneous inflation and economic stagnation — and made distributive policy considerably more problematic, in terms of both the costs of a wide range of measures and the structural rigidities, which consensual distributive policies implemented during the earlier period of prosperity and which were seen to engender and reinforce each other during a period of rapid structural changes at the international level. Secondly, the growing international tension between the Soviet Union and the United States in the mid-1970s, added to the significant worsening of the relative position of the Communist Party within the Union of the Left — especially noti-ceable in the cantonal elections of 1976 and the municipal elections of 1977 — led the PCF to take a rigid line on the renegotiation of the Common Programme when its original five-year term came to an end in 1977. However, the main feature of the Common Programme period was the strengthening of the electoral position of the Left as a whole, and the strengthening of the Socialist Party itself within that coalition. Therefore the PS leadership also took a hard line in the 1977 negotiations, not wanting to be seen to be weak in its relations with its allies at a time when it was widely perceived as the real 'motor force' of a growing left-wing coalition. Negotiations broke off in September.

The net result, however, was to leave the 1972 Common Programme almost intact as the symbolic core of the left-wing coalition — as the legacy of that period of restructuring and the gaining of a new dynamism and appeal. Thus despite the growing estrangement of the PS and PCF in 1978-80, on issues ranging from the minimum wage through the hypo-thetical distribution of cabinet posts to Afghanistan and the Moscow Olympic Games — not to mention the myriad attempts to lay blame for the defeat of the Left in the 1978 parliamentary elections — electoral discipline on the Left continued and it came to be taken for granted that the Communists were becoming more, not less, dependent on the Socialists as time went on. Meanwhile, despite various manoeuvrings within the PS in 1979-80 as faction leaders sought more influence, on the assumption that Mitterrand as a two-time loser in presidential elections (1965 and 1974) would not be the best candidate for 1981, the First

Secretary succeeded in maintaining his dominance of the party apparatus and moved relatively smoothly into the party's candidacy in late 1980. A double shift of voters to Mitterrand in the presidential elections — from the Communists (even on the first ballot), given the symbolic loyalty of many post-1972 Communist voters and militants to the notion of left-wing unity, and from centre-right voters (mainly Gaullists) opposed to the economic policies of President Giscard d'Estaing — clearly demonstrated that the mix of policies inherited from the Common Programme was the basis of the Socialist victory on all three fronts. Indeed, as we shall see the Mauroy Government moved swiftly to implement a great many of these programmes during the 'honeymoon' period of mid- and late 1981.

Thus fundamental coalition pattern has been quite effectively maintained since 1981 despite the many policy shifts of 1982. The Communist Party, in deeper crisis than ever, seems to have no alternative to remaining in the government in its subordinate position; despite reverses in the opinion polls, the Left seems more united than the Right, and one cannot assume even now that they would lose a major national electoral test and the Socialist Party itself, despite groaning from its parliamentary rank and file, seems to be kept in line even more efficiently at the time of writing (early 1983) than was the case in Spring 1982, when a number of disputes between government ministers erupted onto the public scene. More worrying than stresses within the party coalition has been stress within the social coalition, as the Communist-linked trade union, the Confédération Générale du Travail, successfully challenged the government's plans for reductions in the working week along with proportionate reduction of wages (spring 1982) and the continued application of certain of the government's post-June 1982 wage controls, especially in the automobile industry (winter 1982-3). Wage inflation is, of course, the Achilles' heel of social democracy in hard times.

The third contextual dimension is that of the structure of the French economy itself and its problematic position in the international economy. Unlike Britain, which has only been put in this position in the past quarter of a century, France has been what is now called an 'intermediate economy' since the mid-nineteenth century.[7] In the context of the world economy, an intermediate economy is one which is structurally less advanced than the most advanced economies and more advanced than the great majority of less developed ones. This does not refer simply to growth rates — which are relative to existing levels of output and income — nor to macroeconomic indices — which can conceal a wide range of contrasting trends and performances in different sectors and sub-sectors. Rather it refers to the types of goods which are produced and exchanged with (and received in exchange from) structurally different categories of national economies. It means that in those sectors which are economically most advanced in terms of both technological sophistication and productive efficiency (particularly the productivity of capital), there is a structural gap between an intermediate economy and those of the most advanced countries, a gap reflected in the composition and terms of trade not only between those countries but between each of them and third countries; an intermediate economy is thus structurally underdeveloped in such sectors. At the same time, an intermediate economy is considerably more advanced, not only in these sectors but also in a number of other, generally technologically more traditional and more labour-intensive, sectors, than less developed economies.[8]

In the former relationship, the growing structural deficit in French trade with both the United States[9] and West Germany[10] in a number of crucial sectors (industrial capital goods, electronics, more advanced consumer durables, etc.) is seen as a vicious circle, relatively unresponsive to short-term price changes, as patterns of specialisation — with experience of production techniques, marketing networks, economies of scale, etc. reinforcing the market position of those countries already advantaged — are consolidated in investment patterns and purchasing habits. A key component of this pattern is technological exchange (licensing, patents, etc.), which reflects and reinforces the wider structural deficit.[11] In contrast, however, the relative advance in just these areas, in addition to certain more traditional sectors, of France over the underdeveloped world, gives her a structural surplus in such exchanges. However, the growing deficit with the most advanced countries reflects a growing competitiveness in terms of both price and capacity of the latter, with intermediate economies such as the French having to rely more and more on governmental and intergovernmental support — export credits, special agreements (such as that with Algeria over natural gas) at non-market prices, technical assistance and subsidies — to counter the gradual erosion of their competitive position in these very markets and to open up new ones (such as the current French trade offensive in India). In some cases, such measures simply reflect the decreasing rate of profit inherent in such ventures in a context of declining competitiveness, although they do maintain vital trade patterns, provide crucial infrastructural resources, maintain employment in socially or economically critical sectors and hold down the overall balance of trade deficit; but they are dependent on a wide variety of factors difficult to control and coordinate, including the state of political relations between the countries involved.[12] At another level, however — arms sales are a particularly critical example, but industrial capital goods can be another in certain circumstances — the maintenance and favouring of such patterns can have a multiplier effect on the rest of the economy, by providing an alternative to protectionism in the nurturing of sectors which need restructuring or which can provide the source of technological and productive spillover.

In reacting to the policy problems embedded in the 'intermediate economy' structural position, national policy-makers have a range of responses with which to work. Each one of these responses has potential benefits for the national economy, but each can also have severe disadvantages in the context of the world economy. The most obvious is straightforward trade protectionism, the drawbacks to which, in terms of retaliation from those very trade partners whose competitive position is most dangerous, and of potential further loss of competitiveness if traditional industries are 'featherbedded' or new industries nurtured in conditions inappropriate to market conditions crucial to future export potential, are well known. Other forms of what is often called 'hidden protectionism' — government procurement, tax advantages, difficult import regulations, subsidies, financial and political support for exports, etc. — can have the same effects.[13] Broader measures of Keynesian fiscal and monetary 'fine-tuning' are also important elements of any policy response.

Reflation may increase demand, thereby increasing sales and investment; however, in the current world context, given the competitive advantages of the most advanced countries in the most 'upmarket' consumer goods and the advantages of the low-wage newly industrialising countries in 'downmarket' consumer goods, the result is often a greater relative increase in demand for imports than for home-produced products, fuelling the political call for greater traditional protectionism. Problems are thus merely exacerbated. On the other hand, deflation may well hold down imports, but will also hit home demand and undermine investment, leading to falling output. In terms of exchange rate policy, devaluation may have the desired effect in reducing imports and increasing exports, but it will also increase costs and cause a flight of capital, reversing the positive effects in the longer term; revaluation will reduce costs, but make exports more expensive, also hitting output and investment. Countries in a strong structural export position, as in West Germany under the Social Democrats, can, by combining revaluation with a measure of domestic reflation, maintain a certain amount of momentum, increasing investment and managing costs while maintaining an overall favourable trade position; however, this process appeared to have run out of steam in 1982.

Countries in a weak structural trade position have less room to manoeuvre. Policy-makers are continually having to navigate between policy combinations, which, in particular conjunctural conditions, may prove not only to be ineffective and internally incompatible, but also to be counterproductive and to involve significant opportunity costs. 'Stop-go' policies in Britain are archetypical. France avoided such problems during the long boom before 1974 because, starting from a lower economic base than Britain, its economy adapted better to the postwar world market, modernising and expanding at the same time.[14] The state played a crucial role in this process both before[15] and after[16] the coming to power of General de Gaulle in 1958. Of course, in a boom period, such questions are not of the same degree of centrality. Not only is there more money in the kitty with the international economic 'engine' pulling the weaker economies along behind, but in fact the very intermediate position can be an asset, as production can not only add fuel to the engine — complementing its productive repertoire and increasing trade in general — but also provide the essential linkage mechanism to articulate the expansion of the core industrial economies with those of the under-developed world, as the Yaoundé Convention did, connecting global capitalist development with the rising expectations of the Third World in a neocolonial manner, avoiding the more brutal interventionism of the two superpowers. Thus the engine is seen to pull an ever-longer train behind it.

Needless to say, such structural complementarity, in a way which is perhaps analogous, at the world level, to the role of Keynesian policies at the domestic level, becomes a factor of rigidity in the more competitive, zero-sum world of an international recession. What had appeared to be a division of labour turns into competition over stagnant or declining markets. The intermediate economies, as stated earlier, find their positions eroded on both the upmarket and downmarket sides: growth sectors elude them; and captive markets are no longer secure. Trading partners and currency markets pull in opposite directions, as currency speculation follows interest rates. Tight monetary policies, which reduce inflation and costs (in the long run), also hit both investments and exports, thus reducing output and creating unemployment; looser monetary policies and reflation increase inflation and costs in a way which also reduces profitability, thus hitting investments and exports, but also propping up uncompetitive enterprises. The question becomes one of which is the necessary evil: high unemployment and a reduction in output and capacity, in the hope that improving market conditions abroad will pull investment into new, more competitive firms and sectors once the uncompetitive ones have fallen by the wayside; or the maintenance of a large uncompetitive sector, in the hope that improving market conditions abroad will increase overall demand sufficiently that they can find markets anyway and on a broader industrial base too. Experience of the 1970s shows that the second approach, based as it is on the Keynesian principles which sustained the long antecedent boom, tends to be adopted first; this was true in Britain in 1974, with the Social Contract, and in France, too, under the Chirac Governemnt. Its failure leads to the adoption of some version of the first approach, pain-fully at first in Britain under the Callaghan Government but more abruptly under the Thatcher Government, and the other way around in France, with the early austerity of the Barre Government incrementally giving way to a more pragmatic policy of assisted redeployment. Of course, such efforts are constrained not only by external forces but by political and social coalition-building.

A third possible approach, but one which also comes up against serious constraints at all levels, would be to try to get the state to act not simply in response to exogenous conditions — market conditions on the one hand, political conditions on the other — but rather as an efficient, capital-accumulating entrepreneur. States are not accustomed to acting in this fashion, especially in capitalist democracies, where the combination of economic-structural and political-social constraints have confined govern-ments for the most part to manipulating distributive or 'demand-side' policies in a social-democratic or Keynesian fashion. Just what such a structural or state supply-side approach might consist of is, of course, highly problematic.

For example, in responding to the condition of an intermediate economy, it would have to relate a repertoire of 'carrot and stick' policies to a series of strategically coherent choices about what sectors to restructure and how. Should the effort be directed to the downmarket side, emphasising, say, inappropriate technology for the Third World? China has made a success in recent years of such an approach, but the difficulties are obvious, especially in a world where the newly industrialising countries are setting the competitive pace. On the other hand, an upmarket strategy, in a period of tight costs and a position of having to catch up with more advanced rivals, has its obvious pitfalls; for a social-democratic govern-ment, in particular, the counterproductive impact of reflationary policies and labour indiscipline is a clear danger. Building a policy response would require a sufficiently strong internal power base, with the capability of ignoring the pressures brought by loyal supporters as well as by disinvesting capitalists and currency speculators! Nonetheless, as the Mitterrand presidency proceeds, a number of choices have been made which indicate that this is the direction in which the government wishes to go. If anything, the setbacks of conjunctural crisis management have served as a springboard to such an approach, to a state capitalism which is more ambitious than other such experiments in advanced capitalist democracies previously. In the next two sections we shall first trace the path of government policy from May 1981 to the middle of 1982, and, second, consider the attempt to reconstruct economic strategy towards a state capitalist approach both deriving from, yet distinct from, its precursor.

Structure and conjuncture: the path of policy

The repertoire of economic policies pursued by the Mauroy Government following the election of François Mitterrand in May 1981 (for the broad outlines were being set in place even before the parliamentary victory the following month) reflected both the distributive rewards of a left-wing majority, which had been excluded from power for nearly a generation and a broader strategic vision, which had a certain credibility despite the sort of risks considered above. The distributive policies were meant to provide a short-term boost to the economy, which would shortly thereafter be complemented and channeled by means of structural reforms into a virtuous circle of growth; these would feed into the international context in ways which would both strengthen France's structural position and reinforce a more widespread mood — both material and psychological — of recovery, thus minimising the risks of constraint. That these results did not occur does not vitiate the attempt, given the general level of failure in economic forecasting in the current recession; and the failures of the broad strategy at certain levels provides a useful perspective on the way that constraints in the international economy actually work (and on the way that the French government has readjusted its own priorities in a hostile climate).

Essentially, the overall strategy can be seen as consisting of five different types of levels of policy interacting with each other in a dynamic model. The first of these is a rather heterogeneous category of measures of a Keynesian sort, essentially a reflation of demand along with some redistribution of that demand towards the standard categories of recipients of transfer payments: raising of the minimum wage, family allowances, housing subsidies, pensions and the like. A fifth annual week of paid vacation, long a demand of the French Left, was made compulsory. It was hoped that financing for these measures would come from increased tax receipts resulting from subsequent economic growth, as well as the imposition of a wealth tax, another proposal of long standing. Government spending was to be increased generally, officially by 27.6 per cent in the budget proposals for 1982; this required the acceptance of a larger deficit, something which traditional French practice of both Left and Right had long eschewed as a result of the relatively small impact of Keynesian economic practice in France. In the civil service 54,000 new jobs were created. And research spending, aid to industry and regional assistance were all increased — elements which also fall partly under later headings. Unlike the new Social-Democratic governments which were later elected in 1982 in Spain and Sweden, however, the French Socialists refused to devalue the franc, and exchange controls were reintroduced immediately after the May 1981 elections. The impact of these measures was rapidly felt, and along with other reforms in such fields as civil liberties created a 'honeymoon' atmosphere, which lasted into the autumn of 1981.

The second type of policy also looks, at first glance, like one of classic distribution — the attempt to alter conditions of work. The central pillar of this type of policy was the plan to reduce the legal working week from forty hours to thirty-five hours over a period of five years; indeed, the first reduction of one hour per week due in 1982 was, like some of the other measures mentioned above, promulgated by ordinance rather than by law (given the large regulatory powers of the French executive branch under Articles 34 and 38 of the constitution of the Fifth Republic) because of the growing effectiveness of the opposition parties in the autumn of 1981 in using parliamentary manoeuvres to delay the huge amount of legislative work which the Socialist reform programme demanded — especially the nationalisation bill, which will be dealt with later. Essentially, however, this measure was also meant to be the *quid pro quo* for the reflationary measures mentioned above, both by permitting a reduction in wage costs and by leading into a range of measures for increasing productivity, including job-splitting (also encouraged by the Thatcher Government in Britain) and the increased use of shift work. The reduction of hours was also later to be accompanied by a number of measures to increase the rights of workers in the workplace, from a West German-style participation on advisory boards, through better provision for trade-union activity, to the right to influence certain shop-floor decisions such as stopping production lines if workers believe that there is a threat to health and safety.

The third type involved a streamlining of aid to older and declining industries, complemented by restructuring plans for specific industries in return for higher levels of aid, agreed through contracts signed between the government and the industries concerned. Among the more particular measures included in this category were assistance for research and techno-logical innovation, some limited protectionist measures (for example for the leather industry, or quotas on the import of watches from Hong

Kong), and advice and financing for the setting up of industry-wide export marketing organisations to co-ordinate the sometimes non-existent exporting efforts of smaller firms with some of their larger rivals in order to go beyond traditional cartellisation policy and create a wider expansionary dynamic. In some cases, such assistance was an attempt to allow a rapidly declining industry like shipbuilding and ship repairing to retain and develop certain limited, specialised market niches (*créneaux*). In others, like machine tools, it involved an attempt at widespread modernisation of an industry where French structures were efficient in their own terms — in this case, producing to order for particular customers — but not adapted to the areas where markets were expanding most rapidly and setting the pace for future dominance — in this case, the development of more flexible standardised ranges along the lines of the modular systems produced by the Japanese. In the case of the wood industry (everything from forestry to furniture, hardboard and paper), it meant a broad policy starting from the redevelopment of France's own extensive forest resources — not only underutilised but producing trees generally not suitable for industrial purposes — to import substitution in particular areas such as furniture, where import penetration from such market-leading areas as Scandinavia is dominant. In certain chronic problem areas, such as textiles, French policy of attempting to stem the tide of imports, especially from the newly industrialising countries, which now have well over 50 per cent penetration in one of France's most important employment sectors, is little different from that of other industrialised countries, as the long-running saga of the Multi-Fibre Agreement (MFA) demonstrates. These policies were particularly close to the heart of Pierre Dreyfus, Mauroy's first Minister of Industry and the former head of the nationalised Renault automobile firm.

The fourth policy category is one to which we shall be returning at greater length later: the restructuring of the largest industrial firms and the direct encouragement of export-oriented research and development in the most technologically sophisticated sectors. Despite some success for the industrial redeployment policies of the Giscard–Barre years, the downturn caused by the second oil shock of 1979–80 undermined much of the progress made, increasing inflation and depressing investment. The Socialist critique of the Barre policies centred on the lack of overall state direction and the reliance upon unstable market conditions; only a coherent and planned approach, they argued, would enable the stabilisation of conditions sufficiently to compensate for the structural weaknesses of the French position in the international economy and then, in turn, to encourage the growth of private investment (especially in the small and medium business sector, often dependent upon the larger firms for orders). Specific measures in this category revolved around two poles: research and development, on the one hand, and the nationalisation of a number of large firms and the remainder of the private banking sector (most of which had been nationalised in 1945 by the provisional government of General de Gaulle), on the other. These policies, which will be dealt with in some more detail later, were innovatory in a number of ways, and involved an ambitious attempt to create a state capitalist sector, which would serve as a 'locomotive' for the rest of the French economy in the longer term. The actual proposals, however, derived from traditional left-wing demands for public ownership — the list of firms had hardly altered since the 1972 Common Programme, and the nationalisation issue had, as in 1977, been thought of as the preserve of the Communist Party — but their transformation into an anti-recession strategy was mainly the work of the Minister for Research, Jean-Pierre Chevènement, who in June 1982 also took over the Industry portfolio when Dreyfus retired. As Mitterrand pointed out, the 'nationalisation' of these firms was a preventative measure to counter their otherwise inevitable multinationalisation. Important in the early proposals, too, were more extensive measures of employment protection and worker control (crucial to the PCF, which had adopted this stance in the 1970s in the face of the *autogestion* or 'self-management' policies of the CFDT and of sectors of the PS and which had proved attractive to working-class voters).

The fifth level of policy was a broad attempt to find ways to make this overall policy package both more palatable and more feasible on an international level. Of course, much in this area was of a tactical rather than a strategic nature — attempting to reassure the Reagan administration of France's role as a good ally was a particularly salient exercise, although it did fit in with President Mitterrand's acceptance of the *gaullien* consensus on foreign and defence policy[17] — and various specifically economic aspects of the policy were of a traditional pragmatic kind — trade offensives directed at countries like India, the negotiation of gas deals with Algeria and the Soviet Union, arms sales, etc. However,three aspects of foreign economic policy did give it an embryonic strategic character. First, France took a salient role in supporting the developing nations' demands at the Cancun Conference, in particular calling for global negotiations on world trade and aid problems, in the spirit of the Brandt Report, and supporting the proposal to establish an energy subsidiary of the World Bank. Secondly, France has consistently led the European chorus on co-ordinated international reflation, pushing hard, for example, through 1981 and the first half of 1982 for reductions in American interest rates. Thirdly, the Government and the Socialist Party have put forward a vision of a restructured world economy, based on regional co-operation — and thus, within Europe, on an increasing role for the EEC — and with Europe having a particularly important part to play in linking the developed and the underdeveloped worlds.[18]

Common to all of these policy levels was the traditional concern to balance the aims of mitigating inflation, reducing unemployment, increasing profitability and competitiveness and restructuring industry. A number of other policies, more or less successful in themselves — attempts to channel investment away from such outlets as gold and into industry, or the redefining of much of regional policy and ultimately linking it with decentralisation of local and regional government — were meant to tie in with the package. It has often been observed that had the other developed economies experienced an upswing during the course of 1982, then France would have been in an excellent position to play a leading role and to reap more successes than those countries which had attempted to impose far more drastic deflationary policies; not only would a general moderate reflation have complemented France's Keynesian measures, thus releasing more resources for government spending on restructuring, but France's industry would itself be in a comparatively strong position for reacting rapidly to export opportunities in both upmarket and downmarket sectors. As it happened, however, the failure of reflationary measures in a very stagnant world economy threatened to undermine the structural policies and the cohesion of the governing coalition, leading to a second phase of crisis management and a renegotiation within the government of the bases of economic strategy. We shall look first at each of the policy areas mentioned above and briefly consider the obstacles to each — many highly predictable, and indeed widely predicted by financial commentators, foreign observers and the opposition parties — before going on to outline the short-term response of the goverment. In the next section we shall look at the state of play at the beginning of 1983 and the prospects for a revised economic strategy.

Overall, one might identify four sorts of obstacles which this first phase of the Socialist economic strategy encountered, although each is bound up with the others and they are not really separable. In the first place, exogenous economic constraints were strong. The failure of the United States, West Germany and Britain to pursue reflationary policies while the recession deepened was perhaps the most salient feature of the 1981–2 period taken as a whole; strict monetary policies in the United States, centred on high interest rates, reduced output, drastically in some sectors (steel being perhaps the best known), and thus attracted an inflow of foreign funds directed into money markets rather than capital markets, increasing the value of the dollar in particular (also the mark, and to a lesser extent sterling). Added to investors' traditional fear of left-wing governments, the movement of both foreign capital and French capital (despite exchange restrictions) out of the franc further reduced domestic private sector investment (except, ironically, in the compensation-bearing shares of firms due to be nationalised in early 1982). Given the structural position of the French economy mentioned earlier, pressure on the franc, rather than increasing exports to any great extent by increased price competitiveness, in fact increased import costs at the same time when the reflationary measures at home were increasing consumer purchasing power – which fed into demand for imported goods, thus raising inflationary pressures, worsening the trade balance and, in a vicious circle, putting more pressure on the franc. Import penetration levels continued to rise, not only in already troubled sectors like textiles, but also in sectors where France's performance had previously been extremely strong, such as automobiles (where the foreign share of the French market shot up from around 20 per cent in 1980 to over 40 per cent in the worst months of 1982) and in sectors on which the longer-term restructuring strategy was based, such as consumer electronics (where Japanese video recorders, riding, as elsewhere, a sales boom, surged into the French market with no French and little European competition). Reluctant devaluations in October 1981 and June 1982 gave the impression of weakness, and the balance of trade deficit in 1982 was nearly double its 1981 level. Inflation, though reducing in absolute terms, was doing so rather more slowly than in the United States and Britain.

A number of others factors embedded in France's relationship with the world economy reinforced this vicious circle. Unlike Britain, France has little in the way of domestic energy resources, and the combination of an 80 per cent dependency on imported energy with the pegging of oil prices in terms of a rising dollar worsened this structural burden considerably during this period. High levels of interest rates internationally meant that to provide export credits and guarantees, as well as the requisite aid, for the maintenance and expansion of such exports as capital goods to the Third World (which was itself falling to its well known debt crisis) demanded more expenditure while returns were also squeezed. The collapse of the steel industry internationally had already been felt in France as elsewhere, and the combination of high levels of subsidisation plus contracting markets – features of the European steel industry in general – attracted attempts at legal retaliation by American steel producers, working at even lower capacity levels, as European imports ate into declining markets there. These factors, of course, overlapped with a second kind of obstacle, as endogenous economic constraints came into play. The budget deficit rose to over two per cent of Gross National Product — low in comparison to West Germany, Japan, the United States and Italy, but high in comparison to previous French norms (and to Britain) — and was further increased by higher public sector losses and higher-than-expected compensation terms for the new nationalisation measures, following a successful challenge of the original terms by the opposition parties before the Constitutional Council (although other complaints of unconstitutionality were thrown out). The 'social budgets' — unemployment and health — nominally independently funded by contributions from industry and workers, had seen worsening structural deficits for some time (higher costs for such things as health care, along with fewer contributors as unemployment increased), meaning more government aid and, in late 1982, the collapse of the UNEDIC unemployment compensation scheme. Increasing labour costs and 'social charges' — national insurance contributions and the like being higher in France because of the very independence of the schemes, borne in employers' overall labour costs — hit the marginal profitability of many firms in the recessionary environment, especially small businesses of the very type which the government wanted to encourage. Not only did investment fall, but government expenditure increased as the state made concessions in some sectors, for example, reducing social charges by nearly one-third in the textile industry.

The exogenous and endogenous economic constraints examined above — and this can only be a most superficial and partial account of a very complex reality — also interacted with a third type of obstacle, endogenous political constraints, which can only be mentioned briefly. At least three sorts of factors can be seen at work here. To begin with, pressures from opposition parties, although fragmented, did have certain significant effects; the losses for the Left in the 1982 cantonal elections, hitting especially the Communist Party, finally buried the fading traces of the honeymoon period, and the successful partial challenge to the nationalisation measures in the Constitutional Council, after a bruising battle with much procedural wrangling in the National Assembly and Senate, created significant delays and extra costs in the policy area that was to have been the centrepiece of the government's restructuring strategy. Secondly, although the PCF generally followed cabinet discipline, the CGT openly opposed the linking of the reduction of the working week with a proportionate reduction in wages, and in a series of strikes in early 1982 forced the government not only to drop that provision when the first stage of the planned reduction — to 39 hours — was decreed but also to renounce the use of legal compulsion to ensure future staged reductions, leaving it to the 'contractual process'; in addition, strikes in the automobile industry in particular, first in the spring of 1982 (and later, in a different context, in late 1982 and early 1983), served notice to the government that workers' demands were not to be sacrificed easily in the search for industrial restructuring. Finally, of course, some debates were opened within the Socialist Party, not only between those who wanted to go farther in the reflationary and 'workerist' direction — with strong support from sectors of the rank-and-file and within the parliamentary party — and those, particularly the Finance Minister, Jacques Delors, who wanted a 'pause' in the pace of reform, but also between those who wanted a tightened-up strategy to look more to market forces, like the Minister of Planning and Regional Development, Michel Rocard, and those who wanted a more *volontariste* and *dirigiste* (direct state capitalist) strategy based on the nationalised industries, like Chevènement. The government's main asset here, of course, was its thoroughgoing control of the political-institutional levers, and Mitterrand and Mauroy were concerned primarily with the quintessentially political task of not only mediating between but also arbitrating and controlling the disputes among these factions.

The fourth type of obstacle can be termed exogenous political constraints. Some of these were more immediate, such as the American embargo on the export of European equipment for the Siberian gas pipeline, or EEC and German opposition to French protectionist measures. Others were more long term and global in scope, such as American opposition to any general restructuring of development aid and loans, preferring the 'trickle-down' theory; the structural political weaknesses of the EEC, making it an unlikely vehicle for a co-ordinated recovery along the lines preferred by Mitterrand; or the political instability of Francophone Africa, undermining the 'co-operation' initiatives of the Minister for Co-operation, Jean-Pierre Cot, who himself resigned at the end of 1982 as Mitterrand plumped increasingly for a more 'realistic' policy of supporting existing African regimes of whatever provenance in the style of Gaullist and Giscardian neo-colonialism. Overlapping with these concerns, of course, is our first category of obstacle — exogenous economic constraints — as other principal Western economic powers decided predominantly to pursue deflationary economic strategies in a world in which, prior to the deepening of the recession, the major advances in international trade occurred among the highly industrialised nations themselves.

Thus the various elements of the broad economic package pursued by the Mauroy Government in 1981 and the first part of 1982 ran into more and more obstacles. The reflationary policies were introduced rapidly, but their costs and counterproductive effects began to be felt by the end of 1981 as the surge in economic growth began to collapse and pressure developed again on the franc. The measures for the improvement of working conditions were shown by the CGT's opposition to wage reductions to be inadequate as parts of a broader strategy of wage control and productivity improvements; the watering down of the subsequent Auroux Laws in the autumn of 1982 demonstrated the extent to which the government had come to discount the danger of thereby increasing worker opposition, in the face of rising opposition from employers as investment fell and business bumped along in the face of increasing import penetration. The policies for restructuring the traditional sectors were put on the back burner when Dreyfus retired and Chevènement upgraded the high-technology emphasis of economic policy. At the same time, however, delays in the nationalisation process and much higher than anticipated losses in the newly nationalised industries raised costs and put pressure not only on the government but also on the nationalised banking sector (old and new), which was called upon to provide capital on the government's conditions not just for restructuring but for covering losses. The danger of falling into the 'lame duck' syndrome so familiar in West European economies seemed to overshadow the ambitious plans for creating a new 'locomotive'. And the foreign economic policy of the government looked more and more like the bilateral, pragmatic search for energy and export markets, including an emphasis on nuclear technology and arms sales, which had characterised its predecessors. This combination of factors led to the abrupt introduction in June 1982 of a transitional phase of economic policy, one of crisis management, and the beginning of an attempt to reconstruct economic strategy as a whole.

'U-Turn' or 'capitalism without capitalists'?

At this point it must be noted that, despite the bleak picture painted in the previous section, the balance-sheet of the government's original economic strategy exhibited several positive conjunctural results. Inflation, despite remaining at a higher level than that of Britain or the United States — the latter witnessed a sudden and dramatic drop in the inflation rate which had not been widely predicted — came down from around 14 per cent in 1981 to 9.7 per cent in 1982, meeting the government's original target. The budget deficit, despite the additional pressures which have been mentioned, was kept within its 1982 limit of 2.5 per cent of GNP and is likely to be kept within its 1983 target of 3 per cent, well below the United States figure of 6 per cent or the Italian figure of 17 per cent. The rate of bankruptcies stabilised and then began to fall, and the stock market regained its drastic losses of the immediate post-electoral period and moved moderately but steadily upwards during 1982. Most important for the government, however, was the fact that unemployment, having risen to 2.1 million by the end of 1981, stabilised at that figure through 1982 and even dropped slightly in December, at a time when British and American figures were increasing and the West German figure moved up most dramatically of all to 2.5 million by the end of the year. And despite slow economic growth – still higher than most of her partners – and bad trade payments figures, most French people were better off as a result of the government's measures, especially the lower paid.

This contrasting picture highlights the contradictions of a strategy such as the French one; that it can seem such a failure if one looks at certain sorts of indicators, indicators which reflect the concerns of the holders of private capital or of foreign-exchange dealers, and yet look relatively highly successful according to other indicators, indicators which tend to reflect the general level of economic activity. The difference, of course, is the element of profitability, crucial to the first set of indicators but much less so to the second (at least directly). In an international market system – in which broad commitments to avoid general protectionism go along with doubts as to whether protectionist or crude import substitution policies can be either effective in the longer term or politically acceptable given the competitive strength of multinational firms, the transnational nature of technological development, the need for attention to rapidly evolving consumer demand in liberal-democratic capitalist societies, and the huge costs which would be attendant upon any attempt to alter highly interpenetrated trade patterns and currency exchange systems – the state has no choice but to use its influence to improve, maintain or regain conditions of profitability.

This is even more true in an economy in which a large sector is in private hands, and even in Socialist France, with its nationalisation of most of the largest firms (in addition to the large nationalised sector established in the post World War II era) and the rest of the private banks, only about a quarter of production and employment are provided by the public sector. Thus the public sector is not an alternative to a profitable private sector, but, in the unstable conditions of advanced capitalism, an essential factor in its maintenance. This can be achieved in three ways: the maintenance of essential services and infrastructure necessary to general profitability (the health of the labour force, roads, education, energy, etc.); the running of industries and services which are inherently unprofitable, but the collapse of which would put a strain upon the nation's international trading position, create unemployment which would demand less productive forms of public expenditure to avert political unrest and thus further instability, or undermine profitability in other sectors (e.g. steel); or the attempt to improve competitiveness in sectors with longer-term market potential but little short- or even medium-term profitability and thus unable to attract sufficient private risk capital for either restructuring or new technological development.

In each of these cases, however, the purpose of public control and financial support is to underpin or stimulate broader long-term profitability in the national economy as a whole. This is the role which nation-states in the West have been pursuing and developing ever since the dismantling of mercantilism in the nineteenth century. The problem is, of course, that of opportunity costs: first, that expenditure of these kinds can take up funds through taxation which might otherwise have gone into either demand or investment, funds which are in short supply in a period of economic decline and especially short in a severe downturn; and second, that the structures of the public sector will themselves be more rigid and less sensitive to market forces, thus building in rigidities which will be counterproductive in terms of the longer-term goal of profitability in general. Most Western experience has been in the first two types of public sector activity — infrastructure and 'lame ducks' — often aligned, since the 1930s, with Keynesian policies of demand management in order to counteract these opportunity costs. In a period of recession, however, not only is Keynesian demand management often counterproductive in the ways we have discussed earlier in this chapter, but the opportunity costs of public sector expenditure are exacerbated as investment in the private sector is crowded out by the demands of financing public sector deficits, while the market rigidities of public sector firms under pressure undermine international competitiveness in a vicious circle. New supply-side policies are required which can attack the structural causes of these problems, and these run in two directions: the attempt to reduce the public sector deficit by reducing expenditure, as in Britain and the United States; or the attempt to move even more heavily into the third type of spending on the public sector — increasing public investment in longer-term growth sectors — while restructuring 'lame ducks' and making infrastructure more productive and cost-efficient. The latter was always the intention of the French Socialists' economic strategy. But rather than finding such a strategy compatible with (even reinforced by) the demand-side measures which formed the other side of the original package, the constraints discussed in the second part of the last section seemed to demonstrate the conflict between them. Private investment continued to fall significantly in 1982, pressure on the franc continued and the trade and payments deficits ballooned; the political coalition showed signs of strain, too, and the opposition went on the offensive.

The result of all of this pressure was a package of measures announced in June 1982, which combined a realignment of currencies in the European Monetary System – amounting to a 9.59 per cent devaluation of the franc in relation to the deutschmark (although this actually consisted of a 2.75 per cent devaluation of the franc and lira against the European Currency Unit and a 4.25 per cent revaluation of the mark and the florin) – and a thoroughgoing wages and prices freeze until 31 October 1982, to be lifted differentially and progressively in various sectors after that date. The government moved swiftly, using price control powers dating from 30 June 1945 (and often used systematically in concert with the planning process until the liberalisation carried out by Barre in 1978) and introducing new wage control legislation to supplement existing powers dating from the early 1950s. Also frozen were retail and wholesale margins and dividends. Wage indexation clauses were suspended, as were, more problematically, recently negotiated phased wage rises in the automobile industry, which had been agreed after a series of CGT-supported strikes through the late spring, which had demonstrated the newly-conscious force of immigrant workers in the industry, and rises in the minimum wage; these created tensions within the left-wing social coalition. Indeed, the French government (like, in even more compelling circumstances, the Italian) set its sights on the elimination of inflation-maintaining wage indexation altogether. A government reshuffle followed, characterised mainly by the installation of Chevènement in a new super-ministry of Research and Industry and the sacking of the Minister of National Solidarity, Nicole Questiaux (widely regarded as the social-welfarist conscience of the government), and her replacement by Mitterrand's close advisor, Pierre Bérégovoy, in a significantly renamed Ministry for Social Affairs. Chevènement was charged with streamlining industrial policy, and Bérégovoy with reducing the problematic structural deficits in the various social funds mentioned above. Widely regarded as a 'U-turn' in economic policy, comparable to the experiences of Labour governments in Britain in the 1960s and 1970s, the impact of these measures both politically and economically was great.

Of course, to speak of a U-turn is initially misleading insofar as the pace of the reform programme during the first year of the Socialist government had been rapid, and had created a number of *faits accomplis* both in distributive policy and in areas like nationalisation; the unanticipatedly high level of costs which the government had to absorb, however, was a challenge to the as yet unfulfilled promises of the original ambitious Socialist platform as well as to the raised expectations of the electorate. On the whole, the price freeze worked well, with inflation running at 0.3 per cent in July and August and 0.6 per cent in September. The wages freeze also held well, although the inevitable problem arose of dealing with special cases. The troubled automobile industry, for example, was an exception on both levels, as prices were allowed to rise with the new model year and continuing labour troubles over immigrant workers' pay and conditions were fuelled by the government's attempt to delay wage settlements agreed shortly before the freeze. Civil servants' pay was also increased above the norm, and it may not have been irrelevant that the Civil Service Minister, Anicet Le Pors, was not only a well respected *grand commis de l'État* but also one of the four Communist ministers in the government.

Attempts to cut the social deficit by raising taxes on alcohol and cigarettes and by increasing contributions while reducing benefits ran into increasing opposition from both employers (who paid the contributions) and workers (who received the benefits). One symptom of disenchantment with the government from both sides of industry was the breakdown of talks aimed at re-negotiating the UNEDIC unemployment compensation scheme, forcing the government to take a more direct role in the running and financing of the scheme. Another was the decision to impose a new system of payment for hospital care in order to better control accounting and reduce costs, which came under fire both from doctors — who had already been involved in noisy protests against government policy earlier in the year — and a combination of hospital workers, workers who were the beneficiaries of the state health scheme (called Social Security — in contrast to Britain, where 'Social Security' means basic welfare benefits, and the United States, where it means old-age pensions), and — distinctly though somewhat more discreetly — the Health Minister, Jack Ralite, also one of the four Communist ministers. Nonetheless, the government was well pleased with its relative success.

The new atmosphere also took its toll on the planned Auroux Bill for increasing workers' rights in industry, as opposition from employers mounted to measures which they claimed would seriously affect productivity and competitiveness; when the Act was finally pushed through in the autumn it made a number of concessions to management. The Communist Party, however, did not mount any overt opposition to the new policies, careful not to jeopardise their position within the government at a time when internal splits were reinforcing fears of continued declining electoral support — the position of the PCF in local government, crucial to its popular base and organisational structure, being dependent upon co-operation with the PS in the upcoming March 1983 municipal elections — and because of this the CGT, while supporting workers' demands in particular cases, did not adopt an overall strategy of attempting to combat the cuts by widespread strike action. The campaign against gifts to employers, erratically pursued by the PCF and the CGT, however, did find echoes within the PS, particularly within the parliamentary party. The new measures were also characterised by a shift in the thrust of the government's contractual policy, as in several sectors of industry the lifting of the price freeze after the end of November was made conditional upon increased productivity, voluntary price and/or wage restraint, and the like. And despite successes on the inflation front, pressure on the franc continued for a number of reasons, including pessimism as to the long-term effectiveness of wage/price freezes in general, the belief that a further devaluation was inevitable, and the trade balance — which continued to worsen at the same rate as before.

Despite these setbacks on the political, social and economic fronts, however, the government seemed in general to gain cohesiveness and purpose from the exercise. In the first place, despite differences over certain structural aspects of policy (which were decided through the clear relegation of the Planning Minister, Rocard, to a back-seat role, as we shall see) virtually all factions except the PCF, who had little choice in the matter, accepted that a new set of priorities had to replace the *tous azimuts* approach of 1981, and that the core of that set of priorities was the downgrading of distributive policy through reductions in overall levels of real wages and in levels of social benefits, in order to redistribute more of the state's resources into productive activities. Rocard, in a two-part article in *Le Monde* on 14 and 15 July, made clear his position on this, contrasting the sterile 'austerity' of the Giscard/Barre period with a new 'socialist rigour', aimed at improving the economy through negotiation and conciliation in the interests of all, including workers, in the long run.

The Employment Minister, Jean Auroux, writing in the same newspaper on 2 September, emphasised the role of contractual policy in facing the hard choices stemming from 'national and international economic realities' and the need to attack the structural causes of inflation (in rhetoric worthy of any government of Left or Right in the West) by increasing productivity. He identified two themes: first, the need to maintain the *average* level of purchasing power, with some redistribution from the higher paid to the lower paid — but with reference only to levels obtaining at the end of 1983, i.e. allowing for a reduction in the second half of 1982; and the progressive lifting of the freeze in order to wring all tendencies towards indexation from the wage bargaining process, programming wage rises until the end of 1983 and linking negotiations on wages with further reductions in the working week. The Auroux Bills were specifically mentioned as trade-offs for the workers, whom he urged to accept the need for 'a greater sense of responsibility', appealing to them 'to surmount their own short term interests to the profit of the collective interest'. He entitled his new-style contracts *contrats sociaux de compétitivité'* Mitterrand's rhetoric of national solidarity also emphasised the government's new *discours,* while Mauroy announced in *Le Matin* on 12 October that the new rigour 'cannot be brought to an end until we are faced with a proven, vigorous upturn on an international level'.

Complementing this theme of rigour, however, was a reaffirmed emphasis on continuing and reinforcing a number of the government's initiatives on structural reform. These involved several measures on the financial side, including innovations in the incentives for investment in distribution (retailing/wholesaling), measures to increase the level of savings and to direct them into productive investment along the broad lines of the Dautresme Report, the setting up of an unlisted securities market to aid small business and the improvement of credit terms in both industry and finance.[19] Most importantly, however, they involved a continuation of the main lines of industrial policy. As Chevènement wrote in *Le Monde* on 15 September, 'It is necessary to keep repeating that France cannot choose the rhythm of technical progress. She can only choose to be in the forefront or to submit.' Stressing that 'one industrial job pays for three others', he pointed out that long-term employment prospects were dependent on success in industrial policy; that that success would be dependent upon exports; that a campaign against 'anti-industrialist' tendencies in French culture required keeping the rise in the cost of services in line with that in industry so that savings would not be drained towards the former; on better pay for highly qualified personnel in industry; on rewards for professionalism and initiative, etc. He argued that a lack of vested interests or a *rentier* mentality, which had protected inefficient structures, allowed the Socialist majority to transcend old constraints and move towards a new *modèle français*, combining 'a vigorous public *impulsion* and the profusion of decentralised initiatives' in a new collective project based on the complementarity and interdependence of public and private sectors.

This emphasis was continued in the 1983 budget proposals presented in early September, with the maintenance of expenditure on research and industrial policy and the maintenance and extension of tax credits for investment, on the one hand, and ceilings on social spending as well as attempts to reduce the costs of administration, on the other, in order to keep the budget deficit within the ceiling of 3 per cent of GDP.[20] Measures were taken to direct more funds into the nationalised industries, although not as much of this could be used for investment as was once hoped given the high losses of 1982. The new plans for these industries, originally due in the summer of 1982, were finally submitted towards the end of the year and approved in February 1983. At the time of writing it is too early to tell whether the industrial policy will be more successful than distributive policy or than the earlier more all-inclusive approach, but there are several aspects that are interesting to note and may be of importance if this policy is to succeed.

In the first place, the development of the French state itself — combining the long interventionist administrative tradition of *colbertisme* with the experience of nationalisation and planning under both left-wing and right-wing governments of the Fourth and Fifth Republics — provides an organisational structure, which, at both national and local level, is perhaps better equipped than other Western governments to pursue coherent *dirigiste* policies. Not only has the training of public sector elites equipped them for success in private industry, as evidenced in the practice of *pantouflage*, and has public industry in certain sectors (like the Renault automobile firm) or the public banking sector (one of the largest and most successful banking systems in the world) been successful in international market conditions in the past, but even those areas generally regarded as failures in the past, such as electronics in the *Plan Calcul*, have provided lessons which may increase the chances of future success. Despite the crash of an Ariane rocket last year, the French space sector has been immensely successful and has recently been on the verge of being commercially competitive with the American, and in information technology France leads the field in certain specialised sectors of, e.g. computer-aided design. The 'lame duck' mentality is not the dominant characteristic of the French public sector.

Second, the programme of nationalisation completed in 1982 gives the government a wide range of options in a number of sectors, which could move quickly into profitability in a world-wide recovery, particularly, of course, in electronics, but also in pharmaceuticals, aluminium, chemicals and others, particularly if the restructuring and the research and development aid provided by the government is successful in identifying and pursuing new and expanding market sectors and niches.

Third, the methods of finance available to the state, although under pressure at the moment, could provide crucial venture capital once the firms begin to move towards profitability, not only directly through the state budget or indirectly through the nationalised banks but also through the development of new forms of non-voting shareholding now being experimented with or through the small but developing bond market. Thus, if external recovery begins to percolate through the international economy — as recent indicators of the American economy seem to signal — then the French public sector, and the myriad small and medium-sized firms dependent on it for orders, will be well set for the second stage of expansion, attempting to escape from the intermediate economy trap.

And fourth, the actual structures being experimented with do not involve the establishment of giant single enterprises along the lines of British experience with nationalisation or the mixed 'national champions' of the Gaullist period, but rather the setting up of at least two 'poles' (and sometimes more) in each major industry — firms which, though perhaps specialising in different sub-sectors, will overlap considerably in products and technology, and will have to be competitive with each other as well as with foreign firms. In certain cases, such as chemicals, this means that French public firms will not reach the size of their major international rivals, which could still be a competitive disadvantage in terms of marketing and economies of scale; on the other hand, however, the state will be able to compare standards of productivity and efficiency, important in decisions concerning longer-term investment, the results of which are very difficult to predict where there is only one monopoly supplier within a national market. This could be crucial in turning, for example, state procurement orders from a straight choice of a single domestic *versus* a more competitive foreign supplier — in the former case possibly further entrenching an existing lack of competitiveness in the name of the national interest, and in the latter undermining domestic production and longer-term market/export potential — into a situation where such procurement can actually increase the pressures for competitiveness in an effective manner.

And, finally, the strategy will enable the government to directly stimulate development in areas which can have a crucial multiplier effect on broader technological development. Here the prime example is that of cable television, in which, unlike Britain — where the debate is between constraints designed to save the existing television services from competition, on the one hand, and a free market approach which could prove to be both overdependent on cheaper but soon-to-be obsolescent technology and a threat to BBC and ITV, on the other — France is supporting both rapid expansion through seed projects such as the computerising of the Paris telephone directory (eventually involving the PTT telecommunications ministry in providing terminals for subscribers' television sets) and the subsidising of research on fibre-optic technology, which is the future technology of the industry. Provided that such investment is cost-efficient and productive in the long run – and it should be remembered that *all* of the integrated circuits produced in the first three years of their development were bought by the United States Department of Defense in the 1950s[21] – it could provide a sound basis for future development of the French economy as the 'Third Industrial Revolution', based on micro-technology, comes to dominate the world marketplace. Such developments also reflect the experience of earlier industrial revolutions, when wars, government-sponsored trading ventures and the like provided the crucial conditions for profitable capitalist development affecting the private sector. Things are more complex today, but the state, with its very real resources, acting as a capital-accumulating entrepreneur, may have the potential to lead the process of capitalist economic development; indeed, it may prove to be indispensable to that process, producing not exactly a 'capitalism without capitalists' but a state capitalism made safe for the private sector too.

Conclusions: socialism and state capitalism

Where in all this, it may be asked, is socialism? On one level, the difficulties faced by the Mitterrand presidency are reminiscent of those faced by the Wilson Government in Britain in the 1960s, and they bring into question whether currency speculation, import penetration combined with the structural decline of basic industries, and export stagnation, do not obviate any meaningful use of the word. The combination of rising expectations and shrinking capital in hard times may make the dilemma of social democracy into an inescapable trap, feasible only in periods of boom, but even then bringing with it rigidities which undermine the mixed economy in periods of retrenchment. The near-doubling of the French trade deficit in 1982 (from just over 50 billion fr. in 1981 to 93.3 billion in 1982), the need for continued international borrowing to support the currency exchange rate – the French government has arranged to borrow some $9 billion since September 1982, although not all of that has been drawn and, as that which has been drawn has been integrated into the foreign exchange reserves, it is not known whether it has actually been used as such, or how much – and the deficits in the public sector provide the most salient examples of the very real constraints which the international market economy brings to bear on national governments. Redistributive policies, insofar as they can be pursued at all, are characterised not by redistribution towards the workers, but redistribution towards capital, both state and private, in an attempt to restore profitability and competitiveness on a global scale.

This raises real questions as to the nature of public choice in capitalist democracies. State capitalism, as an ideological solution to the problems of advanced capitalist societies, is attractive neither to the capitalists and middle classes which make up the bulk of the electorate of conservative parties nor to the working and lower middle classes who dominate left-wing coalition building. Floating voters, generally middle class, find themselves squeezed from both sides, as their savings are eroded by inflation and taxes, and yet they are also affected by unemployment and wage restraint. Short-run sacrifices are not only difficult to sell electorally but also particularly painful for the Left, who must call for proportionately greater sacrifices from the less well off sectors of the population, who are both their electoral base and their ultimate moral and ideological concern.

At the same time, however, within the narrower framework of pursuing an approach to economic recovery within a capitalist context, the state capitalist policies of a supply-side democratic socialism would seem to contain, if pursued in a sufficiently ruthless fashion, a greater potential for reconstructing a structurally weak economy in the face of recession without the extent of sacrifice of output and employment entailed by the 'cold turkey' of free market monetarism. Further, they may permit a more coherent strategic approach to the problem of reconstituting capital to take advantage of new profit opportunities in the longer term should a new wave of growth emerge. In this sense, the scope for the autonomy of the state within the wider international capitalist framework may be seen to be far greater than admitted in classical market economics or even Keynesianism. Indeed, such an approach, learning from the long-term tendencies of capital towards concentration and internationalisation, may be the most efficient means of capitalist reconstruction available, especially in the structurally weaker national economies, despite the severe financial and political constraints of the shorter term. But, of course, it is neither socialism, nor electorally attractive.

Despite potential setbacks, including losses in the municipal elections and the expected readjustment of the franc within the European Monetary System, the Mitterrand/Mauroy Government is well placed to pursue a longer-term strategy. It controls the political and administrative levers of power in a traditionally *dirigiste* state for at least three years to come, and President Mitterrand will be in office until 1988. The Government has scored a number of crucial political and economic victories despite setbacks already — the stabilisation of unemployment, the maintenance of the franc, with extensive central bank intervention, at its EMS parity of 2.835 to the deutschmark since the previous adjustment of June 1982 and the limitation of the budget deficit as a proportion of GDP. Therefore, should an international recovery take place in 1983–4, the Socialists may have gained a sufficient breathing space to pursue their state capitalist strategy more effectively in the future.

Notes

1   See P. G. Cerny, 'Gaullism, Advanced capitalism and the Fifth Republic', in David S. Bell (ed.), *Contemporary French Political Parties*, London and New York, Croom Helm and St. Martin's Press, 1982, ch. 2.
2   For a more extensive discussion of some of these political issues, see P. G. Cerny, 'Democratic socialism and the tests of power: the Mitterrand presidency eighteen months on', *West European Politics*, 6, no. 3 (July 1983), and P. G. Cerny and M. A. Schain (eds), *Socialism, the State and Public Policy in France*, London, Frances Pinter, forthcoming 1984.
3   See Pierre Birnbaum, 'The state in contemporary France', in Richard Scase (ed.), *The State in Western Europe*, London, Croom Helm, 1981, ch. 2.
4   See Douglas E. Ashford, *British Dogmatism and French Pragmatism: Central-Local Policymaking in the Welfare State*, London and Winchester, Mass., George Allen & Unwin, 1982; also Martin A. Schain, 'Communist control of municipal councils and urban political change', in P. G. Cerny and M. A. Schain (eds), *French Politics and Public Policy*, London and New York, Frances Pinter, St. Martin's Press and Methuen University Paperbacks, 1980/81, ch. 12.
5   See Cerny, 'The new rules of the game in France', in Cerny and Schain (eds), *French Politics and Public Policy, op. cit.*, ch. 2, and 'Democratic socialism and the tests of power', *op. cit.*
6   See Cerny, 'The problem of legitimacy in the Fifth French Republic', paper presented to the Workshop on Normative and Empirical Dimensions of Legitimacy, Joint Meetings of Workshops, European Consortium for Political Research, University of Lancaster, April 1981.
7   The classic study is Charles Kindleberger, *Economic Growth in France and Britain 1851–1950*, Cambridge, Mass., Harvard University Press, 1964; cf. Tom Kemp, *Economic Forces in French History*, London, Dobson, 1971.
8   *Le Monde*, 10 November 1981.
9   *Le Monde*, 18/19 October 1981; see, for background, Robert Gilpin, *France in the Age of the Scientific State*, Princeton, NJ, Princeton University Press, 1968, and John Zysman *Political Strategies for Industrial Order: Market, State and Industry in France*, Berkeley and Los Angeles, University of California Press, 1977.
10 *Le Monde*, 6 October 1981.
11 *Le Monde*, 10 October 1981.
12 Consider, for example, the deterioration in France's position in Franco-Soviet exchanges in the late 1970s: *Le Monde*, 21 October 1981.
13 This is precisely Zysman's argument about the contradictions between the *Plan Calcul* and the conditions for success in the electronics industry internationally. *Op. cit.*

14   See, e.g. Jean Fourastié, *Les trente glorieuses: ou la Révolution invisible de 1946 à 1975*, Paris, Fayard, revised edition 1979.

15   See Richard F. Kuisel, *Capitalism and the State in Modern France: Renovation and Economic Management in the Twentieth Century*, Cambridge, Cambridge Univeristy Press, 1981, chs. 7–10.

16   Cf. Cerny, 'Gaullism, advanced capitalism and the Fifth Republic', *op. cit.*, and Birnbaum, 'The State in contemporary France', *op. cit.*

17   See Jolyon Howorth and Patricia Chilton (eds), *Defence and Dissent in France in the 1980s*, London, Croom Helm, forthcoming 1983; also Cerny, 'Democratic socialism and the tests of power', op. cit., and *The Politics of Grandeur: Ideological Aspects of de Gaulle's Foreign Policy*, Cambridge, Cambridge University Press, 1980.

18   See the report presented by Gilles Martinet and Daniel Percheron to the Valence Congress of the Socialist Party, summarised in *Le Monde*, 23/24 August 1981, and also the interview with the Minister for European Affairs, Andre Chandernagor, in *Le Monde*, 11 August 1981.

19   *Le Monde*, 9 July 1982.

20   See *Le Monde*, 3 September 1982, for a detailed breakdown.

21   My thanks to Dr Judith Reppy of Cornell University for this piece of information.

PART IV LANGUAGE

10 Communist discourse

JOHN GAFFNEY
Roehampton Institute

It is not the aim of this chapter to define the essential characteristics of political discourse or even a variant of it. Indeed, one of the implications of this chapter is that such a definition would be made possible only by a certain reductionism. My own definition of political discourse is wide while it encompasses what I consider to be its essential quality: its ability to draw upon ideas and other conditions ostensibly outside it and thereby transform its own conditions. I shall consider discourse as the verbal equivalent of action: it is, diachronically and synchronically, the set of all political verbalisations, is all the expressible forms taken in response to organisational and ethical imperatives. On the basis of these characteristics it generates response, which may range from indifference through hostility to enthusiasm, and which may or may not lead to political action. Discourse is, therefore, both the name of the linked practices and the form in which individual relation to those practices is elaborated. The significance of any instance of political discourse will change according to its differing relations to all of the above and its overall relation to political action.

Let us look, with this definition in mind, at a section of the *rapport* of the Central Committee of the French Communist Party (PCF), which was given by its general secretary, Georges Marchais, in May 1979.[1]

I mentioned above that a discourse can draw upon its wider conditions. For the PCF, the most severe of these is the presidential system, which is the hallmark of the Fifth Republic. What the study of a moment of discursive activity should demonstrate, therefore, is how, upon its immediate and wider conditions (here, respectively, discourse itself and institutional constraints), the official discourse of a political party effects new orientations and indicates how its self-awareness is modified by its organisation and its goals.

The analysis of the discourse of the Left, and particularly of the PCF, normally involves the comparative analysis of written texts, especially the *projets de résolution* submitted to and amended by congress.[2] By means of these fundamentally syntactic analyses certain semantic rules are developed and the identification of codes made concerning transformations and discursive devices. Two brief and simple examples of this coding are: the use of expressions such as *internationalisme prolétarien* or *le marxisme-léninisme* to mitigate an overtly asserted doctrinal distance between the PCF and the Soviet Communist Party (CPSU); or the quite acceptable denunciation of Stalinism upon condition that mention is made of, and criticism does not go beyond that made by, the 1956 20th Congress of the CPSU.

The approach adopted in this paper should not be seen in contradistinction to this method of enquiry but involves a different perspective in that I consider as crucially significant the spoken word rather than the written text. One of the essential conditions of the general secretary's report is that it is read out to an audience.

Linked to this is a further claim that such attention to the report will enable us to see how the persona of Marchais is imposed upon traditional Communist party discourse and how, through its personal delivery, certain shifts and reorientations take place within it. The person or perceived personality thereby becomes the catalyst of discursive and ultimately doctrinal change. If this be true, the connection between doctrine and the institutional exigencies of the regime makes discourse itself the site of political change.

In terms of institutional changes and the ways in which political organisations cope with them, it is no longer a question for the Left in the Fifth Republic of simply whether or not it should or will put up a candidate for the presidency. This avenue to power has not only been recognised as the main one, it has distorted the organisation and discourse of the political parties involved. The definitive institutionalisation of presidentialism after 1962 did not, however, lead, as many observers expected, to the homogenisation of the parties and the creation of a party system of the American type. The parties have been rapidly and radically transformed in certain ways. They have not, however, disappeared or even been reduced to solely electoral roles. The PCF, because of its organisational structure and doctrine, is perhaps the most dramatic example of this juxtaposition of the pressures of party practices and those of the wider polity.

Perhaps the most pronounced feature of present-day Commuist strategy is the absence of the general line as a measure of deviationism and party integrity. This absence is partly due to the gradual shedding by the party of certain of its tenets and theses: in the 1960s, for example, those of the inevitability of war and the party's irreducible hostility to the regime; in the 1970s, the rejection of the term 'dictatorship of the proletariat' and the substitution of the term 'scientific socialism' for that of 'Marxism-Leninism'. It is one of the contentions of this paper that these two sets of change differ in nature from one another. The changes in the 1960s were specifically designed to adapt the party to the regime and an alliance strategy. In the 1970s, these changes helped the party to adapt in a more subtle way by making it possible for the leadership to exploit certain practices of the regime while at the same time enabling it to appropriate doctrinal justification for such strategic changes as were perceived to be necessary.

French Commmunist Party doctrine now focuses upon immediate issues (activism) and long-term ones (socialist society). The interim period becomes uncharted doctrinal territory and therefore becomes a question of judgement which facilitates the leadership's — and discursively the leader's — appropriation of it.

This is done within the traditional format, modes and styles of PCF discourse. The main formative condition of this is perhaps its own history and its repudiation, after Thorez, of the cult of personality. There are many differences between Marchais's style of leadership and that of Thorez. Here we can mention the most fundamental; that Marchais's is comparatively understated. It is, therefore, through accepted discursive structures and moments that Marchais impinges upon party processes. The report, of course, is only a parallel reading, an echo, of the *projet* itself which, in its most democratic interpretation, is the child of every active member of the party.

This doctrinal shift through discourse is a gradual one. At the 1976 Congress, the diffusion of doctrine and the impingement of the leadership upon party practices was hidden because Marchais at that time led a relatively harmonious party which looked forward, with its leader, to a substantial increase in its power and perhaps governmental alliance with its Common Programme partners. The breakdown of talks on the updating of the Common Programme of Government and the aftermath of the 1978 legislative elections produced a potentially serious expression of discontent within the party and saw in response the near-total appropriation by the leadership of the right to initiate discourse. This was, however, facilitated by the earlier diffusion of doctrine and the shift of focus to the leader. Within this context, the normal cycle within the party of *repli* and *ouverture* was broken in 1979 by the conflation of *repli* and a personified *ouverture* strategy, which would legitimate and inform Marchais's presidential campaign of 1981.

The report of the 23rd Congress is 30,000 words long. In order to illustrate my argument here, I have chosen to examine the shortest section of the report which, incidentally, contains the most famous — or notorious — term used by the party at the time, that concerning the *bilan* of the socialist countries as *globalement positif.* The subject of this section is the nature of the relationship between the PCF and the socialist countries. It combines insistence upon the practical achievements of 'le socialisme existant' (p. 40 of the report) in raising economic living standards, with the affirmation of various principles such as the absence of a single model of Socialist society and the quintessentially democratic nature of socialism. With reference to this latter point, the report asserts the party's own commitment to a plurality of parties and to elections. These points qualify the general argument which is that both practically and morally the socialist countries are superior to their capitalist counterparts.

The central metaphor in this argument is that of *bilan*, which is sustained throughout the section:

> Comme l'écrit notre projet de résolution: 'à la question de savoir quel est aujourd'hui l'apport du socialisme au mouvement historique des pays concernés et à l'humanité dans son ensemble, nous répondons: le bilan des pays socialistes est globalement positif' (p. 40).[3]

The expression *bilan globalement positif* was a contentious one even — perhaps especially — within the party itself. The speaker, by addressing himself to the issue, thus enters the discussion both as *rapporteur* (the term is in the *projet* as well as in the report) and as arbitrator:

> Je passe rapidement sur les querelles de mots qu'a pu susciter, ici ou là, le terme 'bilan'. Quelques camarades on fait l'analogie avec un bilan comptable, comportant une colonne pour l'actif, une colonne pour le passif . . . et ils en ont conclu à l'impossibilité d'effectuer de tels bilans 'en matière de réalisations humaines'! Mais voyons: qui va s'imaginer, si je parle du 'bilan catastrophique' de cinq années de pouvoir de M. Giscard d'Estaing, que je suis un expert comptable? (p. 40)[4]

This scathing dismissal of criticism both discredits external enemies and associates internal dissidence with them. (No longer, indeed, are mere deviationists the internal enemy, but any who challenge authoritative judgement in spite of their own lack of vision and incisiveness and inadvertently threaten the integrity and efficacy of the party thereby.)

What the above quotation actually dies is to admit that the term *bilan* is a metaphor and imply that it was always recognised as such. What it does not argue is whether it is an appropriate metaphor. Given this, Marchais can shift attention to the main element of the argument, which is that it is *positif*:

> Or, je l'ai montré, un examen portant sur l'ensemble de la période historique que nous vivons montre que le sens des évolutions qui modifient notre monde en profondeur est sans équivoque: ce qui avance, c'est le socialisme; ce qui perd du terrain, c'est le capitalisme (p. 40).[5]

The report itself here is used to legitimate the argument. The *examen* that the speaker points out he has demonstrated in fact refers not to a previous document or established party position but to a previous section (pp. 22–4) of this speech. The *bilan* metaphor is thus deemed appropriate because it adequately describes an earlier established position, which involved a historico-ethical justification of the Soviet Union. It is the argument concerning the notion of historical advance as ethical justification which would undermine the speaker's argument, but this lies outside its established terms of reference. In the absence of such a challenge, that which is positive is that which advances. Within limits, therefore, a debate about the appropriateness of the *bilan* metaphor legitimates – and masks – the metaphor of (military) movement which lies behind it.

The speaker then defends the whole expression, *bilan globalement positif* – and thereby instigates another censorship of disagreement – by arguing that it possesses a dialectical truth, in that the adversary and its media make daily play of an imagined negative *bilan*. Thus the more its antithesis is argued (and the verbs used to describe capitalism's methods here are: *endiguer*, *détourner* and *ruiner* (p. 40)), the more such a struggle in its defence will point to a transcendent truth. Partial understanding, therefore, or puzzlement on the part of the activist is, paradoxically – or rather, dialectically – an indication of the truth of the argument. Doubt is thus seen as acceptable, even constructive, continuing doubt as subversive and an indication that the dissidents are the victims of the wider capitalist conspiracy:

> Comment expliquer que les militants d'un parti d'avant-garde en viennent à préconiser, comme position révolutionnaire, que nous nous cantonnions dans une prudente neutralité face à cette campagne de tous les instants? Comment l'expliquer, sinon parce que, peu ou prou, ils cèdent eux-mêmes à la pression énorme de cette campagne? (p. 41)[6]

The point is reinforced by a reminder that the party must not desert the class struggle: 'nous ne pouvons déserter ce terrain essentiel du combat de classe et nous ne le ferons pas.' (p. 41).[7] Supporting reference is made here to a contribution to the *tribune de discussion,* which further associates the leader, without reference to the party proper, with the true site of the struggle, *la base* (the rank and file).

The objections to the use of the term *bilan globalement positif* have therefore been attributed to: (i) a misunderstanding of its metaphorical sense; (ii) the failure to see it as an antithetical moment of a transcendent truth; and (iii), (if (i) and (ii) are not accepted), the dissident's lack of faith and his abandonment of the class struggle. Internal disagreement — in conjunction with the strong and parallel desire for unanimity — is not a disadvantage to this form of leadership, but a necessary feature of it because it distances the speaker from a perceived lack of harmony within the party sufficiently for him to assert and reassert authority within the *rapport.*

This is a feature of most political argument of this kind: that the move away from the particular to the general, from the concrete to the theoretical (here, from struggle to reflection upon it) can involve a move away from simple truth to complex mystifications and that this is the fault of the listener and not the speaker. The implicit allegation is that the listener, aided by the very nature of discourse, has created the conditions for misconstruction in thought and for deviance in action:

> Dans ce domaine, aucune astuce de langage, aucune finasserie tacticienne, qui permettraient tout à la fois d'esquiver la difficulté et d'escamoter le problème, ne peuvent être de mise (p. 41).[8]

Refusing, therefore, others' readiness to do this or their desire that he do it for them, Marchais faces the consequences of his position head-on. Given this courageous stand on the part of the speaker, all hesitation or qualification on the part of the audience becomes equally unacceptable. All doubt must be cast aside as a prerequisite to advance. The argument then focuses upon two alternatives only concerning the routes to be chosen. And the choice is simple and offered with brutal demagogic force:

> Donner une réponse simple et claire à la seule question qui importe en définitive: oui ou non, est-ce une bonne chose que les peuples concernés aient construit le socialisme, ou aurait-il mieux valu qu'ils ne le fassent pas? Notre réponse à cette question est offensive et sans ambiguïté: oui, c'est une bonne chose, pour eux et pour nous (p. 41).[9]

From this example and from several before and after it in the section and speech as a whole, we can see that a rhythmical pattern of collusive advance towards the audience and profitable retreat is established. A problem is raised, its simplicity or complexity stressed. If the problem is defined as simple, a fan of nuance is begun, and, if complex, a categorical response cuts into the apparent complexity. Then, categorical agreement from the audience is implicitly made a condition of the problem's resolution. It is after this that qualification is made, but now it is given exclusively by the speaker, the imagined audience/interlocutor having agreed a moment earlier that the point discussed is resolved. In this case, for example, after the *réponse sans ambiguïté, which as we can see* from the way the argument has developed so far in this section is given in the form of a fundamental and unavoidable moral choice, the speaker continues, 'naturellement, nous devons nous expliquer sur cette réponse' (p. 41).[10]

And so the argument continues upon the diversity of situations, the individual histories of socialist countries, their historical reference points, national diversity, and this at precisely the point where the problem had been answered and its possibilities exhausted.

It is in this context that Marchais mentions the need to formulate *'une appréciation'* (p. 41). In the light of the perpetually renewed complexity of issues it is clear that the appraisal will be the speaker's own and will be revealed to the audience rather than be presented as the reflection of their own deliberations. Let us look first for a moment at how, from the beginning of the section, such an approach was built in to the argument.

The section begins with Marchais naming the subject of the section: 'l'appréciation que nous portons sur le socialisme existant . . . C'est la troisième question que je veux traiter' (p. 40).[11] Not only is the CPSU/PCF connection posited in a conversational manner but there is even, at this level, a priority of *nous* over *les pays socialistes*: our attitude to them rather than our relationship to them. Moreover, the suggestion of urgency and risk is introduced because the speaker is broaching a subject as contentious and ethically significant as human rights, a point which becomes explicit later on in the section. Being prepared to discuss this topic, the speaker is in this way portrayed as giving voice to the unspoken preoccupations of a diffident audience. The speaker is thus — simply through the nature of the subject addressed — presented as both honest and courageous, as well as sensitively aware of anxieties which both exist within the party and are used by its enemies to undermine its faith in itself.

In spite of the fearlessness of the discussion, however, the speaker has guarded against his own deviationism by making 1917 the last sacred/

historical reference point before the immediate 1976–79 period, in the previous section. There is, therefore, an underlying reassurance that *nous* (a non-socialist country) must, in the final analysis, aspire to and become *un pays socialiste.*

The true subject of this section, therefore, is not the traditional one of the PCF/CPSU connection but the speaker's assessment of the Soviet Union, which will involve criticism but only upon condition that the speaker alone undertakes it. The speaker's own standing is reinforced because the contentious issues discussed are moral ones. Marchais is therefore seen as a thinker capable of addressing the problem of and passing judgement upon the Soviet Union and its socialist and humanitarian status. And of course such a discussion will, by definition, involve on the part of the listener, subjective agreement — or disagreement — with the speaker.

In this way, when the speaker comes on to the question of formulating an appraisal he need do so by referring only to the argument so far developed within the report. Having made, in the discussion so far, *les pays socialistes* synonymous with *bilan positif*, the appraisal can be made and the Soviet Union judged, not in terms of its internal conditions, but purely by demonstrating that the *bilan* of the capitalist countries is a negative one. This is done in four stages.

First, the socialist countries are praised for overcoming hunger, misery, illiteracy, under-development and social inequalities. The implication is that these forms of oppression not only existed in these countries before socialism and have been removed, but still do exist in capitalism. Second, the speaker points out the better rate of growth in socialist countries, thus showing that even in capitalist terms socialism is successful. Third, the speaker makes another reference to the *tribune de discussion*, here from the federation of semi-skilled workers at Peugeot-Sochaux, thus allowing the archetypal victim of capitalism to illustrate the point:

Nous qui travaillons en usine, à la chaîne, derrière un four ou une presse . . . , nous échangerions volontiers nos cadences, nos conditions de travail, notre système d'exploitation de l'individu contre celles de nos camarades des pays socialistes' (p. 42).[12]

Fourth, Marchais points out that capitalism often needs to operate through dictatorships. Here he lists South Africa, Uruguay, South Korea, Argentina, Nicaragua (before the revolution), Haiti, Namibia, Rhodesia (before Zimbabwe), Chile, Colombia, Guatemala, Zaire, Indonesia and ends: 'Je pourrais, hélas, continuer l'énumération' (p. 43). We may note here the sweep of countries mentioned. The enumeration goes from Africa to

South America, to Asia, back again to South America, to Africa, to South America again, to Africa. In this way, the speaker assumes the global moral indignation at the tortures and institutionalised murders in these countries and makes them synonymous — because of their joint connection to capitalism — with the parliamentary democracies. By extension, the notion *globalement* in the expression *bilan globalement positif* is itself modified. Not only does it now mean 'globally' in terms of its positive and negative value and its relations to its own past, but also 'globally' in the sense of socialism being the only alternative and acceptable system on the globe.

Having thus described capitalism and explained socialism's practical and moral superiority in terms of the deficiencies of its opposite and having seemingly reduced the problem once more to one of stark choice, Marchais then mentions the crimes of the *époque de Staline* and *les écarts* (p. 43) between what does and what should exist under socialism. Thus once again the persona of the speaker reappears to pass comment at a point in the argument where moral certainty was assured and is now questioned:

Vous le voyez donc, camarades . . . , notre souci est de parvenir à une appréciation lucide, équilibrée, le plus près possible de la vérité (p. 44).[13]

In this way, Marchais distances himself from both capitalism and Stalinism by naming them. He must, however, justify this distance if he is not to be implicated. This he does by recourse to thinly veiled fury:

Voyez-vous, je tiens à garder une expression mesurée dans le cadre de ce rapport. J'aurais beaucoup à dire à ce communiste qui s'abaisse, au détour d'une phrase et pour les besoins de sa démonstration, à assimiler les dirigeants de son parti aux responsables de crimes dont, nous, communistes, sans doute plus que tous autres, nous portons l'horreur en nous. C'est ignoble (p. 45).[14]

Thus, only injustice is seen as capable of moving the speaker to (just) anger.

Immediately before this near-outburst, moreover, such guilt as may be mustered is so directed, indirectly, at the party as a whole by the affirmation that because of the *nouveau rapport de forces mondial* (p. 44),[15] socialism in France is now possible and will be *moins coûteuse* (p. 44).[16] By implication, guilt must therefore be assumed by those now willing to profit from it. Given the logic of the Marxian interpretation of history — that society develops from lower to higher forms of social organisation — the future is irrevocably implicated in the past.

The speaker, if he is to offer an image of the party as guiltless and thereby be seen to release the audience from such responsibility, must simultaneously show that, through his argument, the party need not be implicated. This is done by emphasising, in order to stress the Frenchness of French socialism, the Russianness of Soviet socialism; that the specificities of it stem, in part, from its own Czarist (pre-) history and that this modified the essential characteristic of socialism, its universal democratic impulse. The argument is strengthened, and the Soviet Union protected, by the assertion that the 20th Congress of the CPSU in 1956 recognised this in its denunciation of Stalin. In this way, and in the context of the implicit defence of the Soviet Union, difference, even dissidence, on the part of a sister party can be recognised in that diversity itself — as in democracy — is an indication of a higher level of unity.

Eurocommunism is therefore justified (and named here) and a French road both endorsed and, because of the underlying teleology, seen as the only strategically justified road. Reassurance of this truth — and an indication of the leadership's paternalism — is given:

Les camarades qui, ici et là, manifestent à cet égard des craintes n'ont pas de raisons de s'inquiéter (p. 48).[17]

In conclusion then, we can see that the underlying method of argument in this section is to present the speaker's personal assessment of the Soviet Union as an analysis of the PCF's relationship to it and to appropriate, through a series of alternatingly simplified and sophisticated ethical arguments, the sole position from which to judge the issue and thereby impose a new perspective — or reimpose an old one.

Let us look at the key words and expressions appearing throughout this section that facilitate this personal appropriation. The problem centres upon the interpretation of reality and the manner in which such interpretation is to be made. The method for doing this is *faire un bilan:* making a reckoning, balancing the good against the bad. This, however, is coupled with the notion that this needs delicate and sensitive interpretation. Such a *bilan* consequently leads to the need to *tirer les leçons* (learn lessons) (pp. 46 and 49). It is from these that one must make or formulate an appraisal (pp. 41, 44, 45 and 49). This idea of an appraisal is the crucial one. And 'nous voulons nous garder, et définitivement, de toute apprèciation outrancière' (p. 44).[18] The activist, therefore, may identify the method of enquiry but not draw conclusions from it. However, 'appraisal' itself is linked here to an older notion in Communist discourse, that of *réflexion* (pp. 45, 46, 48 and 49). To reflect is the right and duty of the activist (though we may point out that it is subordinated later in the report to activism); 'appraisal' is the conclusion of 'reflection' and remains the domaine of the speaker. If this is done utopianism, flights of fancy on the part of the unskilled activist, can be avoided (though we may note the manner of the professor in the way it is, *disons un peu,* condoned):

> il ne faut pas cacher que l'expérience et la réflexion nous ont permis . . . de dépasser une vision, disons un peu utopique et abstraite, du socialisme (p. 46).[19]

If we now move in even closer to the text and see the linking words and expressions behind these key terms of *bilan, réflexion* and *appréciation,* we can see the actual structure and dynamics of the argument as very complex, and see how impossible it would be for an activist to know the way forward without guidance. These expressions describe what the leadership has had to do in order to know the correct strategy, which is the subject of the following section. This then, is what the activist or dissident would need to do:

> faire le bilan (p. 40); ne pas déserter le terrain du combat de classe, ne pas cultiver des illusions, donner une réponse (p. 41); prendre en compte, constater, ne pas ignorer (p. 42); répondre (p. 43); examiner, parvenir à une appréciation, se garder de, prendre en compte (p. 44); ne pas atténuer, ne pas modifier, prendre une position, réaffirmer, ne pas céder (p. 45); définir le socialisme, repousser des idées, dépasser une vision abstraite (p. 46); ne pas tomber dans l'erreur, repousser l'idée, proposer, attacher d'intérêt, ne pas se tromper, prendre en compte (p. 47); parcourir un chemin, adopter la démarche créatrice, considérer, trouver le chemin, avoir une vision (p. 48); avoir la volonté, tirer les leçons, porter une appréciation, veiller (p. 49).

Then, and only then, can the party 'mettre en oeuvre la ligne politique' (p. 49).[20]

In these conceptual circumstances, the leader becomes the interpreter of a complex reality for an unsure audience. Marchais becomes a person who can think the unthinkable while displaying unwavering faith. He acknowledges and deplores the crimes of certain forms of socialism and admits the distance between ideal and real socialist forms. He thus presents a material order in moral terms and — drawing upon the *tribune de discussion,* which here operate as fables illustrating the myth of a new socialism which is taking shape — offers himself as having understood it. In this capacity he inducts the listeners into the art of formulating an appraisal, while simultaneously asserting that acceptance of himself is the condition of its success.

Notes

1   G. Marchais, *Pour une avancée démocratique. Rapport au XXIIIe Congrès du Parti communiste français, 9 au 13 mai 1979*, Paris, Parti Communiste Français, 1979.

2   See, for example, J. Gerstlé, *Le langage des socialistes*, Paris, Stanké, 1979. See in particular D. Labbé, *Le discours communiste*, Paris, Presse de la fondation nationale des sciences politiques, 1977, and the various methodological approaches of such journals as *Mots, Langages* and *Langue Française.*

3   'As our resolution projects states: to the question, what is socialism's contribution today to the countries concerned and the whole of humanity, we reply: the overall balance of the socialist countries is positive' (p. 40).

4   'I will refer briefly to the arguments about words caused here and there by the term 'balance' [*bilan*] Some comrades have drawn an analogy with an accounting balance having a credit column and a debit column, and they have concluded that it was impossible to draw up such balances in matters concerning human achievements! But really: who will imagine, if I speak of the catastrophic balance of M. Giscard d'Estaing's five years of power that I am a chartered accountant?' (p. 40).

5   'So as I have shown, an examination of our period of history shows that the direction of evolutions radically modifying our world is unequivocal: what advances is socialism; what loses ground is capitalism' (p. 40).

6   'How can one explain the activists of an avant-garde party coming to envisage, as a revolutionary stance, our adopting a position of prudent neutrality in the face of this incessant campaign? How can it be explained save by the fact that, however little, they are giving way under the enormous pressure of that campaign' (p. 41).

7   'we cannot desert the essential ground of the class struggle and we will not do so' (p. 41).

8   'In this sphere no trick of language, no tactical dodge making it possible both to avoid the difficulty and make the problem disappear, can be employed' (p. 41).

9   'Giving a simple and clear answer to the only question that matters in the end: is it or is it not a good thing that the peoples concerned constructed socialism, or would it have been better had they not done so? Our answer to this question is aggressive and unambiguous: yes it is a good thing for them and for us' (p. 41).

10   'Naturally we must explain this reply' (p. 41).

11   'Our appraisal of existing socialism . . . is the third question I wish to consider' (p. 40).

12   'We who work in a factory, on the production line, at a furnace or a press, we would willingly exchange our production norms, our working conditions, our system of exploitation of the individual for those of our comrades in socialist countries' (p. 42).

13   'So you see comrades . . . our preoccupation is to arrive at a lucid, balanced appraisal, as near as possible to the truth' (p. 44).

14   'Look, I intend to express myself in measured terms in this report. I could say a lot to the communist who lowers himself, by a roundabout phrase or to suit a particular case, to place the leaders of his party on the same level as the

authors of crimes which horrify us communists perhaps more than others. This is ignoble' (p. 45).

15 '. . . new world power structure' (p. 44).

16 '. . . less costly' (p. 44).

17 'Comrades who here and there show their fears in this connection have no reason to be anxious' (p. 48).

18 'We wish to avoid definitively any extreme appraisal' (p. 44).

19 '. . . we should not conceal that experience and reflection have allowed us to go beyond a vision of socialism that was, shall we say, a little utopian and abstract' (p. 46).

20 '. . . draw up a balance, not desert the area of class struggle, not harbour illusions, give his answer (p. 41), take into account, note, not ignore (p. 42), answer (p. 43), examine, reach an appraisal, be careful not to, take into account (p. 44), not reduce, not modify, adopt a position, reaffirm, not yield (p. 45), define socialism, reject ideas, go beyond the abstract vision (p. 46), not fall into error, reject the idea, propose, attach interest, not be mistaken, take into account (p. 47), follow a path, have a vision (p. 48), have the will, learn the lessons, make an appraisal, keep a watch over (p. 49), put into effect (for us) the political line' (p. 49).

11 'Les variables de Solférino' or thoughts on steering the Socialist economy: an analysis of the economic discourse of the French Parti Socialiste

DAVID HANLEY
University of Reading

Le problème des années à venir va être la perception de l'inadaptation croissante du cadre national par rapport aux problèmes à résoudre.[1]

Michel Rocard, 1979

Certes, la France n'est pas une superpuissance; mais son histoire, son rayonnement, sa situation géographique font d'elle un acteur possible entre l'Est et l'Ouest, le Nord et le Sud.[2]

Le Ceres, 1979

In recent years the *Parti socialiste* (PS) has produced much material, official and semi-official, speculative and rigorously analytical, as befits a party whose audience has grown so rapidly. Precisely because the party's growth has been so sudden, however, it is to some extent volatile; and it thus remains far from certain what sort of identity the PS has forged for itself within the French political system. Is it just a catch-all party, picking up whatever crumbs fall its way whenever the Right and the Communist Party (PCF) are weakened? Or is it in the process of carving out for itself a more durable identity? If so, on whom or on what is such an identity based? It seems to me that the texts of the party might be a useful, though not an exclusive aid in attempting to answer such questions, and of course much energy has been devoted to exegesis of PS literature, often from very partisan standpoints. Most such analysis has concentrated heavily, however, on the political dimension of the party's utterances. Yet there is available a wealth of economic material which has received comparatively scant attention — rather curiously in my view, given the centrality of economic analysis to the programmes of any serious organisation. This chapter then will try to analyse the economic discourse or discourses of the PS in the light of the above questions.

It should be pointed out that the word discourse is not used as rigorously as linguistic specialists might like, but in a much more limited and functional sense. That is, it is assumed that within the mass of PS documents dealing with the economy there is an underlying core within a certain logic, which can be rendered explicit for the purposes of analysis. I have taken as my material a wide selection of both official party publications (mainly party programmes and electoral statements) and semi-official ones (mainly texts by leading theorists and the reviews of different tendencies inside the party, both of which usually reflect a clear factional bias and which should therefore permit us to test how elastic is the PS discourse, or to put it differently, how many variations it is possible to play around a given theme.[3]

For convenience's sake is has been assumed that an economic discourse can be broken down as follows: (a) analysis of the current economic position of France, seen as disastrous and therefore implying the presence of an adversary, deemed responsible for the disaster and (b) a strategy to counter this adversary and impose a new type of economic development. We shall, then, look at the core discourse of the PS under these heads as it evolved during the 1970s (it is *not* my intention to examine the actual economic stewardship of the PS since May 1981). But we shall also at the same time examine some of the intra-party debate and thus assess the degree of elasticity within that discourse. It might then be possible to assess the political significance of that discourse and perhaps begin to answer the questions raised above about the party's identity. Clearly this means extensive use of factional literature and, again for methodological convenience, a three-way split within the party has been assumed. On the Left is the CERES, on the right the Rocardians, and the Mitterrandists fill the central, arbitrating position. No one should be taken in by these caricatural descriptions of course, and this chapter will attempt to show how unfounded they are, even though it often suits the protagonists to pretend otherwise. But one has to start somewhere, however crudely and however insensitive to different theorists this may be.

Let us begin with the core PS view of the economic position of France. Using a recognisably Marxist analysis, and one which owes something to the state monopoly capitalism (*stamocap*) types of analysis developed by the Communist movement, the party sees the world economy as an imperialist one. Capitalist relations of production are thus dominant world wide, pivoting round a dominant pole, the US and to a lesser extent the developed states of Western Europe. Within this pole, concentration and centralisation of capital have grown apace, but increasingly the large units of capital are becoming transnational in their scope. The visible symbol of these developments are the multinational companies (MNC) which appear everywhere in socialist discourse as the true enemies of progress.

It is under their aegis that the international economy is currently being restructured, mainly in order to counter the chronic propensity of the rate of profit to fall. The new international division of labour (IDL) which they are sponsoring will in future reinforce the lowly position of Third World countries (sources of raw materials, outlets for the investment of surplus capital and, increasingly, the place where massive low-technology industry will be located). While reserving the 'sunrise industries' for the heart of developed capitalism (i.e. North America, home of most MNC), it will leave less and less modest outlets, in old or new industries alike, to Europe, which must thus descend more clearly than before to a secondary status.

In fact the consequences of such restructuration on European economies are already being felt: structural inflation, chronic trade deficits and worsening currency instability. This latter phenomenon tends to be blamed slightly less on the MNC (transfer-pricing, 'leading and lagging', etc.) than on their natural ally, the US state, whose monetary policies since World War II are seen as having used US military and diplomatic weight to secure privileges in international trade for the dollar, which the normal performance of the American economy could not possibly justify. On another level, much attention is paid to the social and ideological consequences of the rise of MNC, which are held to exert increasing and unacceptable influence on people's style of consumption, thinking and ultimately political behaviour.

Most governments have willingly abetted the rise of the MNC,[4] and those which have other ideas, i.e. the sister-parties of the PS, are increasingly finding their room to manoeuvre closed down. It is almost too late to change.

Such then are the bare bones of PS economic diagnosis, positing a structural crisis of capitalism, with its root cause (alliance of MNC and US government) clearly designated. There is little particularly original about it. What is surprising, though, is how little disagreement it provokes within the party.

First, on a methodological level, all tendencies use a clearly Marxist framework of analysis. CERES has never, of course, made any secret of its Marxism, nor have some of Mitterrand's economic advisers such as C. Goux. What is more surprising is to see the sophisticated use of Marxist techniques made by the Rocardians, who are often accused of being ignorant of or hostile to Marxism. Whatever qualifications they make about the limits of Marxism as an analytical tool (whether in Rocard's own *Questions à l'état socialiste* or in the more recent and more sceptical queries of such as Vivaret and Rosanvallon), it is a fact that the Rocardians wield this tool remarkably well. It matters little if there are some variations of vocabulary (e.g. Rocard talks of an *'économie de domination'* more frequently than of 'imperialism'); the underlying logic is Marxist, even down to the acceptance of the falling rate of profit as the main structural cause of the crisis. In their book on inflation Rocard and Gallus explicitly recognise their debt, going so far as to make a spirited defence of the theory of labour-value, which many neo-Marxists either take as read or attempt to skirt round in various ways.[5]

Moreover the Rocardians accept many of the consequences of such a method, though these are often more readily associated with other currents. The ideological conditioning of consumers by MNC, the way in which these devour small and medium-sized firms (PME, *Petites et Moyennes Entreprises*), the role of the US government and its monetary manipulations are all attacked as vehemently in Rocardian publications as they are in CERES ones.[6] There is even agreement as to the political and economic effects of the new IDL on the French bourgeoisie, which is held to split into an Atlanticist faction (taking whatever place it can on world markets) and a less dynamic, more nationalist fraction tempted by protectionism; politically this is supposed to correspond to a Giscard/Chirac polarity. This is quite clearly recognised in the Rocardian motion to the Metz congress of 1979, though it also warns the PS against seeking alliances indiscriminately with the 'backward' fraction.[7] It is probable in all this that CERES indulges in a more direct anti-American rhetoric than either Mitterrandists or Rocardians, but in terms of the essential, viz. analysis of the movement of capital and its consequences, the Rocardians draw fundamentally the same conclusions. We may thus conclude that within the PS there is a high degree of consensus as regards both the method of analysing the modern world economy and the actual conclusions to which this method gives rise.

Faced with this situation, what is the PS response? The prime aim is to secure rapid economic growth (the nature of which will be discussed below), so as to return to full employment, while increasing living standards and yet holding inflation in check. To achieve this, France must regain her economic independence, i.e. the strategy has a domestic and an international component.

The domestic strategy rests, as all are aware, on the nationalisation of most of the banking and credit sector, plus a number of key industrial groups. As Boublil put it, these were 'rendues inévitables par la crise'.[8] By this means a socialist government would acquire direct influence over the dominant areas of the French economy, thereby widening its field of manoeuvre against the MNC and finance capital generally. Suitably irrigated by controlled credit, the revitalised new public sector (NPS) will then act as a tow-rope for the rest of the economy, i.e. those large firms which still remain private and, more crucially, the hundreds of thousands of PME. By their purchases, their sub-contracting, etc., the giants of the NPS will stimulate the PME, releasing their full potential for job-creation, innovation and productivity gains.

This process will be regulated by the second mechanism of the strategy, a democratic plan. Indicative rather than coercive, based on massive inputs from below (from firms, local authorities, interest groups, etc.), discussed and modified at every level, the eventual national plan which would emerge should give the French economy the organisation and security it has lacked thus far.

Central to the success of the plan is the role of the third piece of the strategy, *autogestion.* There is not the space here to explore the vast definitional problems involved by this concept, endorsed by all tendencies inside the PS and many outside. At minimum and for the sake of brevity, it will be taken to mean decentralisation of decision-making down towards the grass-roots in every context. Thus in the economic context it must include vastly increased involvement of the workforce in the running of firms (the NPS is usually seen as a pilot sector where experiments might be made), together with a political dimension that at the very least would go as far as the administrative decentralisation now being carried out.

Such are the major planks of the domestic strategy. They would be helped by short-term measures to get the programme under way, including notably considerable job-creation in the public sector (by deficit financing), a fairly rapid income redistribution in favour of the worse off and a move against inflation by a fairly *ad hoc* mix of taxation and price control.

The international aspect of the strategy pivots heavily on reform of the international monetary system, which in practice means trying to organise some kind of international pressure against the US dollar. Allied to this is an awareness that rapid expansion of world trade over the past twenty years has rendered the French economy particularly vulnerable to pressure from abroad and that somehow this vulnerability must be decreased. How these objectives of reducing dependence and organising against US monetary hegemony are to be achieved — and these objectives taken together sum up what the PS means by 'recapturing French independence' — is, however, by no means evident, and significantly it is here that the sharpest differences begin to arise.

And yet, on most points of the domestic strategy, convergences between the tendencies still outnumber divergencies. One would not really expect this to be the case *a priori*, however, especially if one took at face value the images these rival groups have of each other.

Thus to take some very obvious points, one might expect to find the Rocardians lukewarm about extending the public sector, preferring to base economic policy on some experimental co-operative sector, a 'third area' halfway between public and private or even − if one listened to the harshest CERES critiques − being ready to endorse fully the liberal market of capitalist economics. Again one might expect the type of growth envisaged by Rocardians to be 'softer', less concerned perhaps with maximising GNP and more attentive to the quality of goods produced, the type of energy used and effects on the environment, compared perhaps with the more productivist aspirations of Mitterrandists and CERES. Turning to the relations of production, we might expect to find Rocardians advocating a *basiste* or semi-anarchist style of management, where firms and local communities were sovereign deciders, to the detriment of any intermediary or national input; this again could be contrasted with the well known beliefs in centralisation of such Mitterrandists as Joxe and Poperen. These myths, for they are nothing less, were frequently and knowingly fostered by the protagonists, especially during the peak period of factional struggle running from March 1978 to early 1981. But my contention is that even during this rather unpleasant phase the underlying convergence in these superficially distinct discourses was very strong.

To illustrate this in more detail we shall look at a number of points within the PS domestic strategy, viz. nationalisations and the role of the private sector, planning and the market, investment and fiscal policy, the type of growth envisaged, and the social and political parameters of such growth. We shall also look at the short-term measures, before approaching the more difficult problem of the international context and foreign trade.

On nationalisations, all tendencies agree that government control of the commanding heights of the economy is vital if the planned economic regeneration is to be achieved. Thus the Mitterrandists: 'sans un vaste secteur public, le gouvernement socialiste, privé du moyen de peser sur les pôles de décision économique, serait vite incapable d'exécuter son programme'.[9] CERES puts it slightly differently, but the logic is the same: 'la nationalisation du crédit et des grands groupes capitalistes est l'instrument nécessaire d'une stratégie autonome du développement. . .'[10] Or, more ambitiously, the group writes: 'les nationalisations peuvent servir de levier pour changer le mode de fonctionnement de l'économie et passer progressivement de la logique du profit à celle des besoins'.[11] The Rocardians agree, albeit with less flourish. In his 1975 work, where Rocard outlines a possible strategy, he begins by taking as read the nationalisations foreseen in the common programme of government;[12] but more crucially, motion C to the Metz congress, written at the height of factional squabbling, reads:

> la planification n'a pas de sens que si la nation est à même de maîtriser les principaux pôles de la vie économique, qu'il s'agisse du crédit, de la banque ou des secteurs industriels dominants.[13]

The Rocardians thus admit the need for state control of the key sectors of the economy, but two points need to be made. First, they undoubtedly talk less about the matter than their rivals, and they usually do so in less aggressive language. Thus it is that perhaps they stress slightly more than the others the fact that under a PS government there will still be a large and vigorous private sector and that they refer more often to the qualities of skill and risk-taking associated with the entrepreneur. But even CERES is full of reassurance for the PME, if sometimes *du bout des lèvres*. Thus it refused in no uncertain terms the threat of *à la carte* nationalisation for PME in difficulty, and envisages the creation of organisms which would enable the PME to organise in groups, thus 'permettant à des centaines de milliers de petits entrepreneurs de concevoir leur avenir avec sérénité'.[14] In appealing to *les petits* against *les gros* and in making reassuring noises, then, CERES can sound quite Rocardian — some of the time, at least.

The second point about the Rocardian view of nationalisation concerns the modalities. The tendency has argued in favour of methods of takeover other than 100 per cent possession of share capital, e.g. majority shareholding or converting existing shares into state bonds so as to avoid excessive pay-outs in the form of compensation. Here, we will merely note this difference of emphasis, but its political meaning will be discussed below.

Whatever the modalities of its ownership, the NPS attracts much consensus as to its management style. It is not to be run in a centralised, East European manner, but with a high degree of autonomy, restricted only by the framework of the plan: its watchwords will be efficiency and competitiveness. If the Rocardians stress this slightly more than the others, these latter do not disagree on basics. Boublil thus argues against having a single statute for the NPS, justifying this by saying that such flexibility accords better with the *autogestionnaire* philosophy of his party! He argues that the big groups should be free to conclude business alliances as they see fit, even with private conglomerates abroad. CERES insists similarly on autonomy, remarking that: 'l'expérience montre qu'une gestion centralisée est inefficace, dilue les responsabilités, réduit la souplesse d'adaptation'.[15] There is similar agreement about the tow-rope of the NPS. *Repères* and *Faire* have both devoted part or all of issues to the PME, showing how vital they are to job creation. While aware that many small employers are most reactionary in terms of pay and conditions, union recognition, etc., socialists of all persuasions recognise none the less that they are probably the main hope of beating unemployment.[16]

So far as planning goes, all tendencies seem to want to go further than what is normally understood by a Keynesian approach (i.e. relying on broad tools of macro-economic management such as interest rates, fiscal manipulation, etc., to regulate the economy). As Boublil argues, these tools are now quite blunt.[17] But although socialist planning is to be indicative and fuelled by inputs from below, and relying extensively on contracts within and between public and private sectors, the plan is to be more than a pious wish. All agree that the full weight of government will be used against employers who deliberately flout agreements to which they are party. One of the fiercest advocates of this line is the Rocardian B. Soulage, often suspected of excessive tenderness towards market liberalism.[18] And it is in this context that we must understand the Rocardian declaration at Metz, which says (in bold type): 'autogestionnaires, nous ne sommes pas anti-étatistes'.[19]

In short, no faction has been proposing either to disengage the state from the economy nor to run it centrally from the offices of the finance ministry. All know perfectly well that they would be in charge of a mixed economy, albeit slightly more *dirigiste* than some. It may well be true that the Rocardians refer more frequently than the rest to the need for a market to assess both consumers' demand and firms' performances; but consider this extract from the CERES motion at Metz: 'une telle planification n'aura pas pour but de supprimer l'économie de marché, mais de l'orienter et de l'encadrer aux lieu et place des intérêts actuellement dominants.'[20]

Moving on to some of the more technical mechanisms for assuring growth, consensus again abounds. All tendencies agree on the need for a vastly increased research and development budget, for attracting savings away from speculative areas (e.g. property) into productive activities in manufactures and tertiary sectors. The means to this end are seen to be a mixture of stick and carrot, i.e. mainly fiscal incentives. CERES' preoccupations with this are familiar, and Chevènement's appointment as Research and Technology Minister gave them due recognition. But Mitterrandists have long stressed these themes also,[21] and the Rocardian J. Rey states clearly that the only way to safety for the economy is 'un effort massif d'investissement'.[22]

The type of growth envisaged is broadly similar. We should not believe that on the one hand CERES and Mitterrandists are out and out productivists, bent on raising GNP at all costs, even oblivious to the dangers of nuclear energy. Nor should we conclude that the presence in Rocardian colours of such admirers of I. Ilich as Viveret means that they are committed to some sort of zero-growth option, where small is beautiful and the only type of economic activity taking place is that of the artisanal community or family — 'des rêveries christiano-champêtres' (Christian-rural reveries), as D. Motchane once suggested in his unique polemical style. All factions are committed to raising GNP via improved industrial performance because they know this is the only way to create jobs and maintain or improve the living standards to which most Frenchmen aspire. All know that this involves many constraints. Thus on energy, no one advocates abolition of nuclear energy because it is vital to reducing dependence on imported energy. But equally, few sing unequivocally the praises of the existing nuclear programme because it was devised by the Right and, of course, because there is a million-strong ecological sensibility to reckon with. What they do is to agree that France must cut her dependence by massive planned economies and diversificiation and development of more indigenous sources of energy.[23]

They also agree, however, that the present quality of life and consumer patterns of developed capitalism must be changed, albeit slowly. One way of doing this and also of regulating demand in the long term is to move towards production of better-quality, longer-lasting consumer durables, many of which might be used collectively rather than be held by individual households. The most enthusiastic champion of such a line, which many would see as typical of the 'American Left' is a man who is often considered a very traditional Marxist, Goux.[24] Rocard and Gallus enthuse about such a trend, for in their view it will begin to change people's attitudes towards objects, which is the key to real long-term social change.

This brings us on to the social conditions of growth, which all strategists see as paramount. By introducing new workers' rights into the NPS and, wherever possible, the private sector, it will be possible to involve the workforce in the running of firms. Just how far such involvement should go is uncertain, but before 1981 all theorists seemed to agree that it should go beyond what has actually been done (i.e. the Auroux labour laws), extending to such key matters as the hiring and firing of staff. It seems hazardous, to me at least, to state that any one tendency demands 'more rights for the workers' than its fellows; at most the Mitterrandists might be slightly more reticent. It is of course this workplace democracy which, together with a more general political/administrative decentralisation, is the core of *autogestion,* but in the specifically economic context, increased worker involvement is supposed to yield heavy productivity gains (cf. the views of British Socialists such as G. Hodgson) as well as an increased understanding of and readiness to support the government's strategy. Where some relative disagreement emerges is on the short-term measures. Everyone agrees on a programme of fairly rapid job-creation in the NPS, to be paid for largely by deficit financing.[25] They also favour a swift narrowing of differentials, by upgrading the lower paid and using a shorter working week — themes particularly dear to the CFDT and its fairly Rocardian leaders. But all these measures cost money, and the question becomes: how quickly can they be carried out before they are paid for by the increased productivity which they anticipate? And, from another angle, what will be the effects of overheating the economy on variables such as the balance of payments (increased revenue tends to suck in imports), and thus on the franc? Again, if taxes on employers are increased to offset the costs, how will employers react? Might they not be tempted to lay men off rather than expand their workforce if taxes and social security contributions are higher? Although no tendency dares neglect these very obvious and important questions, it is a fact thaty they are asked most consistently by the Rocardians, who, when they speak of *parler vrai* and *rigueur*, are addressing themselves precisely to this sort of question. J. Rey is particularly clear.

> Si grand est pour la gauche la tentation permanente d'une sorte de keynesianisme fruste, qu'ill convient aujourd'hui d'en souligner les graves dangers.
>
> Soutenir de manière massive la consommation finale n'aboutit qu'à relancer l'inflation, approfondir de déficit extérieur, accroître le recours à l'endettement extérieur. La baisse de notre monnaie suivrait rapidement . . . et avec elle, la fuite des capitaux . . . Les temps, nous l'avons dit, sont à la rigueur.
>
> Les sacrifices d'aujourd'hui, et eux seuls, nous permettront d'accèder à ce nouveau modèle de développement . . . de desserrer peu à peu les contraintes qui pèsent lourdement sur notre devenir collectif . . .[26]

It is here that the argument about nationalisations could also be fitted in. The Rocardian proposals would allow a government to do with the NPS as much as it would want or need to do, i.e. appoint managing directors and senior personnel committed to its policies and able to run their firms in the framework of the plan. Some of the CERES counter-arguments (e.g. that 100 per cent possession somehow makes nationalisation irreversible)[27] are simply nonsense. What is to prevent a determined right-wing government from hiving-off public utilities whether they are 100 per cent or 35 per cent government owned? The real purpose of such arguments is polemical. They fit into a debate about how much a Socialist government can achieve, and how soon. Within this debate CERES wants to make it clear that its expectations are on the high side, and the Rocardians deliberately aim to arouse less expectation. But this is a question of degree, not kind, for both agree on the fundamental strategy. This can be seen if we look at one or two other aspects of the problem.

Thus non-Rocardians do tend to be rather blithe sometimes about the effects of rapid growth on inflation. Goux, for instance, believes that productivity gains will soon cancel out the effects of a shorter week without loss of pay.[28] More demagogically, the Mitterrand motion at Metz points out that 'l'équilibre de la balance commerciale n'est pas un enjeu de la lutte des classes'[29] (perhaps not, *stricto sensu*, but it could topple a Marxist government, if unchecked), and asks:

> . . . appelerions-nous rigueur économique l'ensemble constitué par la réduction relative des salaires, la dégradation des services publics . . . le transfert de toutes les ressources possibles vers le profit privé, considéré comme le seul stimulant de l'économie?[30]

In other words, Rocard's notion of *rigueur* is associated — without his being named — with Giscard's economic management. But when we read further into motion A we find that 'on ne peut pas consommer plus que l'on ne produit: on ne peut pas acheter durablement à l'étranger plus qu'on ne vend'.[31] Such an appeal to common sense could be endorsed by Mrs Thatcher, never mind Rocard. Behind the polemical smokescreen there is agreement on basic economic objectives and constraints.

One could say the same thing about the whole CERES theory of a *rupture* with capitalism, i.e. the notion that somehow a socialist government could take a series of rapid steps (it is never spelled out just how rapid), which taken together would mean that some irreversible break with capitalist development has been achieved. This the CERES liked to contrast with Rocardian talk of a series of *ruptures*, which made the latter seem less committed to real change. And indeed one could extend this sort of critique to the whole three and a half years of sterile polemic between the 'Totalitarian Jacobins' and the American Left. The only interesting question is: why do the protagonists try to maximise their differences when, underneath, they are in profound agreement? I will propose an answer shortly, but for the moment we still need to consider the one area where there is serious disagreement, viz. the international dimension.

Even here the broad objectives elicit consensus. Thus there is desire for a radical reform of international finance to weaken the dollar, and as a means to this end, a hypothetical alliance of a socialist France, the Eastern bloc and various Third World states, working via the IMF.[32] Goux's old-fashioned attachment to the gold standard is dismissed out of hand by Rocard and Boublil, but this is a comparatively minor difference and in any case one that runs across tendencies.

As regards the Third World, all agree that its position in trade must be improved, mainly by admitting more manufactured imports into France. It is just possible that CERES, aware of the problems this might cause for some of the less competitive PME, is slightly more lukewarm here, but that is a very find nuance indeed. On the trade balance generally, all see the need for reducing the tendency towards deficit. The energy-saving measures referred to are clearly part of such a package. CERES has made this a particular priority and it is largely thanks to their efforts that both the *Projet socialiste* and Mitterrand's presidential programme were committed to cutting foreign trade to less than 20 per cent of GNP. But we should not believe that Mitterrand and CERES are protectionists and the Rocardians out and out free-traders. It is significant for instance that all tendencies accept that the IDL has now gone so far as to compel France virtually to specialise in certain exports, for reasons of comparative advantage: these *créneaux* are usually agreed to be:

> . . . quelques secteurs industriels correspondant d'une part à une forte demande mondiale dans les années à venir et d'autre part à une bonne compétitivité existante ou potentielle des entreprises françaises. La conquête de ces créneaux (matériel de transport, mécanique de précision, électronique de haute technologie, machines-outils, agro-alimentaire — pour lequel la France dispose d'un avantage unique . . .)'[33]

We might conclude thus far that the broad objectives of foreign trade arouse agreement, albeit with differences of emphasis. The real differences emerge when we consider the means for achieving these ends, particularly the role of Europe and the EEC, long a subject of notorious difficulty for the PS, and if anything becoming more so.[34]

While the idea of a Europe unified politically and economically might seem *a priori* attractive to Socialist internationalists the problem is of course that such European integration as has occurred to date has been in the context of expanding multinational capitalism (EEC), the effects of which most socialists see as having been to increase various sorts of inequalities. The question becomes thus: (a) has this process of economic integrations gone too far to be reversed and (b) what can socialists make of the existing EEC? CERES thought on this has always been clear; recognising the impossibility of French withdrawal from the EEC, it aims to stop moves towards further integration or indeed enlargement. The EEC is naturally seen as a framework for the easier development of (mainly US) capital, and within it Germany occupies a privileged role as a staging point for US capital (which does not exclude German/US contradictions).[35] In its talk of a 'DM-zone' and of a German sub-imperialism and its fear of the EMS, which 'locks in' the weaker French economy to its neighbour, CERES displays an anti-Germanism which goes beyond the purely economic to strike at deep-rooted cultural fears. Indeed the whole CERES alternative international strategy has more to do with political culture than with economic assessment.

For much of the seventies the tendency thought in terms of a Southern strategy. A socialist France, it was imagined, might seek privileged economic and diplomatic partners as far as possible in Southern Europe, i.e. the Latin states on the Mediterranean, Balkan states and progressive régimes in North Africa. At the same time economic and political exchanges with Eastern Europe might increase. All this would work to the detriment of US hegemony, but also to that of Northern Europe, which, with its preponderance of social-democratic régimes, was thought by Chevènement and consorts to be 'not mature' for the difficult type of socialism embodied by the PS.[36] It is hard to know how seriously, in economic terms, this alternative strategy was intended. Based as it is on an appeal to deep-seated myths (logical and resolute Latins versus fog-enshrouded traitorous Teutons) it has more in common with some of the less memorable stereotypes of twentieth century literature (Thomas Mann and Camus offer inverted versions of the myth, for instance) than with any economic analysis based on realistic projections of production and exchange. What it does show is that for CERES economic analysis moves over very quickly into considerations of politics and indeed of foreign policy. It is difficult to avoid the conclusion that in the beginning CERES had a vision of the world and France's place in it and that later on the economic pieces of the jigsaw had to be cut so as to fit into the preordained pattern. As Maurras might have said, 'politique (étrangere) d'abord . . .'.

Within this scenario, France is to pursue as far as possible the aim of self-sufficiency. CERES holds that the possibilities for medium-sized states are still large:

La France en effet n'est pas n'importe quel pays. Située au coeur de l'Europe, riche d'une grande tradition de politique extérieure, ayant noué des relations privilégiées avec les pays de l'Est et le monde arabe, disposant par une ancienne vocation autarcique d'un système industriel encore presque complet, en enfin dotée du plus puissant Etat de l'Europe occidentale, notre pays ne se résigne pas à n'être plus qu'un objet passif de l'histoire.[37]

Hence the frequent CERES use of the Gaullian concept of independence, lost economically by Giscard, yet capable to some extent of being recaptured. Thus while never refusing membership of the EEC and never stating openly that France could achieve full autarky,[38] CERES none the less suggests that France should go some distance down that road. How far is of course never specified, but recipients of the message will understand that it is further than Rocard or Mitterrand. CERES obsession with 'complete industrial systems' should be seen in this light.[39]

Rocard is much more sceptical about the room for manoeuvre of a country like France. He believes that capitalist integration has now gone so far that it can only really be challenged by a Socialist response organised at supranational level.[40] This does not imply (at least in the short term) commitment to a Europe integrated economically, politically or militarily, but if it means anything at all it means a willingness to move in time towards such integration. Increasingly structured co-operation between governments of like persuasion (or even ideologically difference ones, if they have short-term interests in common) is the only real way of weakening the hold of the USA and the MNC.[41] On the cultural level, there is no hostility to Northern social democracy rather an admiration for its real achievements compared with the mere verbal edifices built by some of its critics. Nor is there great enthusiasm for Latinity: the enlargement via Spain and Portugal 'could be positive', we are told in a rather dead-pan way. The Rocardian international discours is deliberately low key and refuses to try and tickle nationalist susceptibilities. Autarky is written off summarily.[42] But one strong strand does emerge and that, as readers of *Faire* will be particularly aware, is a growing anti-Sovietism, pivoting on an analysis of the totalitarian character of the Eastern régimes.

As for the Mitterrandists, they are well aware of the cohabitation in their ranks of old-style pro-Europeans and a newer generation of more Marxist hue, for whom Europe tends to equal domination of MNC. Their motion thus expresses frankly the desire for a median position in international affairs, opposed 'également à ceux que tentent le repli sur soi et le rêve nationaliste, comme à ceux qui s'abandonnent aux facilités d'une supranationalité confuse'.[43] In practice they rely mainly on their will to democratise existing EEC institutions and policies, speaking in very general terms and giving little precise idea of what their European strategy might be. This terrain of democratising existing institutions is in fact a convenient and very general one where all tendencies can agree heartily.

If we remain on the level of political culture, then, CERES and Rocardian discourse seem to be at the antipodes. But so far as the programmatic consequences of the different views of Europe go, we are left somewhat in the dark. It is not a question of one group wanting to leave the EEC and another pushing for immediate integration. The likely actions of whichever group took control of the PS or of France were always likely to be rather *ad hoc*, using a mixture of intra-state initiatives, more national strategies and actual common policies, all this despite the vehement denunciations contained in their texts. It may well be the case that the CERES Metz motion stresses that European co-operation thus far has been intergovernmental rather than via common policies, but one would not find anywhere in their texts the wish to demolish successful common policies (for many Frenchmen at least including many of their supporters) such as the Common Agricultural Policy.

The impression persists, then, that structurally the economic discourses of different PS factions are fairly similar in their diagnosis and in their prescriptions. There seem to be important differences in the field of the international economy, but even here the differences seem to be of a political/cultural nature. Moreover they seem to have been maximised. One is led to ask why.

To understand, we must return to the position of the PS in the French political system. The party's political space has always been bounded by, on its left, a PCF which was strong but never really hegemonic and on the right by parties of liberal and more authoritarian hues. As such its clientele was always likely to be volatile, apart from a bedrock of old Socialist support that had never gone over to the PCF when the PS was weak and which, geographically, existed mainly south of the Loire. Hence its appeal — and thus its discourse — had to be flexible enough to accommodate both the old-fashioned *marxisant* type of socialist (plus any PCF deserters), and the newer, more numerous type of voter, mainly from the new salaried middle class.[44] It is my contention that in order to accommodate both types, it was necessary to invent something like the core-discourse analysed here, that is above all a modernising, if not to say technocratic, one.[45] Thus the repeated guarantees of economic expansion and rising standards, based on maximum and efficient use of resources (the Plan) was well calculated to appeal to the life-styles of such classes, and the participatory input could relate quite well to the basically liberal culture into which many of them had been socialised. The only awkward part of the discourse to put across was the nationalisations, which of course are fundamental (both in terms of the actual working of the strategy and politically in terms of reassuring the Marxist voters and activists that the PS is 'really socialist'). It seems to me that the *autogestionnaire* input (which was always used to point out the difference between these nationalisations and the older ones) did this well enough. Now, because all tendencies in the PS know very well that they are working within the above parameters, they know that to diverge too far from the core-discourse is to court trouble. In this sense we have now answered the original question about the PS identity: it is basically a modernising party based on the new middle class, but at the same time it goes beyond this.

For there is a certain real divergence in its discourse, as we saw, and this divergence does have a function. Thus the nationalist divergence of the CERES is an extremely important part of the group's identity, enabling it to appeal to nationalist sensibility inside the PS (more widespread than many believe, perhaps?) and, probably more importantly, to reach out beyond the party activists into the nationalist consensus that Gaullism helped manufacture. Hence in the CERES economic discourse, nationalism (and Germanophobia) must find a place.

In a similar way Rocardism, with its dispassionate playing down of the national factor, its anti-Communism, and its general aura of prudence about the speed of change, appeals to a different sensibility inside and outside the party, more difficult to classify than the nationalist one, but equally important for the PS to win over if it is to progress.

The pattern then is of a modernising core-discourse, necessary to attract a majority-type of voter and activist, on to which are embroidered more subtle discourses aimed at smaller but crucial publics. It is probably possible to demonstrate that the degree of variance or elasticity is proportionate to the imminence of party or national electoral contests. In electoral terms, 1981 showed that the mix could work very well. As to whether the discourse provides a guide to the management of the socialist economy, it can be safely assumed that that is a very different question.

Bibliography

Attali, Jacques (1975), *La Parole et l'outil,* Paris, PUF.
——— (1978), *La Nouvelle économie française,* Paris, Flammarion.
Boublil, Alain (1977), *Le Socialisme industriel,* Paris, PUF.
CERES (1979), *L'enlèvement de l'Europe,* Paris, Editions Entente.
Faire, esp. nos 20, 57–8, 60, 61, 63, 70–1 (the main Rocardian review).
Frontières/Repères esp. nos. 12, 13, 17, 25, 28–9, 31–2, 34, 36, 37, 40–1, 43, 48–58 (the CERES review).
Goux, Christian (1978), *Sortir de la crise,* Paris, Flammarion.

Kolm, Serge-Christophe (1977), *La Transition socialiste*, Paris, Cerf.

Mitterrand, François (1981), *Ici et maintenant*, Paris, Fayard.

Nouvelle Revue Socialiste esp. *Nationalisations* (November–December 1981) and *Quel nouvel ordre mondial?* (May–June 1980 official PS review).

Parti Socialiste (1972), *Changer la vie*, Paris, Flammarion.

—— (1976), *Socialisme et multinationales: colloque de la fédération de Paris du PS*, Paris, Flammarion.

—— (1977), *89 réponses aux questions économiques*, Paris, Flammarion.

—— (1978), *Le programme commun de gouvernement de la gauche: propositions socialistes pour l'actualisation*, Paris, Flammarion.

—— (1979), *Le Poing et la rose* (February issue has texts of motions to Metz congress).

—— (1980a), *Projet socialiste*, Paris, Club socialiste du livre.

—— (1980b), *Socialisme et industrie*, Paris, Club socialiste du livre.

Praire, Lucien and Pierre, Christian (1976), *Plan et autogestion*, Paris, Flammarion.

Rocard, Michel (1972), *Questions à l'état socialiste*, Paris, Stock.

—— (1978), *Parler vrai*, Paris, Seuil.

Rocard, Michel and Gallus, Jacques (1975), *L'inflation au coeur*, Paris, Gallimard.

Rosanvallon, Pierre and Viveret, Patrick (1977), *Pour une nouvelle culture politique*, Paris, Seuil.

Notes

1   'The problem of the years ahead will be the perception of the increasing unsuitability of the national framework in solving the problems facing us.'

2   'Of course France is not a superpower; but its history, its influence and its geographical situation make it a possible intermediary between east and west, north and south.'

3   For a list of material used see Bibliography.

4   It is here that PS discourse usually comes closest to *stamocap* types of analysis, showing up the intermeshing of large private corporations and different parts of the administration, to the exclusive advantage of the former as opposed to any 'general interest'.

5   Rocard and Gallus (1975), p. 136 ff. A Mitterrandist view of the new IDL is in Boublil (1977), p. 23.

6   Ibid. p. 60 ff. for the dollar; p. 54 for the PME; p. 80ff. for ideological consequences. For a Rocardian overview of the international economy, see Part I of their motion C to the 1979 Metz congress of the PS, entitled 'Crise et mutation du capitalisme', *Le Poing et la rose* (1979), p. 14.

7   'Crise et mutation du capitalisme', *Le Poing et la rose* (1979).

8   'Made inevitable by the crisis'.

9   'Without a vast public sector the socialist government, unable to bear down on the poles of economic decision-making, would soon be incapable of carrying out its programme'. (Motion A to the Metz congress, *Le Poing et la rose*, p. 6.)

10   'The nationalisation of credit and the big capitalist groups is the necessary instrument of an autonomous development strategy . . .'. Ibid., p. 27 (part of motion E).

11   'The nationalisations can serve as a lever to change the way the economy functions and gradually move from the logic of profit to that of needs'. (*Repères* (journal of the CERES group), no. 43, May 1977, p. 21.)

12   Rocard and Gallus (1975), p. 172.

13   'Planning only makes sense if the nation is in a position to control the main poles of economic life, whether it concerns credit, banking or the dominant

industrial sectors.' (*Le Poing et la rose*, p. 16.)

14   'Allowing hundreds of thousands of small businessmen to envisage their future with an easy mind.' (*Repères*, no. 38, December 1976, p. 77 and no. 40, February 1977, p. 29.)

15   'Experience shows that centralized management is inefficient, dilutes responsibilities, reduces flexibility of adaptation.' (*Repères*, no. 43, May 1977, p. 31.) For similar views cf. Praire and Pierre (1976), pp. 148–50, and for the Mitterrandists, Boublil (1977), p. 27.

16   *Repères*, no. 37, December 1975, pp. 24–32; *Faire* (journal of the Rocard Group), no. 20, June 1977, pp. 52–62.

17   Boublil (1977) p. 16ff. Cf. also his article in, for once, *Faire*, entitled 'Regulation globale ou politique structurelle', no. 61, November 1980, pp. 36–40.

18   'La sanction socialiste devrait être forte et exemplaire', *Faire*, no. 20, June 1977, p. 5.

19   'We are in favour of worker control, we are not against state control', (*Le Poing et la rose*, p. 15.)

20   'Such planning will not aim to do away with the market economy but to guide and channel it according to the activities and sectors of currently dominant interests.' (Ibid., p. 27.)

21   Goux (1978), pp. 122ff; Boublil in *Faire*, no. 61, November 1980, p. 39.

22   'By a massive investment effort', Boublil in *Faire*, op. cit., p. 41.

23   Cf. the Rocardian motion at Metz (*Le Poing et la rose*, op. cit., p. 17), and for CERES the special issue of *Repères* on 'Energie et Croissance' (no. 47, December 1977), especially the type of energy programme put forward by M. Beaud, pp. 58–9.

24   Goux (1978), p. 118. CERES favours 'une réorientation de la consommation vers la durabilité des biens, couplée avec une politique systématique de recyclage', cf. 'Programme commun et place de la France dans la division internationale du travail', *Repères*, no. 36, October 1976, p. 40.

25   Cf. Boublil's strictures against the fetishism of balanced budgets (op. cit.): Rocard and Gallus (1975), pp. 108ff.

26   'The left is permanently so tempted by a sort of crude Keynesianism that it appears useful today to emphasize the grave dangers of such a policy. Massively supporting consumer spending only stimulates inflation, increases the foreign trade deficit, encourages foreign debt. Thereupon our currency would drop in value with consequential capital outflows . . . As we have said, this is the time for rigorous policies. Only by making sacrifices today will we be able to create a new model of development and gradually lessen the constraints on our collective progress.' (*Faire*, op. cit., p. 43.) Rosanvallon goes deeper when he warns of the difficulty in redistributing income *within* the wage-earning groups because of the sectional and corporate interests injured thereby. Few other tendencies seem willing to grasp this nettle.

27   For the CERES/Rocard argument see 'Nationaliser: pourqui, comment', *Repères*, no. 41, May 1977, pp. 1–65.

28   Goux (1978), p. 117.

29   'A balanced overseas trading account is not one of the stakes in the class struggle.'

30   'Would we call it economic rigour to reduce the relative value of wages, worsen public services and transfer all possible resources to private profit which was considered to be the only stimulant of the economy?' (*Le Poing et la rose*, p. 7).

31   'One cannot consume more than one produces; one cannot go on buying abroad more than one sells abroad.'

32   Rocard and Gallus (1975) p. 220. For the Mitterrandists see Laurent, André (pseudonym of Boublil) in *Nouvelle Revue Socialiste*, no. 48 (1980), p. 51.

33   '. . . some industrial sectors corresponding either to a strong world demand in the future, or good existing or potential competitiveness in certain French firms. The exploitation of these commercial opportunities (transport equipment, precision engineering, electronic high technology, machine tools, food processing equipment) for which France enjoys a unique advantage . . .' This list is from the CERES' Metz motion. (*Le Poing et la rose*, p. 27). Rey has a similar list in *Faire*, op. cit., p. 42.

34   For an informed account of the Left's difficulties with Europe see Joy Bound and Kevin Featherstone, 'The French Left and the European Community', in David S. Bell, (ed.), *Contemporary French Political Parties*, London, Croom Helm, 1982, pp. 165–89.

35   A typical CERES view of this question is in the report of the 10th CERES colloquium, *Repères*, no. 40, February 1977, pp. 64ff.

36   Cf. Chevènement's speech at the Paris federation's symposium on MNC in February 1976 in *Socialisme et multinationales*, Paris, Flammarion, 1976, p. 181. 'L'Europe . . n'est pas mûre aujourd'hui pour trouver elle-même une orientation socialiste. Les bases d'un pôle socialiste peuvent être jetées en Europe du Sud. Et ce pôle peut peser assez lourd pour contrebalancer le poids d'une Europe du Nord qui restera longtemps encore dans la mouvance américaine'.

37   'Indeed France is not just any country. Situated in the heart of Europe, having a great tradition in foreign policy, having established special links with Eastern and Arab countries, possessing, thanks to a traditional policy of self-sufficiency an industrial system which is still virtually complete, and equipped, finally, with the most powerful state of Western Europe, our country is no longer resigned to being the passive object of history.' (Chevènement in ibid., p. 178.)

38   Even in 1976 CERES said that 'l'autarcie n'est ni souhaitable ni possible' and spoke of 'le caractère suicidaire d'une politique systèmatiquement autarcique'. (*Repères*, no. 36, 1976, p. 29.)

39   Cf. for instance *Socialisme et multinationales*, op. cit., p. 117.

40   'Il est aujourd'hui trés clair que le marché mondial n'a rien d'un marché. Il est manipulé et dominé par les interventions des Etats devant le désordre du système monétaire international et par les multinationales. Aucun Etat n'a aujourd.'hui la possibilité d'y résister seul, les socialistes n'ont donc d'autre choix pour mener à bien leur expérience nationale de transformation sociale que de renforcer au maximum les solidarités internationales.' (From the Rocard motion at Metz, *Le Poing et la rose*, op. cit., p. 16.)

41   'Il n'ya plus d'autre solution pour un governement de gauche en France que de participer . . . à la construction d'une volonté politique et économique cohérente, reposant sur une politique planifiée et sur de puissants moyens publics d'intervention.' (Metz, *Le Poing et la rose*, op. cit., p. 16.)

42   'Le maintien d'une économie ouverte sur le monde est en effet une nécessité absolue pour la survie et la possibilité d'une expérience de transformation sociale dans notre pays.' (Ibid., p. 14.)

43   'Equally to those who are tempted by withdrawal and nationalistic dreams as to those who abandon themselves to facile and confused notions of supranationalism' (Ibid., p. 7).

44   This analysis uses the view first put forward in 1977 by Cayrol and Jaffre that there is an old and a new PS electorate, corresponding to a more ideological and a more 'moderate' point of view.

45   The technocratic nature of PS discourse could be demonstrated much better than has been done here, for want of space. Boublil is very characteristic of this mentality, his impatience with liberal theory seemingly relating as much to its sheer inefficiency in terms of economic development as to anything else (e.g. exploitation of workforce, alienation etc.).

PART V   THE STATE OF THE PARTIES

12 The French New Left and the left-wing regime

VLADIMIR CLAUDE FIŠERA
Portsmouth Polytechnic

The New Left in France is very diverse. Some of its component parts date back to the nineteenth century (the anarchist tradition) while others originated in the 1930s and 1960s as splits in the Communist movement (Trotskyism followed by Maoism) or as splits in the socialist party. The latter were joined in the 1950s and 1960s by the emergent left wing of French catholicism and by a growing number of radical student union (UNEF) activists. The PSU (*Parti Socialiste Unifié*) was created in 1960 as a result of this fusion to which were added some former Communists and Trotskyists.

From 1968 to 1981

The most spectacular breakthrough of the New Left in French political and cultural life took place in the 1960s, culminating in the events of May 1968.[1] The May movement started as a mass student protest. The student movement played the role of a mass political movement, reaching well beyond the traditional confines of parliamentary politics, of traditional party politics and beyond the party form itself. The aim was to transform the world, not merely the institutions, and to change life — not merely the realm of power relationships in the 'polis'. This was to be achieved through direct mass action with the young, the students and the activists playing the role of the detonator or of the catalyst of the workers' revolution. It led to the emergence of hybrid political forms, of organisations which accepted at least in part the ideas and the practice of the primacy of action and of collective decision-making at the lowest possible level of political aggregation. At the programmatic level, they reintroduced into socialist politics the 'ultimate ends', proposing to do away *now* with any form of market economy and wage slavery and started even to question the value of science and of progress itself. French Maoism, which started as an arch-authoritarian, archeo-Stalinist split in the French Communist Party (PCF) in the early 1960s was, following May 1968 and until approximately

155

1978, changed beyond recognition by the victory of populist, spontaneist theses and practices in its midst. Similarly, in the same ten years, French Trotskyism saw the domination of analogous hybrid forms and the same can be said of French anarchism, of the PSU[2] and of the CFDT trade union.

Anti-authoritarian ideas and practices are in themselves antagonistic towards the pure expression of party forms, which require a necessary degree of professionalisation of politics based upon a division of tasks, a stable hierarchical line of command and delegation of power. The horizon of the party form is always the occupation and the use of the state be it only as a tool for achieving a stateless society. During and after May 1968, Radical, New Left or Extreme Left stances were adopted not only by political parties or 'semi-parties' (mixes of authoritarian and libertarian ideas and practices on a small scale) but also by a whole host of new movements, sometimes called social movements even if only a few had a social basis. These shared the ultimate aims of their more authoritarian predecessors but not their pretentions to globality and theoretical self-sufficiency, as theory, especially of the Marxist ilk, had by that time become suspect of totalitarianism. These new movements of the 1970s — such as the women's movement, ethnic minorities' movements, radical trade-unionists (the CFDT 'basists' especially in the public sector, new general practitioners' and lawyers' unions etc.), immigrant workers and 'second generation' immigrants, sexual minorities, radical cultural associations (from artists to residents' associations such as the *Confédération Syndicale du Cadre de Vie*), communes, squatters, conscripts, and, after 1974, ecologists — were exclusively concerned with a sectional aspect of society and with the task of changing radically their own lives, of experimenting with totally different forms.

However, all insisted on a refusal to divide politics from society in general and would not accept a vision of change limited to the political sphere, leaving unchanged the economic, social and cultural dimensions. Such 'old left' visions assumed that capitalism was eternal in its principle (the social-democratic ethos) or that politics — via the state — should ultimately absorb all the other dimensions of life, as the Communists would have it. Conversely, the leftists' maximalist rhetoric integrated more and more daily life and subjectivity into politics and put forward the values of equality, autonomy and diversity (*la notion de différence*).[3] By the mid-1970s, all these were subsumed under the concept of self-management (*autogestion*) as a newly found globalisation, contradictory with capitalism but also with any state form including the 'pure' socialist one, not to mention the Eastern Leviathans.

The New Left in 1981

By 1981, the New Left would always favour radical demands having fundamental social implications such as the refusal of both the civilian and the military use of nuclear energy. This, in turn meant the reference to an alternative society, fundamentally anti-productivist, egalitarian and frugal.[4] Its means ranged from electoral activities — which were less and less successful after 1974 — to extra-parliamentary actions. Direct action changed between 1968 and 1981 from central, often violent, demonstrations based on metropolitan universities and secondary schools to peripheral, 'instant' action focusing on limited local objectives such as protest action against the extension of the Larzac military camp, the closure of the Lip factory or the site of the Plogoff nuclear plant in Brittany; on alternative production, which evolved from occupation strikes and work-ins; on neo-co-operatives ('social experimentation') and shifting from 'political' action committees to community politics (*Mouvement associatif*). In the process, the new New Left abandoned most of its references to traditional left-wing theory and political culture, i.e. Marxism. No new all-encompassing and explicitly formulated world-view took its place although, in 1977-81, political ecology, CFDT qualitative claims and the references to self-management did indicate a general rejection of the consumer society based on productivism.

Both the flight into the concrete in the 1970s and the flight into theory of the 1960s reveal a constant absence of the strategic, 'middle-range' level of political intervention. This explains why the New Left ignored the Common Programme of the Left (1972-1977) and underestimated the immediate effect of the world economic crisis which started in 1973. Both also indicate an attempt at bypassing the core, the heart of the working class represented by the sub-culture of the French, qualified, adult, male, industrial workers and of their 'natural' political and trade-union organisations, the PCF and the CGT. Similarly, they ignored the emergence of the middle and low strata of public and private employees who were turning *en masse* to the new Socialist Party (PS). Furthermore, part of this New Left constellation abandoned organised politics altogether, settling in the margins of society while remaining outside the ideological consensus. Consequently, the organisational forms of the most libertarian, *autogestionnaire* movements tended to limit themselves to an *ad hoc* protest movement, single-issue type of activity. Their structures would remain light and disappear without trace.[5] What would remain is a global attitude, well described by the sociologist Pierre Bourdieu, of non-integration, of suspicion and bitterness — an alienation both from the Left and from the

Right. However for most, the Left is still perceived as the original political reference while, the Right, at least for the *'soixantehuitards'*[6] remains the 'other side'.

Unfortunately, these new values/behavioural types did not give rise in France to an articulate alternative political culture[7] as they did in West Germany. Hybrid organisations which benefited most from the 1968 wave suffered most in membership terms when the wave subsided. This is true of the Trotskyist Ligue Communiste Révolutionnaire (the French section of the Fourth International), Comités Communistes pour l'Autogestion and Alliance Marxiste Révolutionnaire (both Pablists), of the Maoist Parti Communiste Révolutionnaire Marxiste-Leniniste and Organisation Communiste des Travailleurs, but also of radical student trade unionists such as the Mouvement d'Action Syndicale, of the PSU and of Radical trends, *basistes*, in the CFDT. They found themselves squeezed between, on the one hand a reborn classical Left, especially the new PS, which had adopted a modernist stance including utopian slogans such as *'changer la vie'* and *'autogestion'* itself, and on the other hand the more solid, highly centralised, authoritarian, orthodox and 'invariant' Lutte Ouvrière, Parti Communiste Internationaliste (both Trotskyist) and Parti Communiste Marxiste-Leniniste (Maoist). The latter did not owe their existence to the May movement or to the cultural dissent of the 1970s. They possess coherent and closed ideologies and organisational structures. They exist outside the social movement, displaying an autonomous, if ghettoised, capacity for action. They belong to the centralist, Leninist tradition and share many common structural and behavioural features with the PCF and the CGT.[8]

At the other extreme of the New Left constellation, we find the inheritors of the cultural dissent of the 1970s. These are very suspicious of party politics as a whole and work preferably in local associations or in parallel, underground structures: communes, environmentalist groups, including the very few who are tempted by terrorism such as some radical local ecologists' groups, the neo-anarchist *autonomes* and *Action Directe* militants. These claim to reject equally the Right and the Left. The electoral clientèle of the Extreme Left and of about half of the ecologists[9], which constitute altogether about 7 per cent of the electorate, had, by 1978, become clearly distinct from the PS modernist vote. Their voters are younger, more educated, more urbanised than the national average. The majority of their young voters are either not integrated into the world of work or are only in part-time employment. They are often teachers, social workers, office workers and technicians while their parents often belong to a higher social group. This new downward mobility creates what

Daniel Boy called a *non-lieu social*,[10] which tends to alienate them from both the political culture of the classical Left and the Right. Recent studies by R. Cayrol and C. Ysmal of this trend (*sensibilité*) in public opinion have shown definitively that there has existed,since approximately 1978, a stable group which 'feels closest' to the Extreme Left and to the ecologists even if they vote, eventually, for more credible parties (the *vote utile* in favour of the PS) or do not vote at all. They are all much more pluralist, egalitarian, libertarian and permissive than the PS and PCF supporters. However, the PSU-Trotskyist sub-group appears to be more politicised, more revolutionary — sanctioning the use of strikes, of illegal procedures and of violence — more anti-capitalist — i.e. not only anti-productivist — and more in favour of left-wing unity than the PS and PCF supporters and also more than the ecologists' clientèle. On these issues, the ecologists are more moderate than the PS and PCF group itself. The ecologists are indeed, as their leader Brice Lalonde put it, both *auto-gestionnaires* and liberals. They have a higher percentage of women and of very young people and seem to constitute a sub-group of their own. Fundamentally they are more in favour of a revolution in personal daily life than in the system of production.

After May 1981

This New Left by May 1981 was in a situation of general decline as regards membership and votes. After the surprise victory of Mitterrand, most groups tried to ride the wave of political enthusiasm, hoping with Alain Lipietz (in *Parti Pris*, 15 June 1981) that a door had been 'half opened'. For instance, the strongest New Left organisation, the PSU, in December 1981 switched towards a pro-governmental position, including the acceptance of the principle of ministerial participation. However, two-fifths of the organisation remained in a position of clear detachment from the Socialist regime, hoping to build via mass mobilisation an alternative that would be left of the Left. Similarly the PCI, the LCR and LO (Lutte Ouvrière) situated themselves as the Left of the *peuple de gauche* and did not oppose the regime openly in their discourse at least until the end of 1981. The 'punctual' rejection of the previous right-wing regime was mistaken by some on the New Left for an enthusiastic support for or at least confidence in the new Mitterrand regime. Some underestimated the underlying general social and political fragmentation and apathy. More-over, the radical promises of the new regime lured the Radical Left especially as some structural reforms were indeed rapidly introduced: nationalisations, regionalisation, in human rights and in part, in womens' rights and workers' rights. The traditional Left also used in part the vocabulary of the New Left: rupture with capitalism, quality of life, self-management, the right to work and live locally, new international order, 'class front' and 'popular unity', including trade unions and associations as well as parties.

The new regime did away with some symbols of state political repression such as the Larzac camp, the Plogoff nuclear plant and military courts, which were traditional targets of New Left dissent. Furthermore, the new regime promised to introduce proportional representation, which would help the New Left considerably to establish itself in institutional politics; a full proportional representation would have given, in 1978 and 1981, five MPs to the PSU and nine and five respectively to the ecologists. Their share of seats in the future regional assemblies would seem certain to be even larger than in the future parliament. What is more, Mitterrand had also promised to introduce a system of local referendums of popular initiative. As L. Jospin, the first secretary of the Socialist Party put it in *Paris Match* of 23 September 1982, the function of the ecologists is 'to find or help to find new practices at the local level' (*sur le terrain*). But for him, they should not try to become an 'ideological or electoral' alternative. For the Socialists, the New Left, through the CFDT, the PSU and the new social movements should play the role of a supporting force, giving its full backing to changes, even very moderate ones, initiated by the institutional sphere. Ministers for Women's Rights and of Justice, for instance, attacked the New Left for being neutral, hyper-critical or even hostile to them while their timid reforms were found to be too audacious by a very backward public. Indeed relations between the government and the New Left turned sour: the former reneged on its promises concerning the nuclear energy programme and proved to be more in favour of the Western Military Block than its predecessor. Some reforms were only half done: proportional representation, the thirty-five hour week, reduction of the military service to six months, extension of workers' rights, etc.

However, the main stumbling block seems to be the prevailing climate of crisis, which proved stronger than the initial 'honeymoon period' (*état de grâce*). The deepening crisis seemingly broke down society into beleaguered, mutually hostile interest groups. Political life seemed by the spring of 1982 to be reduced to the mass apathy of the majority and the episodic violent revolt of the threatened social or ethnic minorities.[11] Social mobilisation in favour of change never existed, trade union activity remained at a low ebb, all parties and trade unions on the Left kept losing members. In 1982, opinion polls showed a growing distrust of national politics and of politicians in general, especially among the young. People reserved their confidence to their families and to their local mayors. Political ideals — a value most treasured by the Left, particularly the New Left — came out at the bottom on the list of values.[12] Unemployment and wage inequalities were the main preoccupations of the French. They also rated high in their order of priorities the management of the economy in general, the inflation rate in particular and wanted a reform of the tax system and of the national health service. The French thought that the Left was more able to achieve these aims than the Right but the margin of confidence kept decreasing throughout the year 1982. Conversely, threats to world peace, foreign affairs, social problems, the increase in workers' and trade union rights, even the reduction in the working week came bottom of the list in poll after poll.[13] Job sharing, the idea of a reduction in wages in order to give work to the unemployed — the 'new solidarities' proposed by the re-centred CFDT — were almost universally rejected. The problem is that all these unpopular themes happen to be central in the New Left ideology.

This state of affairs prompted Jean Poperen, national secretary of the PS, to conclude that the Left could not 'do everything at once' or else it would 'succeed in nothing at all'. Addressing himself to all maximalists, he pointed out that the French were more interested in 'stopping the inflationary process', in 'winning the battle for economic up-turn' (*re-dressement*) and in the 'reduction of inequalities' than in the extension of workers' rights.[14] The fact is that the latter is the cornerstone of the New Left intervention, the incarnation of self-management, which has been abandoned now, even in the rhetoric of the governmental, 'classical' Left.

Conclusion

The above data show that the New Left has to convince public opinion first if it wants to convince Jean Poperen. They show also that the type of priorities currently favoured by public opinion and by the leaders of the PS and of the government can best be put into practice by the inherited political institutions based on delegation of power and a strict division between a few professional, competent politicans and a passive and atomised majority of citizens. Such priorities correspond to the absence of popular mobilisation. The latter, precisely, happens to be — in all New Left theories — the condition *sine qua non* of an advance on the road to socialism. Moreover, it seems unlikely that even these limited aims (economic recovery and the reduction of inequalities) can be achieved without popular pressure from outside the institutions, without a change in mentalities, without the cultural revolution — the 'realist utopia' the New left has been speaking about for so long.

But the Socialist government will also need the New Left and the ecologists for more prosaic reasons: the socialist electoral landslide of May-June 1981 has given way — as indicated by all by-elections, the *cantonales* (district) elections of March 1982, 'professional' elections in private industry and agriculture and all opinion polls — to a return to the traditional fifty-fifty equilibrium between Left and Right. This gives an additional leverage to the New Left and to the ecologists, both as sectional pressure groups and as electoral partners. The Socialists will need PSU, Réseau des Amis de la Terre, Confédération Ecologiste, Union Démo-cratique Bretonne and Choisir (feminists) participation on joint slates at municipal and regional elections — now that a form of proportional representation has been introduced — and their votes at the second ballot at all elections. The non-Trotskyist New Left and the left-wing ecologists hope that this line of 'critical support' will save them from marginalisat-tion.[15] In exchange for this institutional recognition and legitimisation, both radical trade unionists and the radical political Left will have to exercise self-restraint in their demands.[16] Recent by-elections and opinion polls demonstrate that the New Left and radical ecologists' vote, just like the PCF vote — because they are still perceived as protest votes — remain constant in percentage terms, suffering only from the average general increase in abstentions. The latter are particularly important among the young, (often first-time voters), among workers and women.[17] There is a much larger decrease in votes for the apolitical ecologists and for the PS. The latter is being abandoned by its new, right-of-centre or floating voters, who are transfering their allegiances directly to the reunified right-wing opposition at the first ballot.[18] At the same time part of the New Left, radical ecologists as well as some Communist voters, tend to abstain at the first but also at the second ballot, refusing to transfer their votes to the Socialists as a sign of protest against economic austerity and the lack of radical change; However, these same 'maximalists' do not seem prone to engage in extra-parliamentary activities which would challenge the govern-ment or private employers directly and at the national level. There is not even much sign of the emergence of a radical wing in the traditional left-wing parties and trade unions. As Alexandre Bilous, the editor of *CFDT Aujourd'hui* put it,[19] at the end of a debate on the balance of the first year of left-wing rule: 'our project of self-management was situated in the problematic of a seizure of power in a context of rupture. However, the Left came to power without popular mobilisation. Neither the conditions of accession to power nor the conditions of the exercise of power correspond to our theoretical approaches. We must start thinking afresh.'

Notes

1   See V. C. Fišera, ed., *Writing on the Wall, May 1968, A Documentary Anthology*, London, Allison and Busby, 1978.

2   See V. C. Fišera and Peter Jenkins, 'The unified Socialist Party (PSU) since 1968' in David S. Bell, ed., *Contemporary French Political Parties*, London, Croom Helm, 1982, pp. 108-19.

3   See interview with Henri Lefebvre in *Le Monde*, 19 December 1982, pp. IX-X, and the Appeal carried at the 'Etats Généraux sur le travail des femmes' on 26 April 1982 in *Cahiers du féminisme*, June-August 1982, p. 7.

4   See, for example, the programme of the *Amis de la Terre* in Alain Jaubert, *Guide de la France des luttes*, Paris, Stock, 1974, pp. 143-5 and the introduction of Roland Biard, *Dictionnaire de l'extrème gauche de 1945 à nos jours*, Paris, Belfond, 1978, pp. 11-12.

5   See Henry Nadel, 'A propos du maoisme' in *Les Temps Modernes*, September 1982, pp. 494-515.

6   Recent polls indicate that it is also true of the 14-20-year olds of today as opposed to their more nihilist predecessors of the 1970s (see *Phosphore*, May 1982).

7   See Bruno Mattéi, 'Les grandes vacances de l'alternative', paper read at the October 1982 *Forum de l'Autogestion*, in *MAD Gazette*, No. 8-9, 1982.

8   On the latter, see Jean Michel Gilles, 'Les propositions économiques de la CFDT' in *Résister, revue de débat syndical*, No. 9, October 1982.

9   For those who identify with the New Left and vote for the Left at the second ballot see J. Capdevielle *et al.*, *France de gauche, vote à droite*, FNSP, Paris, 1981, and Louis Harris-France opinion poll of 7–20 September 1977, tables in *Tribune Socialiste*, 27 October 1977, pp. 6-7 and *Politique Aujourd'hui*, No. 7-8, 1979, pp. 16-17.

10   Daniel Boy, 'L'électorat écologiste en 1978', AFSP, Paris, 1980.

11   See V. C. Fišera, 'The French Left in power: one year later' in *Labour Leader*, June 1982, pp. 6-7.

12   *Le Nouvel Observateur*, 28 August 1982.

13   See Gallup poll in *L'Express*, 12 November 1982, the bi-monthly *Paris Match*-BVA polls, IFRES poll in *Le Quotidien de Paris*, 27 December 1982, 'Trois sondages . . .' in *Le Monde*, 18 December 1982 and SOFRES–*Figaro* poll of 10 November in Louis Pauwels, 'La corde sentimentale peut aussi casser' in *Le Figaro Magazine*, 11 December 1982, p. 25.

14   *Le Monde*, 9 September 1982.

15   See PSU internal bulletin, *Directives/Courrier aux Fédérations*, spécial municipales, 21 December 1982, p. 2.

16   See Pierre Chapignac, 'Austérité de gauche, faut-il pratiquer l'auto-limitation?' in *Résister*, op. cit., pp. 9-10. Compare with the more radical statement of the CFDT New Left minority at the 39th CFDT Congress in May 1982 in *Lutter*, July-August 1982, pp. 14-21, in particular p. 16, declaration of the 131 CFDT-affiliated unions.

17   See, for instance, Louis Harris-France, *Les 14-20 ans et la politique* – sondage Paris, 1982, and *Phosphore*, May 1982, op. cit., in particular table, p. 27.

18   See the very revealing results of the Givet *cantonale* (district) by-election of 12 December 1982. In this constituency where the closure of a steel plant at La Chiers and the construction of a nuclear plant at Chooz have met with a

persistent popular and radical opposition, the PS vote collapsed, the PCF vote and the New Left vote remained stable and were ahead of the PS. By contrast, in March 1982, the PS had more votes than the New Left candidate and the right-wing ones; the Communist candidate, representing the whole Left at the second ballot, was defeated by a few votes. This time, the RPR candidate — the sole candidate of the Right — was elected at the first ballot (*Le Figaro*, 11, 12 and 13 December 1982).

19   In *CFDT Aujourd'hui*, No. 54, March-April 1982, p. 13. The whole issue is entitled, 'Le changement, c'est pour quand?

13 The Communist Party and the government of the Left in France*

FRANÇOIS HINCKER

It is my intention to outline an analysis of the official position of the French Communist Party (PCF) regarding the left-wing government in France since 10 May 1981 and of the present state of that party's influence, in order to answer the question: what are the consequences of that position and that influence for the Left?

I wish to state at the outset that the PCF of 1982 can only be understood if one bears in mind the history of its relations with the rest of the Left since the death of Maurice Thorez in 1964.[1] Between 1964 and the 21st Congress in October 1974 (occurring a little after the signing of the Common Programme) the PCF gradually, but by no means completely, detached itself from a bolshevik conception of its role and came gradually but very incompletely to regard itself as an integral part of the Left, whose social base, values, ideology and fundamental programme were considered to be common to socialists and communists alike. There would be considerable differences between the two partners but they could be dealt with in friendly rivalry without daggers being drawn. However, since 1974, the PCF has gradually returned to a bolshevik conception of its role and come round again to regarding the Socialist Party (PS) as a bourgeois party. It began again to consider — I can testify to this since I was a member of its leadership at the time — that he principal danger to be avoided at all costs was the accession to power of the PS in a dominant position with respect to the PCF. The culminating point of that development occurred during the presidential election campaign when the PCF repeatedly proclaimed: 'the gang of three, Chirac, Giscard and Mitterrand: their policies are all the same'.

At the end of that election campaign the leadership of the PCF found itself in the precise situation that it had above all wished to avoid: the PS was in power and in an extremely dominant position on the Left. The PS, expecting opposition from the Right and wishing to avoid communist opposition, and wishing also to retain the left-wing line that had brought it to power, proposed participation in government to the PCF, although

* Translated by Stuart Williams

simple parliamentary arithmetic would have shown that it could manage without the PCF. For reasons that will be developed later the PCF accepted and thus communists found themselves sharing government with the very persons that they had been attacking most fiercely some weeks before. If this paradox, further accentuated by occurring when the influence of the PCF was at its lowest since 1936, is not understood, then it is impossible to understand the strange policy of the PCF since 10 May 1981. The present period succeeds sixteen years in which the PCF has followed two contradictory policies at the same time, with one or other being dominant at different periods. Its partnership in government has in no way removed that contradiction: the PCF is after the 10 May what it was before the 10 May, the party which sought and signed the Common Programme and the party which ditched it.

However, the two elements of this contradiction do not counterbalance each other exactly. In fact, the bolshevik conception is the determining one, and by virtue of it the Communist Party as an organisation has top priority and must be preserved at all costs. The second priority is to prevent the PS succeeding in achievements that might make the PCF superfluous in the long run. It should be made quite clear that, according to the dominant communist ideology, the ideal would be realisation of changes corresponding to the spirit of the Common Programme and under the direction of the PCF. The worst that could occur would be the achievement of such changes under the direction of the PS!

Between these two extremes the PCF leadership hopes and tries to ensure that the party will not appear to hinder the carrying out of limited changes; if it did so, its diehard and sectarian attitude would again be punished as it was in the presidential elections. At the same time, it strives to be in favour of taking these changes further, while the PS is dragging its feet — this is to avoid the PS getting the credit for introducing far-reaching measures. This is the dominant ideology of the communist apparatus as it has emerged from the stormy period 1977-81 and it is one that is shared by a considerable section of the public which has continued to have faith in the PCF. These questions will be returned to later.

My first thesis then is that the PCF in respect of the government and the policies of the Left in power has two faces. Whether it presents the one or the other depends upon the place, upon whether it is being shown to the public or to left-wing partners or internally to its own adherents.

The first face has the following features: the PCF is part of the ruling majority and sharing in government in order to carry out the policy defined by the joint declaration of the PS and PCF on the 23 June 1981, the day before the present government was formed. It is true that this declaration is very different from the proposals of candidate Marchais in the presidential election and it is a great pity that those proposals were not approved by the electors. However, the Communists are playing the game, participating in the government and striving for its success. During the first six months, the PCF leadership did not accept responsibility for government policy (Roland Leroy said at the *Fête de l'Humanité* in 1981: 'we are a party in the government but not of the government') except as far as the four Communist ministers were concerned. Since summer 1982, however, the leadership has tended to assert its 100 per cent involvement in ensuring the success of the government. There are two reasons for this; the first is that a left-wing union in the municipal elections, which the PCF is keenly in favour of, would be inconceivable if the PCF only supported the government half-heartedly; the second reason is quite paradoxical — the economic measures of the government are unpopular — they could rebound on the PS (so the PCF leadership thinks), the PCF could then appear to leap to its aid and win credit for its spirit of unity and commitment in bringing about any success the government has. This first face of the PCF can be summarised by the oft repeated phrase: 'the government is going in the right direction'. This face is presented in major speeches, official communiqués and (in somewhat attenuated fashion) *Humanité* articles.

But this first line of official communist discourse appals the tens of thousands of Communists who constitute the party apparatus as it now exists after the eviction by different means of those who were the most in favour of left-wing unity and who made the greatest effort to debolshevise the party. The present members of the apparatus were promoted after the break-up of the Common Programme and they carried out a very anti-socialist presidential election campaign, being persuaded that between Giscard and Marchais there was no third way, that Mitterrand's policies were those of the Right and that it was therefore unthinkable that the PCF should share in a government intending to do no more than carry out the detestable policies of the socialist candidate; frequently between the two ballots they campaigned within the party against voting for Mitterrand in the second round.

So the second face of communism, only for internal use, is as follows: the activists are told 'you are basically right, these are not our policies and they will fail'. But the French will take a long time to come round again. Of course we should do nothing to save the Socialist Party's bacon but leaving the government and taking arms against it would be criticised by the workers, who would consider that our lack of support had brought it down rather than Mitterrand's bad policies. Also, if we left the government the local alliances would break up and the PCF would lose strategic positions in the country, which are quite indispensable to its structure.' This second face of communism producing mistrust, criticism, even opposition, emerges, as we will see later, in the tactics and strategy of the CGT.

At this point I should like to emphasise that in my view there is no doubt that both the leadership and the militant nucleus of the PCF do not wish the left-wing government to succeed because it would be a success for the PS, but at the same time they do not wish to leave the ruling majority and the government because in the present circumstances such a break would be disastrous for the party. I am constantly asked, in France and abroad, how long will the PCF remain in the government? I reply now as I always do: a long time. For the factors explaining the communist presence in the government will persist for a long time: on the one hand, the need of the PS to tie the communists into the majority and on the other, the impossibility of the PCF to attain a position of strength allowing it either to orient the left-wing experience according to its views, supposing that the PS will let it, or to put an end to the experience in a way advantageous to itself.

What are the consequences of this position, which is quite logical if one views events from the bolshevik viewpoint which currently dominates the PCF and which is, I agree, quite bizarre if viewed from outside?

Firstly, the consequences for the PCF itself. The impact on public opinion and political life of a mass communist party generally comes from its aptitude for activism, for somewhat thunderous propaganda, for the dissemination, which may be simplistic but is at any rate clear and popular, of analyses which in other parties are not discussed outside of the apparatus and the professional politicians. This makes a communist party different from other parties. However, the contradictory, ambiguous and embarassed situation in which the PCF finds itself today, straddling two policies of which the more visible one is not the one that corresponds to the fundamental strategy, inhibits it and renders it lifeless.

Some examples:

In all circumstances in which writings or statements have a national impact, for example in *Humanité*, government measures judged to be positive are mentioned in the most neutral way possible, while measures judged to be negative are given a mere mention. For if the former were praised, public opinion might give the government and the PS too much credit and if the latter were too severely criticised, this might jeopardise the necessary collaboration with the PS. On the other hand, local newspapers and tracts, more designed for agitation than information, less likely to be picked up by political observers and reflecting more directly the very anti-socialist state of mind of the middle-rank officials of the party, make a big thing of the unpopular measures, like the wage freeze, or those measures likely to arouse the anger of communists, like the aid given to business. However, local and national publications join together to publicise the work of the four communist ministers and those communists working in the state apparatus, although they have to be careful not to go too far in case they create the illusion that the communists are really influential. That would contradict the idea that the government and the socialist party are basically the same thing and that the communists have only a supporting role because of their electoral weakness.

Since party statements cannot attack the government or the PS without compromising the solidarity of the parliamentary majority, they relentlessly attack the employers. However, as we know, since autumn 1981, the government has been compromising with employers and supporting small and medium firms in particular in order to encourage investment and combat unemployment.

Concentrating on attacking the employers has led to an undeniable eclipse of the party as such by the CGT and to the accentuation of a characteristic that emerged after the break-up of the Common Programme. At the present communists see no political prospects and have fallen back on the economic struggle. But, until 1981, with the presidential election in prospect, the CGT took a back seat and it even seemed as though the party was playing the role of a fifth union federation. I remember very well that between the elections of 1978 and 1981, apart from short electoral periods (European and cantonal), Communists assembled under the party banner for struggles normally led by the union. Since the 10 May, the party has remained incapable of developing a political strategy, since the one it would like, controlling left-wing policies, is impossible, and its second choice of preventing the left-wing experiment from going too far has to remain hidden. Nor can it participate openly in economic struggles between labour and employers since they are bound to adopt a critical tone towards the government. So, it pushes the CGT to the forefront since it has greater freedom *vis-à-vis* the government and yet retains close links with the communist grassroots. But the party cannot let the CGT go too far in its criticism for it would then be forced either to fall in behind or to seem to disown it. At every political turn the PCF oscillates between two poles: it must remain in the government and it must preserve its links with that very special social, political, ideological, cultural *milieu* that I call the 'communist people'.

In other respects the PCF has difficulty in producing an acceptable analysis of the political situation in France. Either it retains its pre-10 May attitude to the PS, François Mitterrand and the whole left-wing experience that they are controlling — that they represent a fundamentally right-wing policy with a socialist face; doing this it would no longer be feasible to remain in the government or the majority. Or else it recognises that the PS and Mitterrand have managed to bring about interesting and positive changes, in which case it is incomprehensible that the communists do not commit themselves further. This would necessarily involve it in 'self-criticism' in respect of its attitude before the 10 May, which would shake the confidence of the faithful in the infallibility of the leadership.

So the PCF adopts a policy of evasion of which the 24th Congress offers a curious example. Although this was the first congress after the communists joined the government, there was very little discussion of the present situation. The congress refused to commit itself about the situation and was even more unwilling to indulge in speculation about possible future developments. It took refuge in the past — blaming it for the party now being weak — and in a utopian future, a model of socialism for France. It could not and would not say what was the concrete link between what the Left was doing here and now and that future dream. So the PCF finds itself for the first time with no political analysis, strategy or programme with any bearing on concrete reality.

Inaction is the corollary of this lack of policy. Any action might after all cause the PCF to fall to one side or the other of the tight-rope it has to walk along. Since the 10 May, there have been two occasions when the workers were ready to respond to a call and join in a mass movement. In January 1982, when the Constitutional Council held up the promulgation of the nationalisation bill, no call was made, for such action would have meant an open display of support by the working class for a socialist government. By contrast, in June 1982, when the government decided to freeze wages at the same time as prices, still no call was made, for taking action then would have been a declaration of war on the government.

No analysis, no plan of action, brusque changes of line in previous years, easily perceptible examples of double talk, electoral failures — it is easy to understand why the PCF is undergoing a crisis of confidence and credibility. But this crisis is not in itself the subject of this chapter.

The second part of this chapter concerns the consequences of this situation inside the PCF for the left-wing experience of France. In other words, what is the present influence of the PCF on French society and public opinion?

The answer to this question causes observers much difficulty. On the one hand, there is no doubt that quantitatively, especially electorally, the PCF has suffered a marked decline. On the other hand, it continues to play a considerable part because of the very passivity that I have described. It functions like a force for inaction and inertia, depriving the government of support that no other organisation can provide in replacement of this faltering, deliberately faltering, PCF. I will develop these two ideas.

The great electoral reverse of the PCF in the presidential election, which was confirmed in the general election, in the cantonal elections, and in various by-elections is well known; it has lost between 25 and 30 per cent of its previous electoral support. As in 1958, an entire section of the 'communist people' has irreversibly broken away. Less easy to measure, but politically very serious for the future of the PCF, is the loss of its influence. Beyond its traditional supporters the PCF now has hardly any fellow travellers and the prestige that it enjoyed among intellectuals has been almost completely eroded. For myself, who knew the period 1956 to 1958, the present damage in this regard is infinitely more serious; at that time a young generation of intellectuals, attracted by the fact that the PCF seemed the only alternative to Gaullism, filled the gap left by the generation traumatised by the 20th Congress of the CPSU. Today, I can see no replacements. In a broader sense, I was struck by the fact that the presidential election campaign was more acommunist than anticommunist and I am struck by the fact that the campaign of the Right and the Extreme Right are more antisocialist than anticommunist, as though smiting the PCF was not worth the trouble, as though it were a paper tiger.

Based on information from various sources, I can state that since the beginning of 1980 the PCF has lost about a third of its members: that is to say a number estimated with a good degree of certainty at 600,000 members in 1980 has declined to 400,000 today, still a considerable figure. But these remaining two-thirds refuse to play an active role, leaving seventy or eighty thousand activists, which is approximately the number of officials of the party itself, its elected representatives and union officials. A sign of this contraction (which is clear to a Communist knowing the internal workings of the machine) is the reduction in party organisations, due to activists being too few to man the original number of cells and sections. This reduction of the party to its officials is a worrying sign of ill-health for an observer. For the party itself, it is less so; for a bolshevik party existing in a democracy needs an electorate and needs officials, it does not need numbers except perhaps as a source of new officials.

But the officials are more homogeneous since the eviction of the officials most in favour of left-wing unity and party modernisation. They essentially control the CGT especially since it undertook an analagous purification at its recent 41st Congress. So that the PCF still has the ability to orientate, set in motion or stop millions of workers, even if this ability is considerably reduced. That it is reduced does not, however, mean that the PS or the CFDT will gain what the PCF has lost; the PS has working class electors but its organisation within firms remains virtually non-existent; the CFDT is a think-tank of ideas but its ability to mobilise the workers remains weak. So it is not so much what the PCF is doing that handicaps the Left, more what it is not doing. Those who leave the PCF are not activists, those whom it retains are activists, but it restrains them because their militant action could help the Left, and therefore the PS, more than the PCF itself. Except for a few years after 1968 and occasional particular actions today (in ecology, for example), the only militant action in France is communist. If the communist movement is keeping its head down then French political life takes place at the summit only, in government or in party apparatuses. Thus, we have a surprising situation which is quite different from that of 1936 in which the arrival of the Left in power has not caused any mass movement and not even any semblance of grass-roots unity between parties.

It would be erroneous to attribute this passivity of the communist people solely to manipulation by the party apparatus. One saw the apparatus disowned, despite its strenuous efforts, at the presidential election. But what remains of the communist electorate, 15 per cent of the electorate or four million voters, is spontaneous in its mistrust of the PS and in its reticence towards any acceptance of responsibility for national management or management of firms and spontaneously attached to a vision of a socialist revolution which would be a great leap forward, or an earthquake, in the manner of the French or October revolutions. Bolshevism is not at all the prerogative of a party apparatus: an important minority of the French, not just workers, sympathise with it. Thus, at certain moments, the PCF has had to emphasise governmental solidarity, call upon the workers to accept hard facts, to join in efforts of running the economy, to take account of economic reality. It has to do this to contain a spontaneous leftism which would otherwise spread among the 'communist people' and could cause the party to fall from its tight-rope into criticism of the government. We always come back to this.

If one adds to this the fact that some other communists, who are in favour of left-wing unity and no longer vote for the PCF, also do not vote for the PS except on great occasions since they do not feel at home in the PS, then one can understand that at least in secondary elections or by-elections or in opinion surveys, the Left can lose overall. What the PS gains does not make up for what the PCF loses.

I have restricted myself to the PCF but it should not be deduced from this that I consider the PCF solely responsible for the difficulties of the Left eighteen months after its accession to power. It is simply that someone who still considers himself a communist naturally feels more responsible for what is happening among his own people. I am anxious about the gap left by the PCF and its followers, a gap which I regret to say the PS is incapable of filling. For it exposes the government and the Left to attacks from the Right, to the consequences of its own mistakes, without the possibility of a spontaneous and constructive popular movement correcting them.

Notes

1   My own reflections on this period are treated more fully in *Le Parti Communiste au carrefour*, Paris, Albin Michel, 1981.

14 The French Socialist Party today*

ROGER FAJARDIE

The present situation, with a socialist president, an absolute socialist majority in the National Assembly and two-thirds of the seats held by the Left, has never occurred before in France. In 1936 the Socialist Party was the largest group in a left-wing majority and Léon Blum was able to form the Popular Front government, but the hostility of the senate put an end to the entreprise. (Today's senate, also in opposition, cannot do likewise.) In 1946 first Felix Gouin formed a coalition government with socialists in it (as well as communists and MRP) and then Léon Blum formed a purely socialist government. However it was a minority government and only filling in until Vincent Auriol was elected president by the parliament. In 1947 the socialist Paul Ramadier dispensed with the communist members of his government but only had a minority group of *députés* to support him. Guy Mollet was in virtually the same position in 1956.

François Mitterrand's Government, with the parliamentary base we have mentioned, has in it thirty-six socialist ministers, four communists, two left-wing radicals and one member of the Movement of Democrats. In the course of the election he tendered a list of 110 proposals most of which, after a year of government, have already been enacted or are well under way. Commitments in respect of housing, employment, nationalisation, the minimum wage, taxation, the death penalty, decentralisation, Corsica and retirement at the age of 60 have been kept. Despite this immense amount of legislation, the state is still on an even keel and inflation (not our fault if we inherited 14 per cent) is slowing down. It is a testimony to the authority of Pierre Mauroy that these changes have taken place without any major unrest. Negotiation and co-operation have been the watchwords — in some areas we have seen the first negotiations for ten or fifteen years.

Learning to govern after twenty-three years is not easy. Nor is it an easy task to explain the Government's policy to the party members, 210,000 of them at the present time. The *lettres de Matignon*, roneotyped notes

* Translated and edited by Stuart Williams

174

from party headquarters, the bulletin *Le Poing et la rose* and the news-paper *L'Unité* have helped, as have the many meetings, courses and appear-ances in the media of party leaders. In July 1982, after a year in govern-ment, the socialist ministers met with the Executive Bureau of the party and the leaders of the parliamentary group to consider progress to date. In a friendly atmosphere Pierre Mauroy justified the policies being applied, in particular the price freeze to combat inflation. The success of this policy showed in the 0.3 per cent inflation of July and August, leading to an annual rate of 10.9 per cent at the present time.

With reference to general policy I should like to quote Pierre Mauroy at the European Press Club on 9 September 1982.

The Left has come to power . . . aiming at growth, progress and social justice. As always we are joyful at the prospect of government, and we are faced with three main questions. This was so in 1936, in 1945-6, and now again in 1981-2. The first question concerns the state; in 1936 the Republic had to be defended, in 1945 it had to be restored and now we seek new means to give power to the people, which is the intention of our policy of decentralisation. The second question concerns social progress; there has always been social progress when the Left has come to power. In 1936 we had paid holidays, at the Liberation we had the social security system and now the forty-hour barrier has been breached together with the granting of a fifth week of paid holidays and retire-ment at sixty. The third question concerns the mixed economy which our nationalisation programme sets out to strengthen. But it is not enough to have objectives, rigour is also required. . . . For we 'inherited' two evils, unemployment and inflation. And we must show the greatest rigour if our policies are to be effective and if the Ninth Plan, beginning January 1984, is to succeed. We must combat unemployment and inflation.

The productive effort of the country must be reinforced and it is to this end that the newly nationalised companies will have ten times the funds that they received from the shareholders previously (140 billion francs have been set aside over five years for the electronics sector). The economy will be developed in various areas (energy, chemicals etc.) but there must be supervision of prices and incomes, public and social expenditure. The government of the country will be progressively changed in line with our policy of decentralisation, as Paris, Lyons, Marseilles and other cities acquire a new status. Our society will change as our policies for youth, women, the handicapped and consumers take effect. But the changes will not all have an immediate effect. As Bertrand Delanoë stated recently: 'the government is engaged is a long-distance race; the organisation of the whole is more important than the performance in any one stage'.

It has been said that public opinion is anxious, but the opinion polls, though not good, are more favourable than they were a year ago. One should also note with Claude Estier (*Unité*, 10 September 1982): 'it is significant that the opposition is still not benefitting at all from the weakened support for the governing majority and even more significant that the Socialist Party is the only political group with a largely positive image.' The party must remain popular and strong especially in view of the local elections in March 1983. It is however difficult to see how it could do better than 1977 when it captured 80 of the 221 towns of more than 30,000 inhabitants (the Left as a whole won 154 of them). The members of the party have their role to play, not one of accusation but of participation. An example of this was the establishment of committees for price stability throughout the country.

As I have said society will not change overnight but some measures have been taken and they will gradually bear fruit. The economy is undergoing difficulties due to falling competitiveness and pressure from international financial circles, but there are signs of recovery as unemployment levels out and prices rise less quickly. The stubborn struggle to reconquer the domestic market has begun. A socialist civilisation remains to be created and we must each play our part. We know that we shall never complete this task but at least we will make some progress towards it. In international politics (expressed here briefly because the subject has been dealt with elsewhere), we have four aims: to support European unity in the face of American demands, to pursue aid policies towards the Third World as a moral necessity, to defend freedom everywhere, to support peace in the world based upon the right of all people to recognition of their national existence.

The socialists determined at Epinay-sur-Seine in 1971 to unite to change society. The party, the government and the President are as one in this aim. I close with the words of François Mitterrand in April 1982: 'if one wishes to have an economic and social revolution and one loses the principle of democracy on the way then socialism will disappear. . . . We have therefore created a form of socialism which is democratic, which accepts universal suffrage, which accepts alternation of governments, which desires pluralism, but which intends to transform society by popular consent.'

NOTES ON CONTRIBUTORS

Margaret Atack is a lecturer in French at the University of Leeds, having previously taught at the universities of Cardiff, Southampton and London. She has written on Jacques Lacan, on Doris Lessing, and is working on the fiction of the Occupation.

Philip G. Cerny has been Lecturer in Politics in the University of York since 1970, and is currently Visiting Associate Professor of Government at Dartmouth College (New Hampshire, USA). He is the author of *The Politics of Grandeur: Ideological Aspects of de Gaulle's Foreign Policy* and editor of *French Politics and Public Policy* (with Martin A. Schain), *Elites in France: Origins, Reproduction and Power* (with Jolyon Howorth) and *Social Movements and Protest in France*, as well as having contributed to various edited collections and scholarly journals.

Tony Chafer is a senior lecturer at Portsmouth Polytechnic. He has an MA from Reading and a *Licence ès Lettres* from Nantes. He has written and translated articles on literature and area studies appearing in *Nottingham French Studies* and *The Journal of Area Studies*. His current research is in the anti-nuclear movement and political ecology in France about which he has recently had an article published.

Roger Fajardie was National Secretary of the *Jeunesses Socialistes* from 1958 to 1961, has been a member of the *Comité Directeur* of the Socialist Party since 1963 and of the *Bureau Exécutif National* since 1973. From 1975 to 1979 and again since 1981, he has been National Secretary of the party with a particular interest in electoral questions. Since May 1981, he has been a Member of the European Parliament where he is vice-chairman of the Committee for Culture, Information, Education, Youth and Sport. He is *en mission auprès du Premier Ministre* with responsibility for questions concerning *Francophonie*. He has been mayor of La Groutte (Cher) since November 1982. He participated in the editing of a collective work on Social Democracy (PUF).

Vladimir Claude Fišera is Professor of Contemporary European Studies at Portsmouth Polytechnic. He is the author of *Writing on the Wall: May 1968, a Documentary Anthology*, co-editor (with Eric Cahm) of *Socialism and Nationalism: Studies in Contemporary Europe* (three volumes) and author of books and articles on east European and British history and politics. He has contributed to a number of collections of essays on French affairs and written on French politics in *Encyclopaedia Universalis, Journal of Area Studies, Labour Leader, ASMCF Newsletter* and others.

John Gaffney is a lecturer in the Department of Modern Languages at the Roehampton Institute of Higher Education in London. He is completing a PhD thesis on the relationship between political organisation and discourse in the French Fifth Republic.

David Hanley is a lecturer in French Studies at Reading University. He is co-author of *Contemporary France: Politics and Society since 1945* and has contributed to several collective works. He has published articles in *Political Studies, Réflexions Historiques, Pouvoirs, Projet* and others.

François Hincker is senior lecturer in Modern History at Paris I University. He is the author of several books about the *Ancien Régime* and the French Revolution. He was a member of the Central Committee of the French Communist Party. He is today the leader of *Rencontres Communistes*. He is the author of *Les communistes et l'Etat* and *Le Parti communiste au Carrefour*.

Jolyon Howorth is senior lecturer in French Studies in the Department of Modern Languages at the University of Aston. He is the author of *Edouard Vaillant et la création de l'unité socialiste en France*; and has edited *La Correspondance entre la SFIO et le Bureau Socialiste International 1900-1915* (with Georges Haupt); *Elites in France, Origins, Reproduction and Power* (with Philip Cerny); *Defence and Dissent in France in the 1980s* (with Patricia Chilton). He has published numerous articles in *Le Mouvement Social, International Review of Social History, Journal of Modern History, Annali, The World Today* as well as in various edited collections.

Jean-Noël Jeanneney is a professor of Contemporary History at the Institut d'Etudes Politiques and at the present time Director of Radio France. He is the author of various works on the political history of France in the twentieth century, on relations between various milieux and governments and on the history of the media, in particular *François de Wendel en République, Le Monde de Beuve-Méry, Leçon d'histoire pour une gauche au pouvoir, La faillite du cartel 1924-1926, Télévision nouvelle mémoire. Les magazines de grands reportages 1959-1968.*

Brian Jenkins is senior lecturer in French Studies in the School of Languages and Area Studies at Portsmouth Polytechnic. He has published articles on French politics and on Socialism and Nationalism in the *Journal of Area Studies*, and is currently collaborating on a book on Socialism and Nationalism in contemporary Britain and Europe.

Douglas Johnson is President of the Association for the Study of Modern and Contemporary France. He is Professor of French History and Head of the History Department, University College, London. He is the author of *France and the Dreyfus Affair* and most recently of *Le Coq et le Lion: dix siècles d'histoire franco-britannique.*

Pascal Petit is a senior research officer of the CNRS working for the Centre d'Etudes Prospectives d'Economie Mathématique Appliquées à la Planification, Paris. This is a research centre for the Commissariat au Plan. His work relates to macro-economic modelling, education, employment and productivity. He has published articles in the *Cambridge Journal of Economics, The Cambridge Economic Policy Review, La Revue Economique* and *La Revue d'Economie Politique.*

Keith Reader is a senior lecturer in French at Kingston Polytechnic. He is the author of a book on the cinema, *Cultures on Celluloid*. He has also published various articles on French literature, cinema and culture appearing in *Media, Culture and Society* and *Stendhal Club*. He is currently working on a book on the intellectual left in France since 1968. He is a member of the committee of the Society for French Studies.

Madeleine Rebérioux is a Professor of Contemporary History at Paris VIII University (Vincennes), *Chargée de Conférences* at the Ecole des Hautes Etudes en Sciences Sociales and Vice-President of the Musée d'Orsay. She regularly does work for the *Mouvement Social*, which she directed until 1983, the *Revue Historique, Annales* (ESC) and the *Bulletin de la Société d'Etudes Jaurésiennes* of which she has been president since 1982. She is directing the publication (by Poirat) in twenty volumes of Jaurès's works and, with Antoine Prost, she runs a CNRS study group entitled *Travail et Travailleurs en France au XIX et XX siècles*. She has published in particular *Les Idées de Proudhon en Politique Etrangère, Jaurès contre la Guerre et la Politique Coloniale, La Deuxième Internationale et l'Orient, La Republique Radicale?, Jaurès et la Class Ouvrière, Les Ouvriers du Livre et leur Fédération.* She has contributed to numerous collective works in France and Italy. Her works have been translated into Italian, Spanish, Russian and Chinese.

Walter Redfern is a professor of French Studies at Reading University. He is the author of *The Private World of Jean Giono, Paul Nizan: Committed Literature in a Conspiratorial World, Queneau: Zazie dans le Métro.* He is the editor of *Jules Vallès: Le Bachelier.* He has published articles in *Romanic Review, NRF, French Review, Mosaic, Journal of European Studies, Europe* and *Revue des Sciences Humaines.* He has contributed to *France Today* and to *Fiction in the First World War.*

Stuart Williams is principal lecturer in charge of French Studies at Wolverhampton Polytechnic. He is Treasurer of the ASMCF and organised its 1982 annual conference at Wolverhampton. He has written an article on languages and area studies in the *Journal of Area Studies* and some reviews in the *ASMCF Newsletter.*